AMICABLE AGREEMENT VERSUS MAJORITY RULE

AMICABLE AGREEMENT VERSUS MAJORITY RULE

CONFLICT RESOLUTION IN SWITZERLAND

JÜRG STEINER

REVISED AND ENLARGED EDITION

Translated from the German by
Asger Braendgaard and Barbara Braendgaard

Foreword by Stein Rokkan

THE UNIVERSITY OF NORTH CAROLINA PRESS
CHAPEL HILL

Originally published as
Gewaltlose Politik und kulturelle Vielfalt
Hypothesen entwickelt am Beispiel der Schweiz
Mit einem Vorwort von Stein Rokkan

Library of Congress Catalog Card Number 73–4688

Library of Congress Cataloging in Publication Data

Steiner, Jürg.
Amicable agreement versus majority rule.
Translation of Gewaltlose Politik und kulturelle Vielfalt.
1. Switzerland—Politics and government.
2. Political parties—Switzerland. 3. Social groups. 4. Power (Social sciences) I. Title.
JN8783.S7413 1973 320.9'494 73–4688
ISBN 9780807897867 (*pbk.*)

To our children Beat, Markus, and Niklaus, who move back and forth between the Swiss and the American cultures. May they become world citizens.

CONTENTS

TABLES

FOREWORD

Switzerland presents a microcosm of Europe: linguistic and religious diversities, regional contrasts in economic growth and in settlement patterns, stubbornly defended pockets of autonomy in a system of increasing interdependence and accelerated interdependence.

For all these reasons every serious study of the politics of Switzerland is a contribution to the study of the political structure of Europe. This goes for historical and institutional studies: it applies with even greater force to a systematic theoretical study such as Jürg Steiner's. A number of descriptive studies have given us solid bodies of information about parts of the Swiss political system: Jürg Steiner's is the first formal analysis of the crucial variables of the system, the first *theory-oriented* case study of Switzerland. One may quarrel with a number of hypotheses in this formal presentation and wish for a fuller exposition of the interlinkages among the variables: what is important is that Jürg Steiner has made this first attempt at a systematization of the available evidence for this one country. Other political scientists may prefer to present their analyses in a more conventional literary form: what is important is that Jürg Steiner has developed a scheme of variables and hypotheses which will inspire parallel case studies for other countries and possibly even direct cross-national comparisons.

As a theoretical case study Steiner's work poses problems of research strategy surprisingly similar to those raised by Harry Eckstein's controversial study of my own country, Norway: how can we know where a country stands on the different variables without comparing it with another or others? What can we conclude from a single configuration of values on the given set of variables? Steiner grapples valiantly with these problems and shows how far it is possible to move in an in-depth study of a single country. He has one great advantage over Eckstein: even if he can adduce only very few and superficial comparisons with other countries of Europe he *can compare the cantons with each other*. Switzerland offers extraordinary opportunities for such intracountry comparisons and Steiner points to a number of concrete possibilities of this type. There is every reason to hope that he will push on further in this direction in the years to come. In developing my model for the explanation of variations in the growth of mass politics within western Europe* I have again and again been struck by

*S. Rokkan, *Citizens, Elections, Parties* (Oslo: Universitetsforlaget, 1970).

the possibilities of transposing the model to the level of the Swiss cantons. In reading Jürg Steiner's book I have again been struck by these isomorphisms: Switzerland *is* a microcosm of Europe and anyone seeking to understand the structure and the dynamics of European politics will do well to immerse himself in this study by Jürg Steiner, both in the data and the evidence he has pulled together and in the general framework he has tried to construct.

Yale University STEIN ROKKAN
New Haven, Conn.
March, 1970

ACKNOWLEDGMENTS

In preparing the English translation I have extensively revised the manuscript. Several reviews of the German version, especially those by Gerhard Lehmbruch and Henry H. Kerr, Jr., were of great help in the preparation of this revision. I have also learned much from discussions with Karl Deutsch, William Keech, Arend Lijphart, Val Lorwin, Duncan MacRae, Jr., Frank Munger, Jeffrey Obler, and Alan Stern. My special thanks go to Asger and Barbara Braendgaard for their translation.

I am grateful to the Swiss National Science Foundation for its support of most of the research on which this volume is based. My German publisher, Paul Haupt (Berne and Stuttgart), has charged nothing for his copyright. Without this friendly gesture an English translation would probably not have been possible.

Chapel Hill, N.C. JÜRG STEINER
January, 1973

PART ONE
THE PROBLEM

CHAPTER I

Theories, Definitions, and Methods

1. THE THEORETICAL QUESTION

Switzerland is strongly segmented into subcultures, yet hostility among its subcultures is relatively low. This low hostility contrasts sharply with high levels of hostility in many other subculturally strongly segmented political systems. This study hopes to contribute to the explanation of these variations.

The *theoretical universe* of this study will consist of all political systems with strong subcultural segmentation. In attempting to explain the level of intersubcultural hostility in such systems, I will begin with as many hypotheses as I can find in the literature. I will use the national system of Switzerland and its subculturally strongly segmented cantons to test these hypotheses. On the basis of the empirical evidence I will develop an interlinked system of hypotheses. In a last step I will apply this theoretical model in a tentative way to the European Community.

All political systems are probably segmented into subcultures to a certain extent. Robert A. Dahl defines subcultures as "distinctive sets of attitudes, opinions, and values that persist for relatively long periods of time in the life of a country and give individuals in a particular subculture a sense of identity that distinguishes them from individuals in other subcultures."[1] In the present context I am interested only in political systems with strong subcultural segmentation. To determine the strength of subcultural segmentation, one must measure the intensity of self-identification of the different subcultures. Possible indicators are responses to attitudinal survey questions, frequency of interactions among the members of a subculture, and organizational ties within a subculture.

The concept of *subcultural segmentation*, as it is used here, is different from the concept of *cultural diversity*. By the latter I mean simply that the members of a political system differ with regard to cultural attributes that have a potential political relevance. The main attributes that I have in mind are language, religion, race, tribe, social class, and region. To measure the cultural diversity of a political system, the computation formula developed by Douglas W. Rae and Michael Taylor may be used.[2] Strong cultural diversity does not necessarily lead to strong subcultural segmentation. In Switzerland before the nineteenth century, speaking the same language had little relevance in the development of a sense of identity.[3] Among the scholars who have done work on the theoretical relationship between cultural diversity and subcultural segmentation are Stein Rokkan[4] and William R. Keech.[5]

My dependent variable (*explanandum*) is hostility among subcultures. I speak of intersubcultural hostility if two or more subcultures perceive one another in such negative terms that they have a desire or at least a readiness to damage one another. Indicators that measure intersubcultural hostility are, for example, responses to attitudinal survey questions and content analyses of political speeches and mass media information. I differentiate the concept of *intersubcultural hostility* from the concept of *intersubcultural violence*. The latter implies that physical coercion is actually used between subcultures. Possible indicators of intersubcultural violence would be the amount of material damage and the number of persons wounded and killed. Intersubcultural hostility does not necessarily lead to intersubcultural violence. Eric A. Nordlinger is among the scholars who have studied the theoretical relationship between the two variables.[6]

These definitions should clarify my theoretical question and how it is delimited from other questions. I am *not* trying to explain why political systems are subculturally strongly segmented. I take strong subcultural segmentation as given and try to explain the level of intersubcultural hostility in such systems. Whether intersubcultural hostility erupts into violence is another question that is outside the focus of this study.

2. THE INITIAL HYPOTHESES

What are the independent variables *(explanans)* that can explain the level of intersubcultural hostility in political systems with strong subcultural segmentation? Scholars such as Gerhard Lehmbruch[7] and Arend Lijphart[8] have argued that the predominant *pattern of decision-making* has to be considered as a *key explanatory variable*. They hypothesize that deliberate efforts of the leaders of the different subcultures to attain unanimously accepted decisions may prevent strong subcultural segmentation from erupting into intersubcultural hostility. Lijphart uses slightly different terms when he writes that "political stability can be maintained in culturally fragmented systems if the leaders of the subcultures engage in co-operative efforts to counteract the centrifugal tendencies of cultural fragmentation."[9] He attaches to this peculiar type of decision-making the terms *consociationalism* and *accommodation.* Other concepts used to describe roughly the same decision-making model are *contractarianism,*[10] *amicable agreement,*[11] and *Konkordanzdemokratie.*[12] In this study I use Lehmbruch's concept of amicable agreement.[13]

I conceptualize amicable agreement as one of the two basic models of democratic decision-making, the other model being *majority rule.*[14] In the Anglo-American tradition the *majoritarian model* is often considered the only democratic one. Thus, Anthony Downs describes one of the characteristics of democratic regimes: "Any party (or coalition) receiving the support of a majority of those voting is entitled to take over the powers of government until the next election."[15]

In the majoritarian model there is no concern for enlarging the agreement beyond the number required to win. Whenever a majority is reached, a vote is taken and the majority position wins. In the *model of amicable agreement* discussion goes on until a solution is found that is acceptable to all participants in the decision-making process. If a vote is taken, the purpose is only to ratify a commonly accepted decision. Amicable agreement corresponds in many ways to the method of *palaver* traditionally used by some African tribes.[16] The two types of decision-making patterns—majority rule and amicable agreement—should be considered as the two extreme points on a *continuum.* In a pure majoritarian situation there is a minimum-winning coalition which, according to William H. Riker, "is rendered blocking or losing by the subtraction of any member."[17] In a pure amicable agreement situation literally all participants in a decision-making process agree with the final decision.

It should be possible to determine whether a political system operates mainly by majority rule or by amicable agreement. There are, to be sure, many problems of *measurement.* It is certainly not sufficient to look at the pattern by which the government is formed; from this narrow perspective Great Britain would have to be classified as a rather pure majoritarian case. This could be fairly misleading because it seems that in Great Britain many decisions are made not by majority rule but by amicable agreement. Thus, Richard Rose writes: "In deliberating upon many major political problems, the government is involved in *bargaining.* It cannot unilaterally determine and enforce its preferences; its officials recognize that they need the assent and cooperation of others in order to obtain a more or less mutually satisfactory outcome."[18] I do not want to argue that the political decision-making process in Great Britain corresponds to the model of amicable agreement. My point is that it is not sufficient to look at the process by which the government is formed, but that it is necessary to study carefully all aspects of the political decision-making process. On the basis of such a fuller analysis Great Britain may or may not be classified as a majoritarian case.

I am aware that many *weighting problems* will arise. If we want to classify a political system on the continuum from amicable agreement to majority rule, we will have to determine, for example, what emphasis we want to give to the decision-making processes on the national and the local levels. Conceivably, majority rule might prevail on the national level and amicable agreement on the local level. How should one classify such a system as a whole? Or it may be that the relations between the political parties are characterized by majority rule, whereas amicable agreement is the prevailing pattern among the economic interest groups. How should one solve the weighting problem in this case? The answer to such questions will necessarily be rather arbitrary. But I think that some solutions can be found. I do not believe, however, that it will be possible in the near future to classify a substantial number of political systems on a finely graded continuum from amicable agreement to majority rule. Probably a more realistic approach is to begin with a three- or four-fold classification: a model with a dominance of amicable agreement, a model with a dominance of majority rule, and one or two mixed models in between.

This study will attempt to determine whether the national system of Switzerland tends more toward the model of amicable agreement or more toward the majoritarian model. The key hypothesis to be tested reads as follows:[19]

*Hypothesis 1**:

> In a political system with strong subcultural segmentation, the more often political decisions are made by amicable agreement, the more probable is a low level of intersubcultural hostility.[20]

Along with Lehmbruch and Lijphart I consider the predominant pattern of decision-making the key explanatory variable. At the same time, however, I wish to test other hypotheses. The literature contains a fair number of hypotheses that deal in a general way with conditions of hostility. It is legitimate to test these general hypotheses with regard to the special case of intersubcultural hostility in subculturally strongly segmented political systems. Most of the hypotheses that I have found in the literature are probably not mutually independent. For the moment, however, I will list them individually. A linkage among the different hypotheses will follow at the end of the study.

Hypothesis 2*:

In a political system with strong subcultural segmentation, the higher the number of autonomous intermediary groups, the more probable is a low level of intersubcultural hostility.[21]

Hypothesis 3*:

In a political system with strong subcultural segmentation, the more the major cleavages crosscut one another, the more probable is a low level of intersubcultural hostility.[22]

Hypothesis 4*:

In a political system with strong subcultural segmentation, the less one of the subcultures has a hegemonial position, the more probable is a low level of intersubcultural hostility.[23]

Hypothesis 5*:

In a political system with strong subcultural segmentation, the less frequent the interactions among the nonelite of the various subcultures, the more probable is a low level of intersubcultural hostility.[24]

Hypothesis 6*:

In a political system with strong subcultural segmentation, the more frequent the interactions among the elite of the various subcultures, the more probable is a low level of intersubcultural hostility.[25]

Hypothesis 7*:

In a political system with strong subcultural segmentation, the lower the political participation at the mass level, the more probable is a low level of intersubcultural hostility.[26]

Hypothesis 8*:

In a political system with strong subcultural segmentation, the higher the political participation at the mass level, the more probable is a low level of intersubcultural hostility.[27]

Hypothesis 9*:

In a political system with strong subcultural segmentation, the more congruent the role expectations between politics and other social fields, the more probable is a low level of intersubcultural hostility.[28]

*Hypothesis 10**:

In a political system with strong subcultural segmentation, the greater the opportunities for the articulation of dissent, the more probable is a low level of intersubcultural hostility.[29]

*Hypothesis 11**:

In a political system with strong subcultural segmentation, the lower the input of demands, the more probable is a low level of intersubcultural hostility.[30]

*Hypothesis 12**:

In a political system with strong subcultural segmentation, the higher the educational and economic development, the more probable is a low level of intersubcultural hostility.[31]

*Hypothesis 13**:

In a political system with strong subcultural segmentation, the higher the pressures from the international system, the more probable is a low level of intersubcultural hostility.[32]

*Hypothesis 14**:

In a political system with strong subcultural segmentation, the stronger the norm of nonviolence, the more probable is a low level of intersubcultural hostility.[33]

*Hypothesis 15**:

In a political system with strong subcultural segmentation, the greater the number of traditional institutions that continue to exist, the more probable is a low level of intersubcultural hostility.[34]

*Hypothesis 16**:

In a political system with strong subcultural segmentation, the earlier the right to participate in the making of political decisions is extended to the whole population, the more probable is a low level of intersubcultural hostility.[35]

3. METHODS

As I have mentioned in the first section of this introduction I want to test the hypotheses listed above for Switzerland and for some of the Swiss cantons. One way to do this would be to describe successively the individual variables of the different hypotheses. This procedure would have two disadvantages: first, one would never get an idea of the interrelations among the individual variables if they were described separately; second, one would not be able to discover new hypotheses since the description would be restricted to the variables to be tested. These disadvantages can be avoided if the political system of Switzerland is described in its entirety. This procedure would relate the individual elements of the system to one another from the start. Furthermore, there is the hope that variables that are useful for the formulation of new hypotheses may be discovered.

The description of a total political system creates major conceptual problems. Traditionally, political systems are described in an institutional framework. For instance, one finds descriptions of the government and the parliament and of the interrelations between these two institutions. A distinction based on institutions would be of only slight relevance to most of our hypotheses. Furthermore, Switzerland has already been frequently described in this manner and another description within this framework would provide relatively little likelihood of discovering new variables. I consider it appropriate instead to choose a conceptual framework oriented to empirically determinable interactions. Institutional structures will be taken into consideration only to the extent that they influence the interactions within the system.

The interactions of a political system can be categorized according to their functions. Gabriel A. Almond and G. Bingham Powell proposed six categories for these functions: "We need to look at the ways in which (1) demands are formulated (interest articulation); (2) demands are combined in the form of alternative courses of action (interest aggregation); (3) authoritative rules are formulated (rule making); (4) these rules are applied and enforced (rule application); (5) the applications of rules are adjudicated in individual cases (rule adjudication); and (6) these various activities are communicated both within the political system, and between the political system and its environment (communication).[36] With this scheme in mind one might wonder whether it is necessary to have communication as a separate category, since interaction as the constituent unit of the scheme already implies interpersonal communication. I will treat communication, then, only as a particularly important aspect of any interaction.[37] I will also differentiate more sharply within the category of "rule making" by distinguishing between the gathering of information, the articulation of innovation, and decision-making itself.

In another context Almond and Powell also refer to those interactions that have the function of articulating consent and dissent vis à vis the system.[38] This is a category of interactions to which David Easton has also given a great deal of attention, using the terms *positive support* and *negative support* rather than consent and dissent.[39] In view of these modifications and amendments, I have developed the following classification scheme of interactions: the articulation of interests; the aggregation of interests; the gathering of information; the articulation of innovation; decision-making; rule application; rule adjudication; the articulation of consent and dissent; and the aggregation of consent and dissent. The individual categories of interactions can be described not only separately but also interrelatedly. Thus, for instance, it is possible to investigate how the method of gathering information influences the opportunity for innovation, or how the rule application affects the articulation of consent and dissent. Through such a description, the individual sequences of the political process can be made visible. This procedure presents a dynamic, rather than a static, picture of the political system, since the system can now to some extent be shown in action. This might be a fruitful beginning for the gradual development of a systems theory, which, in the words of David E. Apter, "shows a 'circular' flow of causes and consequences."[40]

Next it should be determined what kinds of observational data are available to answer the questions in my descriptive scheme. In four previously published studies I have dealt with various aspects of the political participation of the citizens: the interactions between the cantonal legislators and the voters from the city of Berne and a few rural districts in the canton of Berne;[41] the participation of the citizens in the politics of the local community of Belp, a suburb of Berne;[42] the interest in politics at the federal level among voters from eleven local communities with very different social structures;[43] and the participation of 20- to 35-year-old voters from eight towns in three federal referenda and one election for the federal Parliament.[44]

In studies that are yet unpublished I have dealt with two cases concerning Swiss university policy: (1) the decision of the federal Parliament of June 16, 1966, to give a total of two hundred million francs in federal "grants-in-aid" to the cantons for their universities in the years from 1966 to 1968; and (2) the popular decision in the canton of Aargau in 1970 to finance the first phase of the establishment of a university. Whereas the participation studies were mainly based on surveys of representative samples from the electorate, the method of disguised participant field observation was used in both case studies concerning university policy. According to Florence Kluckhohn this method presupposes that the researcher "has to act in a given constellation of roles," and "all members of the group to be investigated have to recognize him as a participant."[45]

Because of the contingencies of my professional career, I have had the opportunity to participate twice in the making of Swiss university policy. From the spring of 1962 to the fall of 1964 I held the full-time position of secretary to the Federal Commission of Experts for University Advancement. This commission, which consisted of one member from each of the nine institutions of higher learning in Switzerland, was to prepare proposals for the federal government for the financial requisitions of the cantonal universities. In the fall of 1964 I became a consultant on university affairs to the government of the Aargau canton and, in cooperation with several commissions, dealt with the question of founding a university in the canton of Aargau. I performed this function full time up to the summer of 1967 and in a part-time capacity until the referendum in May, 1970. In both of these roles I had the opportunity to follow and record the making of the above decisions of university policy.

René Koenig rightly calls attention to the danger that the participant observer may identify too strongly with the observed: "One usually speaks of 'over rapport' as excessively close relations. The observer goes from being participant observer to being observing participant, which is something entirely different, and in certain cases the analytical perspective of the observation may be displaced by practical points of view . . . , at least the question arises, if the observer in the case of the most complete identification will still be able to act as an observer at all."[46] At least two factors counteracted this danger in my research. First, I did not assume my roles until the beginning of the observation period and abandoned them as soon as the study period ended. This diminished the possibility of too strong an identification with the observed group. Second, it may be hoped that Maurice Duverger is right in stating that "unconscious bias is frequent. . . . The technical training of a political scientist, as advanced as possible, can enable him to a certain extent to make up for this difficulty by developing a sense of objectivity in the observer."[47] Koenig believes that "today adults with a certain level of education certainly have enough understanding concerning the needs of scientific research to behave naturally in a laboratory."[48] This leads him to hope that the sources of error in participant observation can be increasingly eliminated by a transfer to laboratory conditions. In my experience, this hope is not justified (at least for the time being) in a study of the political system of Switzerland. I believe, therefore, that participant field observation is the best observational method for the present.

I was also able to employ participant field observation in the Free Democratic party as (1) a member of the ad hoc working group of the federal party instituted to prepare for the elections in 1967 of the federal Parliament; (2) a member of the standing Committee for Political and Cultural Affairs of the federal party; (3) a member of the Press and Public Relations Committee of the Berne canton party; and (4) a member of the Executive Committee of the district party in the Bernese Oberland. In these roles I followed the development of two decisions: the decision of the federal party convention in May, 1967, to prepare a platform for the election of the federal Parliament in the fall of 1967; and the decision of the federal Executive Committee in June, 1967, to state its opinion about a draft for a federal law for the furtherance of higher education. In both these cases the danger was even greater that I might identify too strongly with the observed groups since I had been a member of the Free Democratic party prior to the period of observation and continued to be a member during that period. However, I hope that my training as a social scientist enabled me not to succumb to the danger of too strong an identification.

In addition to the unpublished empirical data based on participant observation, I can also cite new data on electoral behavior. In the winter of 1968–69 I did a survey in the greater Lucerne area, sponsored by the Swiss Society for Practical Social Research, in which I drew a random sample of 20- to 50-year-old male voters in the local communities of Lucerne, Emmen, Horw, and Kriens, based on the voter register. The sample consisted of 508 voters. Of this sample, 325 interviews were completed, representing a return of 64 percent, which roughly corresponds to international standards.

In this volume I am also able to use some of the data from a study about the decision-making process in all the committees of the Free Democratic party in the Berne canton. In this case the participant observation, which lasted from January, 1969, to September, 1970, was an open one in the sense that my role as participant observer was not disguised by any other role. A fuller description of the data of this research project will be given in a later publication.[49]

In addition to my own data I will use the secondary literature to fill out my frame of reference. It might be argued that the empirical basis is not broad enough for a description of the political system of Switzerland in its entirety. Against this objection two considerations may be offered. First, it is never possible for reasons of time and finances to get reliable and valid observational data about all aspects of a political system. If one were to wait until the empirical material were completely collected, one would never get to the point of a systems analysis. Second, and even more important, only a systems analysis will show where the largest gaps exist in our knowledge and where new detailed studies are most needed. The optimal research strategy might be an alternation of detailed studies and systems analyses, in which case, of course, a division of labor among different research teams might take place.

PART TWO

THE POLITICAL SYSTEM OF SWITZERLAND

CHAPTER II

The Input of Demands from the Political Parties

1. THE PARTY SYSTEM OF SWITZERLAND

Typologies of the Party System of Switzerland

According to Giovanni Sartori there are only four politically relevant parties in Switzerland.[1] He takes into consideration only those parties that are needed as coalition partners or that have a sufficiently great "power of intimidation" to influence the tactics of party competition. Sartori formulates the first criterion as follows: "A minor party can be discounted as irrelevant whenever it remains superfluous over time in the sense that it is never needed or put to use for any feasible coalition majority. Conversely, a minor party has to be counted, no matter how small, if it finds itself in a position to determine at least one of the possible governmental majorities."[2] Sartori's second criterion is that "a party is 'big enough' to qualify for relevance whenever its existence, or appearance, affects the tactics of party competition, and particularly when it alters the direction of party competition (e.g., by determining a switch from centripetal to centrifugal competition) of one or more of the major governing oriented parties."[3]

In Sartori's typology the Swiss party system would be characterized by moderate pluralism; he counts all party systems with from three to five relevant parties as belonging to this type. In a moderately pluralistic party system the parties are "likely to be 'moderate' in their platforms and behavior."[4] Such a party system would furthermore be characterized "by a unilateral opposition, by the absence of relevant antisystem parties, and hence by a bipolar mechanism of competition between governing oriented parties."[5] The four politically relevant parties in Switzerland referred to by Sartori are obviously those which, since 1959, have distributed the seven seats in the federal government among themselves according to the so-called magic formula, 2:2:2:1. They are the Free Democratic party, the Christian Democratic party, and the Social Democratic party with two seats each, and the Swiss People's party with one seat.[6] As is shown in table 1 these four parties have an overwhelming majority in the Federal Assembly, which is composed of the National Council and the Council of States, and occupy 83 percent of all seats. Are the small parties which are without representation in the federal government, actually—as Sartori assumes—

TABLE 1. DISTRIBUTION OF SEATS IN THE FEDERAL ASSEMBLY AFTER THE FEDERAL ELECTION IN 1971

Parties	National Council	Council of States	Federal Assembly
Free Democrats	49	15	64
Christian Democrats	44	17	61
Social Democrats	46	4	50
Swiss People's party	23	5	28
Independents	13	1	14
Liberal Democrats	6	2	8
Republicans	7	0	7
Communists	5	0	5
Anti-Aliens	4	0	4
Protestants	3	0	3
Total	200	44	244

Source: *Statistisches Jahrbuch der Schweiz 1972*, p. 558.

without political relevance? At first glance one might be tempted to agree, since these parties are not only small but also extremely heterogeneous. Thus the Communist party is situated on the extreme left of the Swiss party continuum, the Anti-Alien party and the Republican party on the extreme right. Because of this heterogeneity the nongovernment parties have never acted in unified opposition. If Switzerland were a centralized state with a "normal" parliamentary system, Sartori would no doubt be right in his assertion that only the four government parties are politically relevant. For in such a case the heterogeneous nongovernment parties would hardly be in demand as coalition partners or exert sufficiently great "power of intimidation" to influence the competition among the major parties in a decisive way. But Switzerland has a strongly federal structure and a parliamentary system that includes the institution of *direct democracy*.

By direct democracy at the federal level we mean that all constitutional changes are subject to a referendum. In addition, the electorate has the right to initiate constitutional changes by a petition of 50,000 signatures. A petition of 30,000 voters or eight cantons can also require a federal law or a general federal decree to be subjected to a referendum.[7] If, according to Sartori's hypothesis, only four parties in Switzerland have political relevance, it would indicate that the other parties either could not gather the necessary signatures for an initiative or referendum, or that they at least always lost in the referenda. However, the history of Swiss referenda shows that not only the parties of the Federal Council, but also the lesser parties have been able to collect the required number of signatures, and have been successful in referenda. The most remarkable example of success by a lesser party in recent years is the referendum on May 27, 1962, concerning a proposal for an increase in the compensation for the members of the National Council. This referendum was necessitated by the intervention of the Free Citizens party, a party so small that it is not even represented in the Federal Assembly. Its activity is restricted to the canton of Aargau, where it occupied only five out of two hundred seats in the cantonal Parliament at that time. This tiny party succeeded in collecting the necessary 30,000 signatures. Furthermore, the referendum was successful, and the proposal to increase the salaries of the members of the National Council was defeated overwhelmingly. Even though the proposal had the support of all the parties represented in the Federal Council, the referendum against the proposal succeeded by a vote of 381,229 to 176,737.[8] Larger nongovernment parties, notably the Independent party, make use of the right to initiatives and referenda fairly frequently, and not simply on questions of secondary political matters, as in the referendum of the Free Citizens party.[9]

However, it must be said that the right to popular initiative and referendum is restricted by financial constraints. The introduction of an initiative or a referendum and the management of the subsequent campaign is a rather costly affair. François Masnata estimates that the costs might be somewhere between 100,000 and 1,000,000 francs.[10] The wide range of the estimate is justified because the costs vary greatly with the subject of the referendum. If it is a popular matter, it is relatively easy to collect the necessary signatures, and the referendum propaganda can be kept within moderate limits. These preconditions might have existed for the referendum of the Free Citizens party, which was able to count on the support of widespread antiparliamentary sentiments.

If, in contrast, a referendum concerns a matter that is not yet that popular, the financial outlay has to be considerably larger. Therefore, although it is technically possible for a small party to make use of the right to initiative and referendum, it is improbable on a practical level. One must conclude that these small parties, because of the institution of referendum, do have some political relevance, but it is limited to certain political situations. Yet the significance of the small parties may be greater than can be inferred from the number of initiatives and referenda they have called for. The fact that a small party may make use of the initiative or the referendum often influences the large parties to anticipate the demands of the small parties.

In order to determine how many politically relevant parties there are in Switzerland, not only the federal subsystem, but also the subsystems of the cantons and the local communities must be analyzed. Because of the strongly federal structure of Switzerland, the twenty-five cantons and more than three thousand local communities are administrative units as well as independent authorities in many areas. Some parties without representation in the Federal Council have governmental responsibility at the cantonal and local levels and therefore cannot be considered politically irrelevant. At the cantonal level the Liberal Democratic party has the strongest government representation of any of the parties: it participates in the government of the cantons of Basel-City, Geneva, Neuchâtel, and Vaud. The Democratic party is represented in the governments of the cantons of Glarus and Graubuenden, and the Independent party in the canton of Zurich.[11] At the local level the picture is even more varied. Here even the Communist party assumes governmental functions. For example, it is represented in the executives, or city councils, of the local communities of Geneva, Chaux-de-Fonds, and Le Locle. At this level the picture is particularly complex because the local executives often have representatives from parties whose activity is limited to the community. For instance, in the city of Berne a party called the Young Berne is represented in the executive.

It seems to me that it has been possible to disprove Sartori's proposition that there are only four politically relevant parties in the political system of Switzerland by recognizing the influence of the federal structure and the institution of the referendum.

An intensive analysis of the party system of Switzerland would have to examine the subsystems of the federation, the twenty-five cantons, and the more than three thousand local communities. In a study of the party system on all three levels, Roger Girod makes a distinction between two types, or, as he calls them, *formulas of party systems.*[12] One type includes systems in which *one* party has had the absolute majority for a relatively long period of time (the *formula of the dominant party*); the other type is one in which no party has an absolute majority (the *formula of multipartism*). A two-party system in which the absolute majority alternates between the two parties exists nowhere in Switzerland. Girod breaks down the dominant-party type into two subtypes, the *solitary-party type* and the *predominant-party type,* by investigating the existence of parties other than the dominant party. Appenzell Inner Rhoden is the only solitary-party type canton, with the Christian Democrats being the single party. It hardly seems possible to classify Appenzell Inner Rhoden in a meaningful way within Sartori's typology. Appenzell Inner Rhoden can be classified only as having a one-party system. According to Sartori this category only includes systems "which do not permit the existence of any other party . . . whose peculiar feature is to veto—both *de jure* and *de facto*—any kind of party pluralism."[13] These characteristics, however, are not applicable to Appenzell Inner Rhoden: by law as well as by fact any other party would be able to be active.[14] Indeed, at one time the Free Democratic party was active, but it ceased to function as a result of continued lack of success. Girod argues that the homogeneity of the canton explains the one-party situation: "The solitary party formula of this very old, small mountainous republic of Catholic faith (with a total population of 13,000, of whom nearly 5,000 inhabit the main town which is simply a large village) is the result of its marked religious unity, of the economic and social homogeneity of its people, and of the simplicity and cohesion of its traditional hierarchic structure."[15]

The Christian Democratic party has a very rudimentary organization in Appenzell Inner Rhoden. Essentially it limits its activity to an annual meeting that is attended by only thirty to forty members.[16] The party is so insignificant that the Federal Statistics Office declares in its publications that there can be no differentiation according to party in the Parliament of Appenzell Inner Rhoden.[17] The Christian Democratic character of the canton can be seen only in the fact that both representatives in the federal Parliament belong to the Christian Democratic parliamentary group.[18] The Christian Democratic party, then, does not dominate the political life of Appenzell Inner Rhoden as in the one-party system in Sartori's typology. The main characteristic of political life in the canton is not that only one party exists, but that all political forces cooperate. Because of the homogeneity of the canton the different political forces have not organized as separate parties. The only existing party circumscribes political life in a way hardly noticed by the public. Girod correctly calls this party system embryonic.[19] If we compare Appenzell Inner Rhoden with the other cantons, we notice great similarities, although it is the only canton with one party. As is yet to be seen, all cantons show a trend toward the cooperation of all political forces. As Girod suggests, the Swiss party system is a "party system which tends towards an overall alliance of all political forces."[20] Appenzell Inner Rhoden is "but one incomplete . . . variety of that system."[21]

The example of Appenzell Inner Rhoden implies that the number of parties is not as great a factor in the formulation of an effective typology of party systems as Sartori assumes. It is difficult to classify cases such as Appenzell Inner Rhoden in a meaningful way if we rely only on a quantitative criterion. A typology of party systems is, in my opinion, not so much a question of the number of parties as it is of other characteristics. For example, Gerhard Lehmbruch has suggested another typology of liberal democratic political systems.[22] It is composed of the following elements: (a) a competitive pattern of conflict management (of which the fundamental device is the majority principle); (b) a noncompetitive "cartelized" pluralist pattern that works by *amicabilis compositio* (amicable agreement); and (c) conflict management by an interaction of bureaucratic arbitration (that works by hierarchy) and democratic control.

Appenzell Inner Rhoden can be classified relatively easily in Lehmbruch's typology. Based on Girod's analysis we can say that it approximates the type in which political conflicts are regulated primarily by amicable agreement. According to Lehmbruch, "This [type] refers to political systems, which—along with a democratic and parliamentary constitution—are characterized by the predominance of a peculiar pattern of conflict regulation among the most important political groups: The majority principle is to a large extent replaced by the principle which was called *amicabilis compositio* in the Peace of Westphalia. Such an amicable agreement is as a rule made institutionally secure by the fact that the most important groups are represented in the government and assert their influence on political decisions by extensive patronage in the distribution of office."[23] In Appenzell Inner Rhoden all important groups are represented in the government in accordance with the type described by Lehmbruch. It is of relatively little importance that all these groups belong to the same party, for the degree of organization of this party is so low that it hardly has any weight as a reference group. The type of democratic system described by Lehmbruch in terms of a "noncompetitive, 'cartelized' pluralist pattern" corresponds roughly to Arend Lijphart's *consociational democracy*. Lijphart considers an "overarching cooperation at the elite level with the deliberate aim of counteracting disintegrative tendencies in the system" as the principal characteristic of a consociational democracy.[24] For the time being these references to the typologies of Lehmbruch and Lijphart will suffice. I will repeatedly return to them in more detail below.

Although Appenzell Inner Rhoden is the only case of the solitary-party type at the federal and the cantonal levels, its characteristics are not uncommon at the local level. Unfortunately there is no systematic analysis available of the party systems of the more than three thousand local communities in Switzerland; nevertheless, I have been able to study some communities in the canton of Berne. It appears that in small isolated rural communities with an agrarian structure the Swiss People's party is frequently the only party.[25] The party system in communities of this kind is usually structured like that of Appenzell Inner Rhoden: it is characterized above all by the cooperation of all the political forces of the communities. Thus the different regions and occupational groups of the community are usually represented in the local executive. It is not important in the regulation of political conflict that all members of the local executive belong to the Swiss People's party because the party hardly ever acts in a decision-making capacity with regard to local political affairs. The party becomes active almost only when it is a question of proposing candidates from the community for cantonal or federal office. A typology primarily oriented to the number of parties cannot clearly characterize the essential features of such communities. It is almost accidental that there is only *one* formal party in these communities inasmuch as different political groupings in local politics have, to a large extent, the character of quasi-parties. Thus in many areas the farmers and the artisans form two separate groups that pursue their own policies independently. I should like to suggest that there would be no decisive change in local politics if farmers and artisans were not united in the same party, but formed two distinct parties. After all, the principal characteristic of these communities is that the regulation of conflict conforms to the pattern of amicable agreement. No great change in that pattern would result if the political groupings of the community were organized as separate parties.

If we assume that the number of parties is the main feature of a typology, then the solitary-party type in the canton of Appenzell Inner Rhoden and in various rural communities deviates markedly from the party systems of the rest of Switzerland. If, on the other hand, we assume that the primary attribute of a typology is the method of conflict regulation—an assumption that seems to be more appropriate—we can see a wide-ranging similarity between Appenzell Inner Rhoden, the various rural communities, and other party systems because the principle of amicable agreement in Switzerland is ubiquitous.

In Girod's predominant-party type, *one* party has an absolute majority in Parliament for a long time. Girod finds this type of party system in the cantons of Appenzell Ausser Rhoden, Lucerne, Nidwalden, Obwalden, Schwyz, Uri, Wallis, and Zug. The Free Democratic party has the absolute majority in Appenzell Ausser Rhoden, the

Christian Democratic party in the rest of these cantons.[26] In applying Sartori's typology to these cantons we encounter difficulties once again. Sartori does indeed provide for the case of the predominant party, but restricts it to such an extent that it is no longer applicable. He defines the predominant-party system as "the type of party pluralism which is characterized by the fact that no alternation in office occurs over time, even though alternation is not ruled out and the political system provides all the opportunities of open and effective dissent, i.e., for opposing the predominance of the ruling party. . . . it simply happens that the same party manages to win, over time, an absolute majority of seats (not necessarily of votes) in parliament."[27] It is crucial to Sartori's argument that in the predominant-party system "no alternation in power occurs (de facto) for a considerable length of time."[28] Sartori obviously assumes that the party with an absolute majority in Parliament is the only government party and thus is able to exercise power. This assumption, however, does not hold for the Swiss cantons listed by Girod, in all of which the predominant party shares the executive power with other parties. Moreover, the distribution of posts in the government is always roughly proportionate to the strength of the parties in Parliament. In many cases the small parties are even favored. For instance, the Social Democratic party has one seat in the seven-member government in the canton of Lucerne although the party had won only 6 percent of all parliamentary seats after the election in 1971.[29]

The crucial aspect of the party system in these cantons is evidently not that *one* party has the absolute majority in Parliament. Sartori's typology is not tenable because it assumes that the regulation of conflict conforms to the majority principle. He concludes that in a predominant-party system power must be exclusively with *one* party. This is not true in the Swiss party systems of this type because the primary pattern of conflict regulation is amicable agreement.

Girod's second main type in the Swiss party system is the formula of multipartism, in which, in contrast to the formula of the dominant party, no party has an absolute majority of seats in Parliament. Girod attempts to differentiate the formula of multipartism according to the dominance of either three or more than three parties in politics. With the "three-party formula . . . three parties dominate the political life of the canton, none of the three having the majority in the cantonal parliament, all three (and only they) being represented regularly in the Executive Council."[30] Under this type he lists the cantons of Berne, Schaffhausen, Solothurn, St. Gallen, Freiburg, and

Ticino.[31] According to the typologies of Lehmbruch and Lijphart the principle of amicable agreement is also predominant in the party systems of these cantons, for the three parties are represented in the government roughly according to their parliamentary strength, and there are no attempts—as would be the case in the type conforming to the competitive pattern—to form a coalition of two parties against the third. In the canton of Solothurn the *three-party formula* was for a long time to be found in its pure form, since there was no fourth party either in or out of Parliament.[32] In the other cantons mentioned by Girod there is, however, at least *one* small party besides the three government parties. After the election in the canton of Berne in 1970 the three government parties—the Swiss People's party, the Social Democratic party, and the Free Democratic party—held 179 of the total 200 seats in Parliament, the 21 remaining seats going to four smaller parties.[33] In his typology Girod does not take the nongovernmental parties into consideration because he only counts the parties that dominate politics. Girod defines the rather vague "dominate" in terms of participation in the government. This criterion would presumably be justified in a pure parliamentary system, for 21 representatives would hardly be able to accomplish much before a government majority of 179. However, in the Berne canton, where the referendum exists, it is a somewhat different matter. The canton of Berne is, at the present time, confronted with the question of whether to build an airport. The Independent party, one of the small nongovernment parties, is violently opposed to this project. In a pure parliamentary system this opposition would not be relevant, for the Independent representatives could not possibly have their way in Parliament because of their low number. By referendum, which is obligatory for such a project in Berne, the propaganda of the Independent party could, on the other hand, have a decisive effect in some circumstances. In fact, it happens not infrequently that the voters in a referendum about a specific case do not follow the recommendations of the party for which they usually vote. As I learned through participant observation, the government parties are quite aware that the opposition of the Independent party may be important to the outcome of the referendum.[34]

Since small parties using the referendum may become politically relevant under certain circumstances, one cannot ignore them in a typology of party systems. To be sure, Girod's typology does not refer expressly to a party's political relevance, but to whether it belongs to the dominant parties. In a system in which influence by referenda is crucial, however, this criterion is so difficult to measure that it does not appear useful to me. Furthermore, it remains unclear precisely what Girod intends the concept of the dominant party to mean. To what extent must a party influence the political events to qualify as dominant? This is a question he does not answer clearly. At least in view of the importance of referenda in the Swiss system, it seems strangely rigid to consider participation in government as the only criterion for party dominance.

Girod includes systems with more than three parties under the type of the *pronounced multiparty formula.* According to his counting method this type covers the party systems of the federation and the cantons of Zurich, Glarus, Basel-City, Basel-Country, Graubuenden, Aargau, Thurgau, Vaud, Neuchâtel, and Geneva. In Zurich the government consists of five parties: the government of the federation is represented by four parties as are the other cantons. With the exception of Geneva the composition of the government is roughly proportionate to the strength of the parties in Parliament. Only in Geneva is a party with a proportionate claim to representation in government affairs excluded. This is the Communist party, which, after the election in 1969 had 18 percent of the seats in Parliament, a percentage that should have given it a right to one of the seven positions in the government. That it was denied this by the other parties for ideological reasons indicates that in the canton of Geneva the principle of amicable agreement does not apply to the Communists. This makes the party system of Geneva a remarkable exception to that of the other cantons. It is not that the other cantons are more friendly to the Communists, but that the party does not have the parliamentary quota needed for participation in government in the other cantons. The case of Geneva shows that there is a limit to the principle of amicable agreement even in Switzerland. This limit is evidently reached when a party does not adhere to the basic democratic principles. Such a party is then excluded, for all practical purposes, from the common pattern of political cooperation. At present these sanctions apply only to the Communist party.[35] All other parties may participate in government if they have the necessary percentage of seats in Parliament.

After having surveyed the party systems of the federation and the cantons with a few side-glances at the local communities we can return once more to Sartori's typology. It is representative of typologies that fail to account for party systems in which the principle of amicable agreement is the primary pattern of conflict regulation. Sartori tacitly assumes that the majority principle is the rule in party systems. Under this assumption it is understandable that he primarily investigates party systems with respect to the number of relevant parties and majority conditions. The fixation on these two quantitative criteria makes it impossible for Sartori to place the Swiss party systems in his typology in a meaningful way. I have already stated that Sartori is able to imagine only one-party systems in which the solitary party has eliminated competition from other parties by suppressing them. To Sartori, then, one-party systems are always authoritarian or totalitarian regimes. With this perspective Sartori cannot account for such party systems as that of Appenzell Inner Rhoden. To classify such systems meaningfully one has to realize that for them it is the principle of amicable agreement and not that of party competition which has primacy. Therefore the existence of only one party does not necessarily mean that other parties have been eliminated. The examples given above show that it may be strong social homogeneity that prevents the formation of more than one party.

We have also seen that Sartori's typology does not do justice to the party systems of those cantons in which there are several parties, with one having the absolute majority in Parliament for a long time. Since Sartori assumes that the parties are in a permanent state of competition, he can only present a type in which the majority party is continuously in power. Such a type, however, ignores the realities of Swiss politics in which the party with the absolute majority lets the minority parties participate in government according to their strength in Parliament. This fact is probably the clearest evidence that amicable agreement and not the majority principle has priority in Switzerland.

Neither is Sartori's typology useful in classifying those party systems in Switzerland in which no party has the absolute majority in Parliament. In the case of such multiparty systems it makes a decisive difference to Sartori if the number of relevant parties exceeds five. If there are five or fewer parties, it is a case of *moderate pluralism*: "The parties are likely to be 'moderate' in their platforms and behavior. . . . the political system operates, at base, according to a bipolar alignment of the government-opposition kind."[36] If, on the other hand, the number of parties is in excess of five, it is a case of *extreme pluralism*: "[There is] party 'fragmentation' . . . in the sense that extremistic appeals largely condition the overall drift of the polity. . . . The system no longer has a dualistic configuration, its structural mechanics pivot on three poles (at least) and hence the system is multipolar."[37] In differentiating between moderate and extreme pluralism Sartori evidently assumes that there is competition in the formation of the government so that the party coalition with the absolute majority in Parliament always comes out as the winner. Sartori furthermore assumes that the character of this competition depends on whether the number of relevant parties is more or less than five. Amicable agreement and participation in government according to parliamentary strength do not present themselves to him as alternatives. Had he consciously limited his typology to party systems with a competitive pattern (as defined by Lehmbruch), this omission could not have been held against him. However, Sartori characterizes Switzerland as a four-party system and consequently an example of moderate pluralism. I have already shown that Switzerland as a whole, in view of its federalism and the institution of direct democracy, has more than four relevant parties. Even if the concept of political relevance were defined narrowly with the inclusion of only the two largest nongovernment parties, the Independent party and the Liberal Democratic party, there would still be six parties, and consequently the party system of Switzerland would fall under the type of extreme pluralism. According to Sartori's typology this would lead to the expectation that the Swiss parties held extreme views. However, just the opposite is the case. As Girod states, with the exception of the small Communist party, there is a strong consensus among Swiss parties: "This consensus is absolute with respect to the political regime [federalism, direct democracy]. It is almost equally strong concerning the relations between Church and State. . . . We have seen how far this consensus has come in socio-economic affairs. . . . Under these conditions it is hardly possible for the parties to be in opposition about anything but strongly technical questions of application and dosage. The great controversies over basic principles have no current interest."[38] I will try to describe in detail the reasons for this consensus among Swiss parties. At the moment the task is to show that the party system of Switzerland is by no means a case of extreme pluralism.

That Sartori's typology cannot be used in Switzerland at any level is explained solely by the fact that it is far too strongly oriented to party systems with a competitive pattern. This discussion of Sartori's views should have made it clear that Swiss party systems are fundamentally different from party systems in which conflicts among parties are primarily regulated by the majority principle. According to Lehmbruch the decisive characteristic of the Swiss party system is that interparty conflict frequently is regulated by amicable agreement.[39] I agree with Lehmbruch that a typology of party systems in liberal democracies is likely to be more fruitful if one first asks whether the regulation of conflict follows the principle of majority rule or of amicable agreement.

Lehmbruch cites the Anglo-Saxon countries and Scandinavia as examples of majority rule, and Austria, Lebanon, and Switzerland as examples of amicable agreement. He introduces a third category to facilitate the classification of countries like France, the Federal Republic of Germany, and Italy in which the conflict regulation consists of an "interaction of bureaucratic arbitration (which works by hierarchy) and democratic control."[40] In this context we do not have to decide if this third category is meaningful and necessary. The important thing is to keep the two main categories carefully apart and not to confuse them in an inadmissible way as Sartori does.

Like Lehmbruch, Girod considers the cooperation of the parties the principal characteristic of the Swiss party system: "The party system which operates in Switzerland today is without doubt of a particular kind. All the parties, with the exception of certain marginal groups, cooperate on a permanent basis within the executive council. This overall alliance is not in any way disturbed by competition in elections which serve only to record the very small fluctuations in party popularity."[41] In his typology Girod attempts to classify the federal, the cantonal and, in part, the local subsystems. Like Sartori, he bases his typology primarily on two quantitative criteria: the number of parties and the relationships among the majority parties in Parliament. He cites four types in all: (1) the solitary party, (2) the predominant party, (3) the three-party formula, and (4) the pronounced multiple-party formula.

Girod admits implicitly that his typology has little theoretical import for Swiss politics. This can be shown from his distinction between the three-party formula and the pronounced multiple-party formula. He more or less restricts himself to a description of the cantons in these two categories. For instance, he finds that two of the five cantons (Berne and Schaffhausen) in his three-party formula are predominantly Protestant, one (Ticino) is predominantly Catholic, and two (Solothurn and St. Gallen) are religiously mixed. The pronounced multiple-party formula shows an equally diverse distribution so that the religious structure is not a differentiating characteristic of the two types. Girod also tries to determine which parties in both types participate in the government of the cantons. There is no clear difference between the three-party formula and the pronounced multiple-party formula here either: the Free Democratic party and the Social Democratic party are represented in the governments of all these cantons. In the three-party formula cantons the third party is the Swiss People's party in two cases (Berne and Schaffhausen) and the Christian Democratic party in three cases (Solothurn, St. Gallen, and Ticino). In the pronounced multiple-party formula cantons the following parties are represented in the government in addition to the Social Democratic party and the Free Democratic party: the Christian Democratic party, the Swiss People's party, and the Independent party (Zurich), the Christian Democratic party and the Democratic party (Glarus and Graubuenden), the Christian Democratic party and the Liberal Democratic party (Basel-City and Geneva), the Christian Democratic party and the Swiss People's party (Basel-Country, Aargau, and Thurgau), the Liberal Democratic party and the Swiss People's party (Vaud), and the Liberal Democratic party and the National Progressive party (Neuchâtel).[42] A comparison of the party structures of these two categories shows such a diffuse picture that Girod does not even try to determine the distinguishing characteristics. Girod also tries to determine if there are significant differences between the two types with respect to the total number of parties. Here, too, his conclusion is negative: "Those cantons in which there is a pronounced multi-partism do not have more parties than those with a three-party formula."[43] I have carried the comparison between the two types somewhat further than Girod, but have found no significant differences between the two types with respect to electoral participation or the fluctuations in election outcomes.

It seems, therefore, that both groups of cantons suggested by Girod are essentially different only with respect to the number of parties in the government, i.e., the defining characteristic of his typology. This means, of course, that the value of the typology must be assumed to be low. I do not mean to assert that the number of parties in the government has no importance whatsoever, but I do believe I have shown that this criterion cannot have primacy in a typology of Swiss party systems. Girod's typology is not much more useful if we include his two other types—the solitary party and the predominant party—in our considerations. For none of the four types does he give precise characteristics other than the definitions. Consequently, Girod's typology is of a different kind than the one proposed by Sartori. Sartori gives so much substantive meaning to his categories that they become irrelevant within the Swiss context. Girod has avoided this trap by giving them only a formal definition without any substantive content. Hence, Girod's typology is applicable: nothing prevents us from classifying the cantons according to the number of government parties and the criterion of whether *one* party has an absolute majority in Parliament. His classification, however, is not very meaningful because he does not show how the varying types differ except in definition. I attribute this deficiency to the fact that Girod used criteria that are important in party systems with a competitive pattern, but not in those with a noncompetitive pattern. The number of parties and the relationships of the majority parties in Parliament are less important in Switzerland because all parties with the necessary proportional claim are admitted to the government more or less automatically. Therefore, there is no need for coalition talks that might otherwise be occasions for giving importance to the number and strength of parties.[44]

A change of population in the canton of Zurich recently demonstrated that the number of government parties hardly influences the character of the system. Catholic immigration in Zurich had strengthened the Christian Democratic party to the extent that it had become proportionally entitled to a seat in the government. In 1963 a representative was elected to the cantonal government and this meant an increase in the number of governmental parties from four to five. However, essentially no change in the political system of the canton of Zurich took place. It might also be hypothesized that no fundamental change would occur in the federal system, if, for instance, the Independent party succeeded in gaining enough strength to move into the federal government as the fifth party.

It is still necessary to determine the criteria to be used in developing a typology that could meaningfully categorize the various party systems at the federal, the cantonal, and the local levels. We have seen that the number of parties and the majority relationships alone are not the answers. It is more relevant to look at the principal cleavage lines and to determine whether the main antagonisms are between the bourgeois and socialist parties or between the clerical and anticlerical parties. It is also of great relevance to know whether cleavages occur within the parties themselves.

In developing a typology along all these lines, Stein Rokkan's study of the smaller European democracies presents itself as a point of departure. His is a genetic approach that aims "to pin down the crucial differences from country to country in the sequences of the establishment of the rule of the electoral game and in the formation of party alternatives."[45] Rokkan uses two models in this sequential analysis. With one model the crucial factors are "the timing and speed of decision at four '*threshold points*': the protection of the rights of the opposition, the extension of the suffrage, the lowering of the barriers of representation, and the entry into the Executive."[46] With the second model Rokkan attempts to make a classification "of '*systems options*' at four critical junctures in the history of each nation: the Reformation, the National Revolution after 1789, the Industrial Revolution and the International Revolution after 1917."[47] From the behavior of the individual countries in these decisive historical questions and situations, Rokkan develops "a typology of cleavage structures and these again offer a basis for predictions of the salient characteristics of the national party systems."[48]

In order to apply Rokkan's approach to the party systems of the Swiss cantons, it would be necessary to determine the decisive sequences in the history of the cantons. One such sequence could be the struggle between clerical and anticlerical forces in the nineteenth century. The cantons could be classified according to the severity of this struggle. This classification would presumably show that the cantons of Lucerne, Solothurn, St. Gallen, Aargau, and Ticino belong in the group with the most intense antagonisms. If this group is contrasted with the other group, it appears that the relations between the Christian Democratic party and the Free Democratic party differ in each group. In the cantons where there was a hard struggle between the clerical and the anticlerical forces, the present party system is characterized by a strong antagonism between the Free Democrats and the Christian Democrats. This may be caused by the fact that both parties in the nineteenth century—though at that time they were not organized as parties in the modern meaning of the term—confronted each other as clerical and anticlerical. This antagonism has apparently petrified in the party systems of these cantons even if the intense antagonism of clerical and anticlerical forces has died away. In contrast, the cantons without acute antagonisms in this nineteenth century struggle show a tendency to friendly relations between the Free Democrats and the Christian Democrats and a close mutual cooperation within the group of bourgeois parties.

This example has shown how the different responses of the cantons in an important historical sequence may lead to different cleavage structures in their party systems. It is now a question of discovering further sequences that were followed by a "freeze" of party antagonisms. This would gradually lead to a multidimensional typology that would allow for a meaningful classification of the party systems of the cantons. However, this task cannot be accomplished within the scope of this book.[49]

The Historical Development of the Party System of Switzerland

In order to give the proper historical depth to this analysis, it would be worthwhile to inquire if the noncompetitive pattern of the party system of Switzerland is rooted deep in Swiss history, or if it is, instead, a relatively new phenomenon. In 1919, when the elections to the National Council were carried out for the first time according to the proportional system, the Social Democrats won 41 of 189 seats. In the 44-seat Council of States, whose members are chosen in a different way in different cantons, the Social Democrats were not yet represented. Thus they had a total of 41 out of 233 seats in the Federal Assembly, composed of the two councils together, which should have given them a right to *one* seat on the Federal Council. They did not get this seat until 1943, when, with 61 of 238 seats in the Federal Assembly, they actually had claim to two seats. It was not until 1959 that the Federal Council represented all parties proportionally. At this time two representatives of the Social Democratic party were elected to the federal government. This party had previously either been underrepresented, or not represented at all in the national government.

Even among the bourgeois parties the principle of proportional representation was slow in coming. From the founding of the federal state in 1848 until 1891 the Federal Council consisted entirely of Free Democrats who had won a military victory over the Christian Democrats (then called Conservatives). The Christian Democrats were finally allowed one seat in 1891, and in 1919, a second, making the ratio of members 5:2 in favor of the Free Democrats, although in that year they did not even have twice as many seats in the Federal Assembly as the Christian Democrats (there were 86 Free Democrats to 58 Christian Democrats). It was not until 1953 that the Christian Democrats finally reached the number of seats in the Federal Council they deserved according to their strength in the assembly. The Farmer, Artisan, and Bourgeois party, which separated from the Free Democrats after World War I, has had one seat since 1929, which conforms roughly to its proportional claim. (In 1971 the Farmer, Artisan, and Bourgeois party united on the federal level with the Democratic party to form the Swiss People's party.)

This historical sketch shows that it was a long way from the founding of the federal state until the functioning of the so-called magic formula of 2:2:2:1 in 1959, which allows the four large national parties to participate in the government according to their strength in Parliament. Since this is a new phenomenon, one might assume that the principle of amicable agreement has no deep roots in Swiss history. There is, however, a great deal of evidence against such an assumption. One must first bear in mind that the cantons and local communities have had proportional composition of the executive for some time. As early as 1854 the Free Democrats and the Conservatives had formed a coalition government in the Berne canton where governments had previously been formed of either all Free Democrats or all Conservatives. The Social Democrats were first allowed to participate in governmental responsibilities in 1897, when one of their representatives was elected to the government of the Geneva canton.[50] According to Girod's analysis, the cantons had begun to follow the principle of proportional composition much earlier than the federation. By 1959 both of the newly elected Social Democrats in the Federal Council had had previous experience in cantonal or local government.

Economic interest groups, as well as the cantons and local communities, preceded the federal government in their use of the principle of amicable agreement. An important example of its use in industry was the 1937 "peace treaty" between the Metal and Watch Workers' Union and the corresponding Employers' Organization, in which both parties pledged to solve conflicts by negotiations, and to avoid coercive measures such as strikes and lockouts.[51] By the end of 1971, 1,389 such agreements had been made between employees and employers.[52] There were only 28 strikes from 1961 to 1971, involving 102 plants and 4,449 workers, in which a total of 90,681 working hours were lost.[53]

The Federal Council has always represented language groups more or less proportionally. Since the first Federal Council in 1848, which included one representative each from the French- and Italian-speaking parts of Switzerland, the former has always had at least one council seat, while the latter has almost always been represented. It is important to keep in mind that the council, even in the time of Free Democratic "one-party rule" in the last century, has never been a homogeneous group with unified party goals. This can be attributed to the fact that the Free Democrats at that time were a very heterogeneous group, assembled from different geographic areas and from the various language, religious, and occupational groups. The Free Democrats did not organize themselves as a national party until 1894.[54] This heterogeneity was reflected in the composition of the Federal Council, whose chief task was to arbitrate the interest differences among its members and to find compromise solutions. The various political tendencies within the Free Democratic Federal Council seemed at times to be so pronounced that Numa Droz, who was a council member from 1875 to 1892, could even speak of different parties: "According to the epoch, this or that party complained about being represented insufficiently, or even not at all in the executive power. From 1875 to 1883, without going back further in time, the Left was irritated because it had only two or three federal councilors, although it had almost an absolute majority in the two chambers. Later, the Center and Right recriminated, because the Left could count five or six out of seven members."[55] This quotation reveals that some proportionalization of the Federal Council could be identified even in the last century. Gerhard Lehmbruch rightly maintains that "the election of Joseph Zemp in 1891 as the first Christian Democrat in the Federal Council and the consequent demise of the Free Democrats in the composition of the executive does not mean a change in the system, but a consistent further development of it."[56] Erich Gruner asserts that "contrary to common opinion, the Federal Council had no uniform political line, even before the introduction of the proportional formula."[57]

These historical facts indicate that the roots of proportionality reach back to the beginnings of the modern Swiss federation in 1848.[58] If we were to attempt to find further historical evidence, we would see that the principle of amicable agreement was the principal pattern of conflict regulation in earlier Swiss history as well. Decisions that affected all cantons required a unanimous agreement in the Diet, the representative body before 1848. Because of this institutional regulation, there was strong pressure to find compromise solutions that would be agreeable to all cantons. However, this regulation asked too much from the principle of amicable agreement. Since it was often impossible to reach agreement among all cantons, decisions had to be indefinitely postponed for many important questions. The strongest pressure to find common solutions came from the common dependent areas of the cantons (Gemeine Herrschaften).[59] The cantons succeeded in developing for these areas some sort of functioning administrative organization through complicated proportional regulations. Even after Switzerland was split by the Reformation, the proportional administration of the common dependent areas was able to survive.

It is also important to understand that the idea of proportionality succeeded in the political life of the individual cantons. In the rural cantons as well as in the patrician city cantons it was customary that all the important families participated in the government. It was definitely exceptional that in 1732 in Appenzell Ausser Rhoden, Zellweger, the leading family, was ousted from political office by opposition under the leadership of Wetter, the rival family.[60]

If we survey the history of Switzerland since the oath of federation in 1291, we can see a clear tendency toward the regulation of political conflict by compromise rather than by authoritarian decisions or by majority rule. Seen in this historical light, the complete proportionalization of the Federal Council in 1959 appears not as a change or innovation, but as the conclusion of a long historical development. What made for good relationships among the cantons and among the leading families in early Swiss history, and what, since the founding of the modern federation in 1848, has developed into a working model for the various language groups, economic interest groups, and cantonal and local parties, was finally applied in 1959 to the parties in the federal government. We can say, then, that this common pattern, the desire to resolve conflicts by amicable agreement among all concerned parties, has been prominent throughout the history of Switzerland.

The Articulation and Aggregation of Demands in the Party System of Switzerland

In party systems with a competitive pattern, government and opposition parties confront one another. Switzerland has a party system that I have termed noncompetitive because all major parties participate in the government. But what are the possibilities for the opposition's articulation of demands within noncompetitive party systems? First, it should be noted that the government parties themselves can choose to oppose government policies. The principle of amicable agreement is not interpreted so widely that the government parties have to agree to a common policy in each and every case. The principle of amicable agreement among the Swiss parties consists primarily in the participation of each party in government according to its strength in Parliament. Oppositional behavior is made easier for the government parties because the institution of a government platform does not exist in the political system of Switzerland. Some explanation of the way the government is chosen may be necessary to understand this. The Federal Assembly, consisting of the National Council and the Council of States, is the constituency of the Federal Council. At the beginning of each legislative period there is total renewal of the Federal Council for a term of four years. It is not elected on one ballot, but there is one ballot for each of the seven members. Furthermore, the incumbents who run again can usually count on being reelected. There have been only two exceptions to this rule so far and both in the previous century.

This mode of election makes it virtually impossible for the Federal Council to present a platform before its election. As the members of the Federal Council are elected individually, the final composition of the government is not known until the election is over. What functions then do the government parties perform under such an electoral system? It can be stated that the government parties are not compelled to agree upon a platform before the Federal Council is elected. With respect to its personal composition, there has developed a complex pattern of interactions among the government parties. Each government party nominates its candidates independently, but the parties are not always willing to accept one another's favorite candidates. If an official party candidate is not agreeable to the other parties, Parliament will elect another candidate, usually of the same party. In 1959 the Social Democratic party nominated the mayor of Schaffhausen, Walther Bringolf, as candidate for the Federal Council. Instead of Bringolf, who was criticized for his Communist past, the Federal Assembly elected Hans-Peter Tschudi from Basel. The Christian Democratic party had a similar experience when its official candidate Ettore Tenchio was rejected in favor of Roger Bonvin from the canton of Wallis.

The parties try to prevent such misfortunes by anticipating parliamentary reactions to their selection of candidates. This is successfully done in most cases. As a result members of the federal government in office in 1973 were all nominated officially by their party with the above exceptions. In the case of the nomination of a Free Democratic candidate, I observed that the reactions of other parties were indicated primarily during informal conversations with leading representatives of those parties. But there were no formal talks between the Free Democrats and the other government parties. As far as I have been able to ascertain, only infrequently do the parties confer formally on matters of candidate selection.

Accordingly, there are only very loose relations among the government parties at the beginning of a legislative period. No government platform is presented in Parliament as a basis for the election of the Federal Council. The government parties do not even submit a common list of candidates to the Parliament. The contacts among the government parties are usually restricted to informal conversations that explore the qualifications of the candidates that are most likely to be elected. It is evident that such a selection procedure does not give rise to a coalition government in the usual meaning of the term. It is even doubtful that it makes sense to talk about the Federal Council as a coalition government. The government parties do not unite to pursue a specific common policy. They just happen to be those parties whose parliamentary strength gives them a claim to participate in governing. With such a structure of government it is understandable that each party reserves the right to oppose government policies at its own discretion. In a document of the Free Democratic party, for instance, this right is formulated as follows: "If a compromise reached in Parliament is not compatible with liberal ideology, such a case will lead us to present our own proposal to the people to force a clear decision to be made between the liberal alternative and the nonliberal compromise."[61]

In a similar vein the other three parties in the Federal Council emphasize repeatedly that they have a right to opposition. In practice there are various possibilities for the articulation of such opposition. One of these is that a government party assumes the role of ad hoc opposition on a certain question. A typical example of this was the Social Democratic popular initiative concerning land legislation. The Social Democrats demanded that the public sector be allowed the right of preemption. This demand did not meet with the approval of the other parties in the Federal Council, and no generally satisfactory compromise was reached. The Social Democrats would have had to concede to a great deal had they agreed to the decision of the government majority. But they decided to be in opposition on this specific question. In 1963 they launched a popular initiative together with the Swiss Federation of Trade Unions and gathered the required 50,000 signatures. In this case, however, the opposition was not successful; the initiative was defeated in a referendum on July 2, 1967.[62] An extreme form of oppositional behavior on the part of the government parties occurred in the winter of 1966-67. The federation was confronted with the delicate task of bringing its financial affairs back into balance. In the Federal Council a compromise was made: the tax on stock dividends should be retained, and in return for this, a 10 percent increase in income tax and sales tax was scheduled. In the parliamentary deliberations considerable parts of the bourgeois government parties opposed the stock dividend tax with the effect that it was abolished against the recommendations of the Federal Council. The Social Democrats opposed the increase in income and sales tax in a countermove that led to the fall of that part of the government compromise, too.[63] In effect, then, the government parties are able to reserve the right to opposition even if a compromise has been reached in the Federal Council.

A second form of opposition open to government parties is a consequence of the departmental structure of the Federal Council. According to Article 103 in the Federal Constitution "the tasks of the Federal Council are . . . distributed among its individual members following the structure of the departments." But the same article also states: "The decisions of the Federal Council originate with it as a governing body." As will be shown in the case studies below (see pp. 128–225), a major part of the decision-making authority has been delegated to the individual departments. This division of government responsibility is used by the government parties to create opposition to the department heads of the other parties. This type of opposition was articulated clearly in the 1966 annual report of the Free Democratic party in the Berne canton: "The commotion about the Mirage and the deflationary economic measures has calmed down in the past year, but without removing the dark shadows it threw upon the popularity of Free Democratic politicians. To these two important controversies two new ones have been added: the bottleneck in the Federal finances and the weak road construction policy. But here the principle burden of 'guilt' does not fall upon Free Democrats." The Mirage affair was caused by considerable unauthorized increases in the costs of the procurement of fighter bombers. Although the Constitution places responsibility for such matters with the Federal Council as a body, the other government parties attempted to use the increase in the costs against the Free Democrats since the head of the Department of Defense was the Free Democrat Paul Chaudet. Finally, the Social Democrats demanded that Chaudet resign.[64] The second problem referred to in the report also created opposition to the Free Democrats because their man, Hans Schaffner, as head of the Department of Economic Affairs, was in charge of the deflationary measures that were considered by many to have failed.[65]

The above quotation from the annual report also shows that the Free Democrats attempted to attack other parties on account of the failures in their departments. The Free Democrats blamed the federal financial bottleneck on Roger Bonvin, the Christian Democratic head of the Department of Finance and Customs. Similarly, the Social Democrat Hans-Peter Tschudi, in charge of the Department of the Interior, was attacked by the Free Democrats for the "weak policy of road construction." This kind of opposition is not ad hoc in being limited to certain issues; instead it is rather structural in that the departments of other parties can be used as primary targets. Occasionally one almost gets the impression that there are seven federal governments, corresponding to the seven departments, and in each the government party is the party of the head of the department with all the other parties being in opposition. This dispersion of government responsibility among the departments, which may be found in any administrative system, is enhanced by the fact that the Swiss government does not have a prime minister with authority over the other members of the government.

A third opportunity for opposition by government parties follows from their federal structure. According to Gruner the Swiss parties are not "monolithic centralized edifices, but large 'girders' uniting the cantonal organizations."[66] Only the Social Democratic party of the four government parties was founded as a party for all of Switzerland. It is "the only Swiss party with a national origin. From its creation it has been headed by a national leadership."[67] But as Masnata can demonstrate even that party has strong federal elements: "The independence of the cantonal parties does in fact make the elaboration of a common Federal policy very difficult. . . . A party from a French-speaking canton can only with difficulty tolerate criticism by leading Swiss Germans of this or that aspect of their activity, and the same is true in reverse. Each cantonal party has a tendency to consider itself as a whole and not as part of a whole."[68] The federal structure of the Swiss parties is also emphasized by the fact that their leading representatives are not perceived as national party leaders. Girod states that "the role of national party 'great leader' does not exist in Switzerland. On the contrary, parties have cantonal leading figures who are generally unknown to the average citizen in the rest of the country."[69] Masnata confirms Girod's general conclusion with respect to the Social Democratic party. "It is hard to imagine that a member of the Federal Parliament from Zurich (even if he did speak French fluently) would set up a conference in the French-speaking part of Switzerland. Even within the cadre of the cantons, such exchanges are rare."[70]

Girod's observations can be confirmed by another example.[71] Before the federal election in 1967 each party had to provide its own personalities for the election programs on television and radio. The deliberations in the leading circles of the Free Democratic party showed that there was nobody available who appeared to be a national party leader. Long talks were necessary before it was decided who should represent the party. The solution was a group of cantonal party leaders chosen with a view to ensure as good a regional balance as possible. It can be seen, then, that the federal structure of the government parties, which will be described in more detail in the section on the decision-making process in the parties, allows the cantonal parties to take repeated liberties in opposing their federal counterparts.[72] This was the case during the federal referendum of February 28, 1965. The referendum concerned the introduction of deflationary measures, which consisted, on the one hand, of restrictions in the supply of money and capital and, on the other hand, of limits in the construction and building sector. The federal organizations of the four government parties supported both parts of the proposal. At the cantonal level, however, there was a much more diverse mixture of opinions. This is evident from table 2.[73] In the decision concerning monetary restrictions, nine Free Democratic, four Christian Democratic, and two Social Democratic cantonal parties took a position different from that of the federal parties. In the decision concerning the construction and building restrictions, nineteen Free Democratic, five Christian Democratic, two Social Democratic, and two Swiss People's party cantonal parties did not support the economic policy of the Federal Council. These figures show in an impressive way how independent the cantonal parties are from the federal parties. It is, therefore, important to consider the

TABLE 2. RECOMMENDATIONS OF THE FOUR GOVERNMENT PARTIES WITH RESPECT TO THE DEFLATIONARY MEASURES

	Free Democrats		Christian Democrats		Social Democrats		Swiss People's Party	
Cantons	M	C	M	C	M	C	M	C
Ticino	Y	X	N	N	N	N	—	—
Graubuenden	N	N	Y	Y	Y	Y	—	—
Wallis	N	N	X	X	N	N	—	—
Basel-City	N	N	X	X	Y	Y	—	—
Basel-Country	N	N	—	—	Y	Y	—	—
Schaffhausen	N	N	Y	N	Y	Y	Y	N
Nidwalden	N	N	Y	Y	—	—	—	—
Obwalden	N	N	Y	Y	—	—	—	—
St. Gallen	Y	N	Y	Y	Y	Y	—	—
Appenzell A. Rh.	Y	N	—	—	Y	Y	—	—
Zug	Y	N	Y	Y	—	—	—	—
Geneva	N	N	Y	Y	Y	Y	—	—
Solothurn	Y	Y	Y	Y	Y	Y	—	—
Neuchâtel	Y	N	—	—	Y	Y	—	—
Appenzell I. Rh.	—	—	Y	Y	—	—	—	—
Lucerne	Y	Y	Y	Y	Y	Y	—	—
Schwyz	N	N	Y	Y	Y	Y	—	—
Freiburg	Y	N	X	X	Y	Y	—	—
Zurich	Y	N	Y	Y	Y	Y	Y	Y
Berne	Y	N	Y	Y	Y	Y	Y	Y
Uri	Y	N	Y	Y	Y	Y	—	—
Glarus	Y	Y	Y	Y	Y	Y	—	—
Aargau	Y	N	Y	Y	Y	Y	Y	X
Thurgau	Y	Y	Y	Y	Y	Y	Y	Y
Vaud		Y	Y	Y	Y	Y	Y	Y

Source: Reymond, "La votation fédérale," p. 131.
Note: M = monetary restrictions; C = construction restrictions; Y = yes; N = no; X = free vote.

cantonal level if one wants to estimate to what extent the government parties oppose the policies of the Federal Council.

It has now become evident that the principle of amicable agreement is not applied universally throughout the political system of Switzerland. Just as party systems with a competitive pattern do not always regulate interparty conflicts by the majority principle, so amicable agreement is not the only pattern of conflict resolution in Switzerland. The principle of amicable agreement refers primarily to the proportional participation of all parties in government, but this participation is subject to modifications.[74] There is, for example, no generally accepted rule stating exactly what number of seats in Parliament legitimizes the claim to a seat in government. Consequently, the distribution of government posts is more than just an arithmetical problem. The canton of Aargau is a case in point. It has five seats in its government and its legislature has 200 seats. Arithmetically, one could conclude that 40 seats in Parliament would entitle a party to one seat in government. After the 1965 elections the four largest parties had the following number of parliamentary seats: Social Democrats, 62; Christian Democrats, 46; Free Democrats, 43; Swiss People's party, 30.[75] This distribution entitled each party to one seat in government, which the parties agreed to according to the principle of amicable agreement. The problem revolved about the assignment of the fifth seat. Numerically the Social Democrats could claim it because their 62 seats corresponded to 1.55 seats in government. However, the other parties were not prepared to give up the seat to the Social Democrats on the basis of this narrow margin, and an election developed over the contested seat. Though not always arithmetically exact, the principle of proportionality is generally used in the distribution of government seats because the parties mutually acknowledge one another's claims according to the principle of amicable agreement. But there are also important exceptions with respect to the principle of amicable agreement among government parties. It was shown that at the federal level (and the same applies to the cantons and the local communities) the government parties are not afraid to manifest their opposition to government policies. In most other democracies with coalition governments opposition as practiced in recent years by Swiss parties would probably have led to the fall of the coalition. In Switzerland, on the contrary, there has been no overthrow of a national government since the founding of the federation in 1848.

Apparently the Swiss system has built-in mechanisms that make the fall of a government more difficult to bring about. I would even go as far as to propose that the Swiss government cannot be brought down. The main reason for this invulnerability has to do with the manner in which the Federal Council is elected. The members of the council are elected individually for a fixed term of four years, and, according to the Constitution, the legislature cannot stage a vote of no confidence during that period. If a government proposal is defeated by Parliament, it is not necessary for either the member sponsoring this proposal or the Federal Council as a body to resign. This conclusion also holds with respect to the referenda: they do not have the character of a plebiscite so the government does not have to resign in case of a negative result. It was considered contrary to the rules of the system that Social Democrat Max Weber resigned as a member of the Federal Council in 1953 when a financial project he had prepared as head of a department was rejected by the electorate. Weber gave the following reasons for his resignation: "It is not possible anymore for me to prepare and to defend a financial project to conform with the postulates of the opponents of the defeated proposal."[76] However logical this motivation may seem, Weber's resignation still did not conform to the rules of the system. There is only one other such case in the whole history of the federation, and this was in 1891 when a member of the Federal Council resigned because a referendum was defeated. How firmly established the Federal Council is during the legislative period was shown by the Mirage affair. In the case of the acquisition of Mirage fighters, the Federal Council in general and the head of the Department of Defense in particular were considered responsible for such grave errors that a parliamentary investigative committee was constituted. Among other things it concluded that the report of the Federal Council, on which the Parliament based its granting of funds for the acquisition of one hundred Mirage fighters in 1961, was "partially biased, partially inaccurate, and, in some places, even formulated in a misleading way."[77] The parliamentary committee also blamed the Federal Council for the fact that "the execution of the 1961 Federal decree aimed at a degree of perfectionism which did not take sufficient account of the stipulated financial limits . . . [and] that the execution had deviated from the evident intent of the Federal decree in several respects."[78]

In spite of these impressive rebukes neither the Federal Council as a collegial body nor Paul Chaudet, the head of the Department of Defense, had to resign. Chaudet's continuation in office was not due to the fact that Parliament did not consider his mistakes grave enough. It was rather that the institutional framework does not allow for the resignation of a member of the Federal Council during the term of office of the legislature. Under these circumstances the Social Democrats, anxious to punish Chaudet, had to content themselves with demanding his resignation at their party convention, but Chaudet did not resign.

The toppling of a government would be possible only at the outset of a new legislative period. This has not yet happened in the history of the federation, and it presumably may never happen. Since the Federal Council is not elected as a body, but as individual members presenting themselves for reelection, the fall of the government would be possible only if Parliament chose to vote for a different candidate in the place of each incumbent member of the Federal Council. This possibility has never even been seriously considered and seems completely unrealistic in Swiss politics. Although the Federal Council never has been toppled as a body, individual members may fail to be reelected. As shown above, only two members of the Federal Council have not been formally reelected so far.[79] More important, however, is the informal mechanism that was used, for example, in the case of Paul Chaudet. In 1964 he incurred liability in the Mirage affair, at the end of 1966 he was supposed to be elected vice-president of the Federal Council, and in 1967 the general election was scheduled to take place. Chaudet could anticipate from the general sentiments in Parliament that his election as vice-president—which was otherwise only a formality—might never occur, and that his seat might even be at stake in the renewal election coming up a year later. He saw the seriousness of this situation and submitted his resignation "voluntarily" at the end of 1966.[80]

Hughes has found a whole string of cases in which members of the Federal Council resigned because they were afraid that they would not be reelected: "If they are not going to be reelected, they sensibly do not choose to stand."[81] He suggests that, "in the face of these examples, it is not possible to talk as if Federal Councillors were always reelected so long as they choose to stand without qualification."[82] If we acknowledge the possibility of a "forced" voluntary resignation, then we can see that the members of the Federal Council are easier to unseat than could be concluded from the fact that no member has been denied reelection in this century. This informal sanction of "voluntary" resignation applies, however, only to the individual members and not to the Federal Council as a body. Hughes rightly concludes that "there is no procedure for expressing lack of confidence in the government as a whole."[83] There exists in controversies between government and Parliament "a mock battle in which victory is not (as it is in a true parliamentary system) the resignation of the whole cabinet, but the resignation or non-election of an individual Federal Councillor."[84]

In the Swiss political system, then, there are neither formal nor informal mechanisms to cause the government as a whole to fall. The implication of this fact is that a government party does not have to fear a crisis if it opposes a certain government policy. This opportunity for opposition on the part of government parties is directly related to the existence of the proportionality principle in the formation of the government. The Swiss parties may accept this principle so willingly only because doing so does not mean that they lose the right to articulate certain demands in opposition to the government. The real role of the principle of amicable agreement in the Swiss party system gradually becomes clearer. Amicable agreement is not rigidly adhered to in the sense that interparty conflicts are never regulated by majority decisions. For instance, it is the majority principle that is followed when parties that do not recognize the fundamental democratic principles of Switzerland are excluded from participating in the government. Second, the majority principle is utilized when it is not numerically clear and unambiguous to which party a government seat falls. Finally, we have seen that conflicts that arise again and again among the government parties on specific issues are often regulated by majority decisions in Parliament or through referenda. The Swiss party system can therefore be termed noncompetitive only in the sense that amicable agreement is the prevailing pattern of conflict regulation. In this sense the Swiss system also conforms to Lehmbruch's typology, which assumes that a system is noncompetitive if amicable agreement is the *predominant* pattern of conflict regulation.[85]

Thus far we have seen that Swiss government parties relatively frequently articulate demands in opposition to government policies. As a next step the parties not represented in government should be studied. It should be remembered that these parties do not participate in government only because they have too few seats in Parliament. This rather superficial criterion is not a sufficient basis for a common opposition policy. At the federal level the six nongovernment parties—the Independent party, the Liberal Democratic party, the Republican party, the Communist party, the Protestant party, and the Anti-Alien party—constitute a very heterogeneous group compared to the government parties. In Parliament the Anti-Alien party and the Republican party belong on the extreme right and the Communist party on the extreme left, whereas the other three parties can be found more toward the middle of the line.[86] As a consequence of this heterogeneity the nongovernment parties have never been able to act in unified opposition to government policies. According to studies by Erich Gruner only the Communists and the Independents carry out a systematic opposition policy, but their actions are not coordinated.[87] The Communist opposition is a consequence of their antipathy toward the capitalist system. The picture is more complicated with the Independents. This party was formed in 1936 by a dynamic outsider, Gottlieb Duttweiler, who had made a name for himself in business by founding the Migros-Cooperative Society. The Independents do not perceive themselves as a party, but as a movement, and their stated intention is to bring change into Swiss politics. This view is closely connected with the personal opinions of the founder whose influence on the party is still relatively strong even though he is now dead. The oppositional function assumed by the Independent party was formulated in a campaign leaflet for the National Council election in 1967: "In the federal parliament are many representatives of vested interests. According to their party they are the power holders in big business and interest groups. The Independent party is a thorn in the flesh to all these, because it interferes with their logrolling and pork barrel politics. The Independent party represents everybody. Therefore it is free to stand up against malpractice and work for better solutions."[88] This quotation makes it clear that the Independent party does not wish to develop a basically different ideology. Its main goal is to fight abuses in the present system.

The Liberal Democrats and the Protestants do not consider themselves systematic opposition parties. Although they are without representation in government because of their small numbers, their behavior with respect to government policies is almost the same as that of the government parties: they support or oppose the government on the merits of the individual issues. The Anti-Alien party and the Republican party have concentrated their energies on the problems of the foreign workers, an area in which they passionately oppose government policy.[89]

In conclusion it may be said that the Federal Assembly has two parties—the Communists and the Independents—which systematically oppose government policies. For two reasons this opposition is not particularly relevant. First, the two parties do not form a unified front because they pursue different ends: the Communists work for structural change in the political system of Switzerland, whereas the Independents aim at certain changes within the framework of the present system. Second, both opposition parties are very small. Of 244 seats in the Federal Assembly the Independents have only 14 and the Communists only 5. It should not be concluded from this, however, that the Communists and the Independents are without importance. The right to popular initiative and referendum are available to them as ways of articulating politically relevant demands in particular situations. Therefore the Independent party claims during the election of 1967 are probably overstated, but not basically false: "The Independent Party has achieved important things. In spite of the unified counteractions of the other parties the troublesome opposition of the Independents in their untiring struggle has led to a number of important advances—very frequently through popular support."[90]

Finally, we must consider the parties that are too small to have representation in the Federal Assembly at all. They might be called *minor parties*. Even these parties cannot be deemed politically irrelevant a priori. They also have the opportunity to utilize the popular initiative and the referendum. That this right is more than merely formal is substantiated by the above-mentioned successful referendum, which was introduced by the Free Citizens party to deny National Council members an increase in pay. So far there has been no systematic study of the minor parties. It is therefore not known exactly how many of these parties exist. At least it can be determined that the following parties participated unsuccessfully in the 1967 election for the National Council: the Union of Bourgeois parties; the Party for Freedom of Opinion in Parliament; the Party of the Swiss People; the Independent Liberal Radical party; the Unattached Voters; the Action of the Canton of Basel; Team 67; the Free Citizens party; the Unitary Romance party; the Social Independent movement; and Vigilance. These parties polled a total of only 1.7 percent of all votes in the 1967 election for the National Council.[91] Furthermore, the following minor parties are represented in individual cantonal parliaments: Young Berne; the Liberal-Socialist party; the Free Conservatives; the Free Voters for Education and Progress; the Independent Union of Ticino; the Union of Liberal Radical Workers; the Social Farmer movement; and the National Progressive party.[92]

To those parties mentioned so far should be added others which competed unsuccessfully for a cantonal parliamentary mandate. Since there are no systematic studies of these parties, nothing definitive can be said about their positions with respect to government policy. However, I would like to suggest that most of the minor parties oppose government policies. Some fragmentary references in a study by Gruner and Siegenthaler show that there may be some substance to this argument.[93] For example, they call the Free Citizens party "a reservoir of politically frustrated individuals." Yet the Young Berne is an example of a minor party that refutes this notion. The Young Berne sends one representative to the local executive in the city of Berne. The party has recently indicated that it does not systematically oppose government policies when it recommended the proposals about deflationary measures.[94] Technically speaking, each of these minor parties has the opportunity to oppose the government by an initiative or a referendum. But some of them are so poorly organized that they can hardly ever make use of this right in practice. An example of such a politically irrelevant minor party is the Young Thun. It was founded before the local elections in 1962 and returned one representative to the forty-member city Parliament. Its representative was completely ignored by the representatives of the other parties, and since the Young Thun never brought about an initiative or a referendum, it dissolved itself before the local elections in 1966.

The influence of a minor party, on the other hand, should not be measured only by its degree of success with an initiative or a referendum. Its potential political relevance should also be considered. For example, if a government is able to anticipate the kind of initiative that such a party may introduce, the government may be able to retain its political leadership by satisfying some of the party's demands before the initiative is introduced.

Since all relatively large parties in Switzerland participate in government, it would be easy to jump to the conclusion that there are hardly any politically relevant channels through which opposition to the government could be communicated. However, we have shown how government parties are able to oppose the government. Nongovernment parties—even those without representation in the federal Parliament—can oppose the government through the initiative and the referendum. We can see, then, that the Swiss party system has many channels of communication through which opposition to government policy may be articulated.

A second characteristic of the input structure, which in part is related to the first, is that most parties articulate demands conforming to as well as opposing government policies. Only the Communists, the Independents, and some small parties are in opposition more or less continuously. The other parties—government as well as nongovernment parties—support or oppose government policy according to issues and the prevailing political constellation. The political system of Switzerland is thus fundamentally different from the classical model in which, according to Dahl, "opposition is so sharply distinguished that it is possible to identify unambiguously *the* opposition."[95] Dahl finds the largest deviations from this model in the United States and Switzerland. In the United States it is "never easy to distinguish 'opposition' from 'government'; and it is exceedingly difficult, if not impossible, to identify the opposition. In Switzerland the opposition is perhaps even less distinctive."[96]

Whereas the first two characteristics of the input structure follow from the preceding analysis, two others need to be introduced at this point. A third characteristic of the input structure is that the demands of the individual parties never differ strongly. Only the small Communist party distinguishes itself from the other parties by its demand for a fundamental ideological change. The demands of the other parties all conform to the system in that they adhere to the fundamental democratic principles of Switzerland. The consensus does not stop here, but it is extended to a more or less perfect agreement about the ends to be achieved on all important issues. Only the means to achieve these ends cause the differences of opinion. For example, Girod states that there is a strong consensus among the Swiss parties on all important questions—even on the question of the relation between church and state and problems related to economic and social policy. I would like to suggest that the demands of the Swiss parties coincide to such an extent partly because the party cleavages crosscut other important cleavages—in particular, the cleavages of occupational groups, linguistic groups, religious groups, regional groups, cantons, economic interest groups, and voluntary associations. A party that draws its supporters from different social groups cannot afford to cater to the interests of one group only. If it does not want to lose a part of its supporters, it is forced to place itself in the middle and to respond to the interests of the various groups in society. If, for instance, party and language lines crosscut, a party cannot afford to represent onesidedly the interests of a specific language group. On the contrary, every party attempts to articulate demands that pay heed to the needs of all linguistic groups.[97]

A survey made by Gruner in the Aargau canton clarifies the relationship between party boundaries and those of occupational groups.[98] Tables 3 and 4 show that the members of the different occupational groups are not distributed randomly among the parties. The concentration of farmers among the Swiss People's party, of workers among the Social Democratic party, and of independent businessmen, artisans, and retailers among the Free Democratic party is conspicuously high. There is an evident connection between occupation and party

TABLE 3. VOTERS IN THE CANTON OF AARGAU FOR THE NATIONAL COUNCIL IN THE 1963 ELECTION BY OCCUPATION (IN PERCENTAGES)

Parties	Independent Businessmen, Artisans, Retailers	Farmers	Supervisory Clerical Employees	Other Clerical Employees	Workers	Retired Persons
Social Democrats	10	5	15	27	61	28
Free Democrats	36	3	44	28	8	27
Christian Democrats	18	15	20	17	12	17
Swiss People's party	20	72	2	5	7	6
Protestants	2	1	1	3	1	4
Independents	4	1	8	8	3	8
Free Citizens	1	1	2	3	1	4
Lists without party denomination	9	2	8	9	7	6
Total	100	100	100	100	100	100

Source: Gruner, *Der Schweizer Waehler*, p. 10.

TABLE 4. VOTERS IN THE CANTON OF AARGAU FOR THE NATIONAL COUNCIL IN THE 1963 ELECTION BY PARTY (IN PERCENTAGES)

Occupations	Social Democrats	Free Democrats	Christian Democrats	Swiss People's party	Protestants	Independ-ents	Free Citizens	Lists with-out party denomina-tion
Independent Businessmen, Artisans, Retailers	4	22	15	19	14	10	5	16
Farmers	2	1	9	50	7	2	5	3
Supervisory Clerical Employees	3	16	10	1	3	13	9	8
Other Clerical Employees	26	44	37	12	52	51	45	39
Workers	61	12	25	16	17	18	27	31
Retired Persons	4	5	4	2	7	6	9	3
Total	100	100	100	100	100	100	100	100

Source: Gruner, *Der Schweizer Waehler*, p. 10.

preference, which is, however, not so strong that party and occupational boundaries coincide.

In the election of 1963, the farmers gave 72 percent of their vote to the Swiss People's party. On the other hand, however, only 50 percent of the Swiss People's party vote consisted of farmers so that the boundaries of the occupational group do not nearly coincide with the electorate of the Swiss People's party.[99] It should also be taken into consideration that this party is not active in many cantons. It gained its 23 seats in the National Council election in 1971 in the cantons of Berne (10), Zurich (5), Aargau, Graubuenden, and Thurgau (2 each), Basel-Country and Vaud (1 each). It participated unsuccessfully in the campaign in the cantons of Freiburg and Ticino and did not appear in the remaining cantons. There the farmers had to vote for other parties. It can be inferred from Federal Bureau of Statistics data that, according to canton, district, and local community, the farm vote primarily went to the Christian Democrats and the Free Democrats.[100] Nor do the boundaries of workers and Social Democrats coincide. The Aargau study showed that 61 percent of the workers voted for the Social Democrats and that 61 percent of the Social Democratic voters were workers. The boundaries of workers and Social Democrats coincide even less according to a study by Girod in the city of Geneva.[101] Tables 5 and 6 indicate—definite conclusions cannot as a rule be based on aggregate data—that far less than half of the workers in Geneva voted

TABLE 5. VOTERS IN THE CITY OF GENEVA FOR CANTONAL PARLIAMENT IN THE 1961 ELECTION BY RESIDENCE (IN PERCENTAGES)

Parties	Working-Class Areas	Middle-Class Areas I	Middle-Class Areas II	Suburban Areas
Social Democrats	22.2	24.7	19.3	14.8
Communists	23.5	18.0	17.5	10.7
Free Democrats*	25.1	24.5	24.9	26.5
Christian Democrats	18.2	17.2	17.3	18.1
Liberal Democrats	11.0	15.6	21.0	29.9
Total	100.0	100.0	100.0	100.0

Source: Girod, *Milieux politiques et classes sociales*, p. 40.
Note: Girod distinguishes among four types of residential areas: (1) working-class areas (workers, 62 percent); (2) middle-class areas I (workers, 49 percent); (3) middle-class areas II (workers, 46 percent); (4) suburban areas (workers, 28 percent).
* In Geneva the cantonal party of the Free Democratic party is called the Radical party.

TABLE 6. VOTERS IN THE CITY OF GENEVA FOR CANTONAL PARLIAMENT IN THE 1961 ELECTION BY PARTY (IN PERCENTAGES)

Residence	Social Democrats	Communists	Free Democrats*	Christian Democrats	Liberal Democrats
Working-Class Areas	23.0	29.0	21.5	22.0	12.5
Middle-Class Areas I	38.0	33.0	31.0	31.0	25.5
Middle-Class Areas II	22.5	24.0	23.5	23.0	26.0
Suburban Areas	16.5	14.0	24.0	24.0	36.0
Total	100.0	100.0	100.0	100.0	100.0

Source: Girod, *Milieux politiques et classes sociales*, p. 40.
* In Geneva the cantonal party of the Free Democratic party is called the Radical party.

Social Democratic. Thus the Social Democratic party received only 22 percent of the vote in areas with a worker population of 62 percent. This is partly due to the fact that in Geneva the Communist party is a second party that claims to represent the working class. It should also be taken into consideration that the bourgeois parties, particularly the Free Democrats and the Christian Democrats, attract the votes of many workers. The bourgeois parties polled 54 percent of the votes in the working-class areas. The Social Democratic party in Geneva does not seem to be exclusively a working-class party; 16.5 percent of the Social Democratic votes came from suburban areas. It appears from the monograph by Masnata that the Social Democrats cannot simply be called a working-class party even at the federal level. This conclusion is based not on the number of voters, but on the number of party members. Masnata writes that "working-class members of the Social Democratic Party only constitute a small part of the forces of the working class. . . . It is possible to conclude from this with some amount of probability that the Social Democratic Party of the 1960s is not *the* party of the working class."[102] Masnata says further that *the* working-class party does not exist in Switzerland at all. The Communists cannot assume this role either since they have no representation, or only weak representation, in most cantons. In the 1967 election for the National Council their percentage of the votes was 20.9 in the canton of Geneva, 19.3 in the canton of Neuchâtel, 14.3 in the canton of Vaud, 6.8 in the canton of Basel-City, 3.6 in the canton of Ticino, and 2.6 in the canton of Zurich. There were no Communist candidates in the remaining nineteen cantons.[103]

Even if the boundaries of the working class and the Social Democratic party are far from the same, the extent of coincidence is larger than for the farmers and any party. The Social Democrats are firmly established in the working class everywhere in Switzerland, whereas the function of an agrarian party is performed within regions, by the Swiss People's party, the Christian Democrats, the Free Democrats, and in some cases even by the Democrats and the Liberal Democrats. The boundaries of the other occupational groups coincide even less with party lines. According to Gruner's study of the canton of Aargau, the number of supervisory clerical employees and independent businessmen, artisans, and retailers voting Free Democratic was above average (44 and 36 percent, respectively), but these two groups constitute only 16 and 22 percent of the Free Democratic voters, respectively. In contrast to Aargau, there is no such concentration of the Free Democratic vote in the upper social strata in Geneva. According to the study by Girod, their supporters come from all four types of residential areas in rather even proportion. This difference in the social composition of the Free Democratic vote in Aargau and Geneva is related to the existence in Geneva of the Liberal Democratic party, which recruits its members to a large extent from the upper social strata. If we compare the Free Democratic party in Geneva and Aargau and remember that this party in many places polls a considerable part of the agrarian vote, it becomes evident that its occupational composition is very heterogeneous. This occupational heterogeneity also occurs in the Christian Democratic party. It appears to have more working-class votes in Geneva than in Aargau. In other places the Christian Democrats count many farmers among their rank and file. It can be inferred from Gruner's Aargau study that the small parties also tend to be occupationally mixed. The different occupational groups voted in approximately equal proportions for the Protestant party, the Independent party, and the Free Citizens party.

It is hardly a surprise that crosscutting between occupational groups and party lines is weakest among the working class. In all European democracies the interests of the working class have been represented by a special party or at least by a special group of parties. It is noteworthy that the Swiss Social Democratic party is not only the party of the working class. On this point Girod concludes that "the present program of the Social Democratic Party (adopted in 1959) is frankly reformist and pragmatic. It does not refer at all to the principle of class struggle, and there is no allusion to marxism. . . . The party intends to be the party of all, without exclusions."[104] Masnata comes to the same conclusion: "If the Social Democratic Party originally tended towards the type 'class party,' it very soon attempted to rally to its cause not only the workers, but all classes in the population."[105]

It would require a cross-national study to elucidate conclusively why the Swiss Social Democratic party is not solely a party of the working class. Masnata relates the low level of class consciousness in the Social Democratic party to the fact that Switzerland became industrialized in the nineteenth century in a unique way.[106] According to Masnata, "The poverty of the mineral resources has deprived Switzerland of mining and heavy industry both of which demand the employment of a considerable number of workers. . . . The absence of important industrial centers at the same time retarded the appearance of a real proletariat, living under identical conditions and liable to organize."[107] The decentralization of industry led to a high incidence of the worker-farmer type. "They considered themselves only partly as workers and their interest in the problems which could be posed to the working class was slight."[108] That the large branches of the watch and textile industry employed many cottage workers also had a negative influence on the class consciousness of the workers. According to Masnata, "[These workers] lived in isolation, without contacts, and considered themselves more as artisans than as workers. . . . An abyss separated these 'workers' from the proletarians of the big cities of Europe."[109]

That the Social Democratic party is not a distinct party of the working class can be related not only to the particular characteristics of the industrialization process, but also to the fact that Switzerland has become a highly developed industrial society with a corresponding stratified structure. A similar society, the Federal Republic of Germany, is described thus by Karl Martin Bolte: "There is a multitude of status differences in our society, but the status structure of society is not subdivided into clearly differentiated strata. The strongest tendency to distinct boundaries between the strata is found at the top and particularly at the bottom of the status pyramid. Between these top and bottom strata there is to a large extent a fluid transition from high to low, in which many members of society do not even have a clearly definable social status. Depending on context and area of interaction (occupation, residence, etc.) a different status appears and becomes relevant for behavior. . . . With respect to K. Marx's prognoses, there has been no cleavage of society between top and bottom, i.e., no disappearance of the middle, but rather a gradual extension of the middle of our society."[110] Two of my investigations show that the Swiss social structure is also characterized by fluid transitions and concentration in the middle positions. For example, in Belp, a community outside the city of Berne, the voters were asked to place themselves in the following predefined status groups: upper class, upper middle class, lower middle class, farmers, working class, and proletariat. It is interesting that not a single worker considered himself a proletarian; on the other hand, 28 percent of the workers considered themselves middle class.[111] These data show that the workers do not perceive themselves as a proletarian lower class, and not even as a clearly distinguishable working class. The pressure toward the middle positions and the smooth transitions between the social strata are evident. In another study 20- to 35-year-old voters from urban areas were asked to respond to the following statement: "Whether you call yourself worker or clerical employee is without consequence for the status assigned to you by others"; 38 percent agreed with this formulation completely, 10 percent agreed somewhat; 46 percent disagreed completely, 14 percent disagreed somewhat; and 2 percent did not state their opinion.[112] More than a third believed, then, that the social differences between workers and clerical employees are unimportant. This shows once more how little the Swiss workers are perceived by the population as a unitary class.

Three characteristics of the Swiss political system could also explain why the Social Democratic party is not a clear-cut class party. First, the political rights of the citizens are well developed. Masnata asserts that "the class consciousness of the working class is further diminished by the existence of democratic institutions: having the opportunity to participate in the political life of the country, the workers do not feel themselves to be outside the system. . . . Consequently, the mere existence of genuine political rights enables the workers to try to attain their goals by political means rather than by violence."[113] Second, federalism, according to Masnata, has also impeded the development of the Social Democrats as a class party: "The diversity of Switzerland has curbed the exchanges and contacts among the workers so that they were not able to ascertain that their situation was similar if not identical throughout Switzerland. Federalism prevented the Swiss workers from becoming collectively aware of belonging to one and the same class. The rivalry of German- and French-speaking cantons, the fear of the latter that they should be dissolved as the minority in an amalgamation of the whole certainly put some obstacles in the way of the creation of a working-class movement at the federal level."[114] Third, roughly all parties can participate in government responsibility according to their strength in Parliament. "Having made participation in various executives a basic tenet, the Social Democrats are compelled to take this into account to a large extent in the editing of their platform. . . . The Federal Council is . . . a collegial body where all decisions are made by the majority. The collegial aspect of it implies that a member may be obliged to go before one of the houses of parliament and defend a position which is not his own, but that of a majority of his colleagues. More than a politics of compromise this implies a politics of collaboration, a spirit of mutual understanding. This collegiality creates a sort of solidarity among the members of government from which socialism . . . does not appear as more reaffirmed."[115] After the preparation of the present text I conducted a study of the electorate in the Greater Lucerne area: the findings are published here for the first time.[116] Table 7 shows how the voters of the various parties are distributed among occupational

TABLE 7. PARTY VOTERS IN THE GREATER LUCERNE AREA BY OCCUPATIONAL GROUPS, 1968-69 (IN PERCENTAGES)

Occupational Groups	Christian Demo-crats (N = 82)	Free Demo-crats (N = 102)	Independ-ents (N = 24)	Social Demo-crats (N = 39)	Absten-tions or No Informa-tion (N = 78)
Independent business-men and managers	0	1	0	0	0
Professionals	7	6	4	0	4
Supervisory clerical employees	23	18	13	5	13
Other clerical employees	26	30	50	28	36
Independent artisans and retailers	7	11	4	3	5
Farmers	1	0	0	0	0
Overseers and foremen	5	7	0	15	6
Skilled workers	20	18	25	36	20
Unskilled and semiskilled workers	5	7	4	10	8
Students	6	2	0	3	8
Total	100	100	100	100	100

Note: Chi-square = 40.8 not significant. Here and in the following tables the levels of significance are as follows: .001 = very significant; .01 = significant; .05 = not very significant.

groups. It can be seen that the Christian Democrats and the Free Democrats are overrepresented in the higher status groups and the Social Democrats in the working class.[117] But the boundaries of parties and occupational groups are far from being identical. The distribution of parties among the different occupations is such that the chi-square test does not show significant differences. Thus both the Christian Democrats and the Free Democrats recruit 25 percent of their votes from the skilled and unskilled workers. On the other hand, 33 percent of the Social Democratic votes come from the group of clerical employees.

In table 8, the level of education is used as an indicator of social stratification.[118] Here we can also find some overrepresentation of Christian and Free Democrats at the higher level of education and of the Social Democrats at the lower levels. But the chi-square test does not indicate significant differences. The findings of the Lucerne study confirm, then, the results of earlier work showing that party and occupational cleavages crosscut to a relatively large extent.

TABLE 8. PARTY VOTERS IN THE GREATER LUCERNE AREA BY LEVEL OF EDUCATION, 1968-69 (IN PERCENTAGES)

Level of Education	Christian Demo-crats (N = 82)	Free Demo-crats (N = 102)	Independ-ents (N = 24)	Social Demo-crats (N = 39)	Absten-tions or No Informa-tion (N = 78)
Primary school	17	17	21	31	19
Secondary school	40	49	54	56	45
Higher education	43	34	25	13	36
Total	100	100	100	100	100

Note: Chi-square = 13.2 not significant.

Party and language lines crosscut to an even stronger degree.[119] According to the 1970 census the Swiss population (excluding aliens) is distributed among language groups in the following percentages:[120]

German	74.5
French	20.1
Italian	4.0
Romance	1.0
Others	0.4
Total	100.0

TABLE 9. SEATS OF THE THREE LARGEST PARTIES IN THE 1971 ELECTION FOR THE NATIONAL COUNCIL BY LANGUAGE GROUPS (IN PERCENTAGES)

Language	Social Democrats	Free Democrats	Christian Democrats
German	78	70	76
French	20	22	18
Italian	2	8	6
Total	100	100	100

Source: *Statistisches Jahrbuch der Schweiz 1972*, pp. 552–58.
Note: In the cantons that have more than one language, the seats were distributed according to the language of the elected.

As shown in table 9 the seats in the National Council are distributed almost proportionally among the three main language groups. In contrast to the three largest parties, the fourth, the Swiss People's party, is heavily concentrated in the German-speaking part of Switzerland, where in the 1971 election the party won 22 of its 23 seats. The remaining seat it won in the French-speaking part, whereas it ran unsuccessfully in the Italian-speaking part. In spite of this disproportional distribution, the Swiss People's party cannot be considered *the* party of the German-speaking Swiss. There are still thirteen German-speaking cantons where there are no candidates from the Swiss People's party. This pattern shows how little the boundaries of the Swiss People's party are identical with a language group.

Among the small parties without representation in the Federal Council, the Liberal Democrats and the Communists have their stronghold in the French-speaking cantons. Five out of six Liberal Democratic seats in the National Council and all five of the Communist seats come from those areas. On the other hand, the Independent, the Republican, the Protestant, and the Anti-Alien deputies are all from the German-speaking cantons with the exception of one Anti-Alien from Vaud.[121] These five parties are all too small to be able to represent a specific linguistic group. The phenomenon of a party's attempt to represent the interests of one particular linguistic group occurred in the 1967 election for the National Council when the French-speaking Unitary party (Parti unitaire romand) was constituted. However, this party's total lack of success indicated how little inclined the Swiss are to identify parties with language groups.[122]

In order to proceed with an appraisal of the extent to which parties and religious groups crosscut, it is of primary importance to investigate the Christian Democratic party more thoroughly. This party was formed in the last century during the struggle between clerical and anticlerical forces when religious tensions were very high. It was then called the Catholic Conservative party. Today the party is increasingly striving to recast its image from a Catholic party to a Christian party with a broader appeal. In its 1967 election platform its philosophy was articulated clearly: "The Christian Democratic Party of Switzerland has as its goal a structuring of social life in accordance with the values of Christianity. . . . It unites Swiss from all religious groups who explicitly state their goal is a Christian, democratic, federal and social Switzerland." Yet the Christian Democrats are still perceived by their opponents as the political arm of Catholicism. Thus a statement from the press service of the Free Democrats proclaims that "the [Christian Democratic] party is and will be the party of political Catholicism. The thesis that it is a broad Christian union is a blatant invention which grossly

TABLE 10. CATHOLICS AND CHRISTIAN DEMOCRATIC PARTY VOTERS FOR THE NATIONAL COUNCIL IN THE 1967 ELECTION BY CANTONS (IN PERCENTAGES)

Cantons	Catholics in 1970 Census	Christian Democratic Voters
Wallis	95	58
Schwyz	91	49
Ticino	90	37
Freiburg	86	48
Lucerne	85	49
St. Gallen	64	48
Solothurn	59	25
Geneva	53	14
Graubuenden	53	40
Aargau	50	20
Glarus	44	13
Thurgau	44	27
Basel-City	41	12
Basel-Country	39	14
Neuchâtel	38	0
Zurich	37	11
Vaud	36	5
Schaffhausen	32	0
Berne	23	6

Source: *Statistisches Jahrbuch der Schweiz 1972*, pp. 44, 554–55.
Note: Excluded from this table are the cantons where the election for the National Council was a tacit one or where the canton has only one member in the council.

distorts reality. It can only be interpreted as sly party-tactical double-talk."[123] It may not be possible to unify two such different perceptions into an adequate conclusion. It may be more fruitful to compare the percentage of Catholics in the population with the percentage of Christian Democratic voters in the individual cantons as in table 10. Even if table 10 does not show the Catholics and the Christian Democrats to be in the same ranking order within the cantons, there is a clear trend for the Christian Democratic vote to be large in cantons with a large Catholic population. On the other hand, it can be inferred from these figures that not nearly all Catholics vote Christian Democratic, since in all cantons the percentage of Catholics in the population is larger than that of Christian Democrats. Gruner's study in the canton of Aargau also shows that the Christian Democrats have more Catholic than Protestant supporters—36 percent of the Catholics voted Christian Democratic as opposed to only 8 percent of the Protestants.[124] These two figures show, however, that not all Catholics vote Christian Democrat, and that there is also a substantial number of Christian Democratic voters among the Protestants.

Further, it has to be determined whether the interests of the Catholics on religious issues are predominantly articulated by the Christian Democrats. The most important religious issue in Switzerland at the moment is no doubt the possible abolition of the so-called Exception Clause in the Federal Constitution. This refers primarily to Articles 51 and 52, which read as follows:

Article 51. The Jesuit order and societies affiliated with it may not be admitted to any part of Switzerland, and its members are prohibited from any activity in Church and education. This prohibition can be extended by Federal decree to other religious orders whose activity is dangerous to the state or disrupts religious peace.

Article 52. The founding of new monasteries or religious orders and the restoration of abolished ones is prohibited.

These articles became part of the Federal Constitution in the last century and were sponsored by the Free Democrats, who had gained the upper hand over the Christian Democrats in the War of Separation (*Sonderbundskrieg*). From the beginning, the Christian Democrats have been opposed to these articles, which are obviously discriminatory against Catholics. After more than a century, however, support for the abolition of these articles has grown. In the 1967 campaign not only the Christian Democrats, but all larger parties, supported the abolition of the Exception Clause. Even the Free Democratic election platform said: "We propose a partial revision of the Federal Constitution to abolish the religious articles and their substitution by a general article on tolerance." It seems that the religious issue is not a source of conflict among the parties anymore. Under these circumstances one may wonder why there has not yet been a referendum seeking the removal of the Exception Clause. This has not occurred because the political leadership fears that the bridging of the religious gap would only be superficial. A referendum might have a negative outcome, and this would of course deepen the old cleavages. Occasional minor incidents among Free Democrats and Christian Democrats on religious issues indicate that this premonition is not entirely without reason. A typical example of this is given by Gilg and Reymond in their annual chronicle of St. Gallen in 1965:[125]

In Berneck in the Rhine valley an action committee led by young Free Democrats was formed to gather signatures for a popular initiative at the local level to institute a merger of the two religious school systems. Approximately 50% of the voters signed the initiative. . . . The local referendum then rejected the initiative with a narrow margin on December 12. This controversy had consequences for the whole canton; the Free Democrats paid for the attempt to change the cultural status quo with a defeat in the election of a president for the newly constituted administrative court, as in October the Christian Democratic parliamentary group successfully presented their own candidate against the Free Democratic candidate, whom they had originally accepted.

Generally speaking, we may conclude that Catholic demands are no longer articulated exclusively by the Christian Democrats as in earlier decades, but that primarily the clerically oriented section of the Catholic population still has strong links with the Christian Democratic party.

TABLE 11. PARTY VOTERS IN THE GREATER LUCERNE AREA BY RELIGION, 1968–69 (IN PERCENTAGES)

Religion	Christian Democrats (N = 82)	Free Democrats (N = 102)	Independents (N = 24)	Social Democrats (N = 39)	Abstentions or No Information (N = 78)
Catholic	94	59	75	74	73
Protestant	4	33	13	26	17
Other religion	2	1	4	0	3
No religion	0	7	8	0	5
No information	0	0	0	0	2
Total	100	100	100	100	100

Note: Chi-square = 46.8 very significant.

These conclusions have been corroborated to a large extent by a study I have completed in the Greater Lucerne area.[126] As shown in table 11, the religious composition of the parties showed statistically significant differences. Almost all the Christian Democrats were Catholics, whereas the other parties had considerable proportions of Protestant voters. If we distinguish among those Catholics who go to church regularly and those who rarely do, we get differences in electoral behavior (table 12) that clearly show that the Christian Democrats are particularly numerous among those who go to church regularly.[127] But the Christian Democrats in Lucerne are by no means identical with the frequent churchgoers; on the one hand, 19 percent of that group vote for the Free Democrats, and, on the other, 12 percent of the infrequent churchgoers vote Christian Democrat.

TABLE 12. VOTING PATTERNS OF CATHOLICS IN THE GREATER LUCERNE AREA, 1968-69 (IN PERCENTAGES)

Parties	Regular Churchgoers (N = 154)	Nonregular Churchgoers (N = 90)
Christian Democrats	45	12
Free Democrats	19	33
Independents	4	12
Social Democrats	9	17
Abstentions or No Information	23	26
Total	100	100

A few words should also be said about the Protestant party, which attempts to present itself as a counterbalance to the Christian Democrats, but without much success so far. In the 1971 election for the National Council it polled only 1.6 percent of the vote, winning three seats.[128] Other religious parties which shoot up sporadically have experienced even less success. This was the case, for instance, with the Independent Protestant Christian Citizens who polled a mere 0.6 percent of the vote in the 1967 election for the National Council, a total that did not give them any representation at all.[129]

Are there any party boundaries in Switzerland that coincide with those of the cantons? It would not be surprising if there were, since the Swiss federation was founded by independent cantons. Under these conditions it could be imagined that parties appeared having as their main goal the representation of the interests of particular cantons.

However, this potential for cantonal parties has not been realized anywhere in Switzerland. The closest approximation would be to say that the Swiss People's party is the party of the canton of Berne. It was formed after World War I by the splitting of the Free Democrats and was originally active only in the canton of Berne.[130] Its stronghold is still in Berne: 10 of its 23 seats in the National Council after the 1971 election came from that canton. The focus of the Swiss People's party on Berne is also shown by the fact that the general secretary of the cantonal party in Berne has always been simultaneously the general secretary of the federal party organization. It should also be noted that the five members of the Federal Council from the Swiss People's party have all come from Berne so far. On the other hand, this evidence does not allow us to equate party and canton. More than half of the Swiss People's party's members of the National Council are elected outside the canton of Berne, and the party only polled 31 percent of the Bernese vote.

The Federal Bureau of Statistics has analyzed the 1967 election for the National Council to see if party lines divide rural and urban areas.[131] As shown in table 13 the voters of the individual parties are not distributed randomly among rural and urban areas. For the three largest parties—the Christian Democrats, the Free Democrats, and the Social Democrats—the distribution of urban voters ranges from 24 percent for the Christian Democrats to 48 percent for the Social Democrats. This range is not so wide that it constitutes a real polarization into a rural and an urban party. If the smaller parties are included, the range becomes wider, but still not wide enough to talk about an extreme polarization. The Swiss People's party, the most rural party,

TABLE 13. PARTY VOTERS FOR THE NATIONAL COUNCIL IN THE 1967 ELECTION BY THE SIZE OF THE COMMUNITY (IN PERCENTAGES)

Parties	Urban Communities	Rural Communities
Swiss People's party	16.5	83.5
Christian Democrats	23.6	76.4
Free Democrats	37.0	63.0
Social Democrats	47.5	52.5
Protestants	48.3	51.7
Independents	63.0	37.0
Communists	70.6	29.4
Total	40.9	59.1

Source: *Nationalratswahlen 1967*, pp. 35-37.

still received 17 percent of its vote in urban areas, and the Communists, the most urban party, recruited 29 percent of its voters in rural areas.

The Swiss parties also tend to crosscut with economic interest groups such as the employees' organizations. In the 1967 election for the National Council, the Swiss Federation of Clerical Employees' Unions recommended the following candidates: Free Democrats, 10; Social Democrats, 6; Independents, 4; Christian Democrats, 2; and Protestant party, 1.[132] Of the nine parties with previous representation in Parliament only two, the Communists and the Liberal Democrats, did not receive any endorsements. The general secretary of the Swiss Federation of Clerical Employees' Unions gave the reasons for these recommendations in the following statement of principle: "This is less the outcome of a particular orientation, but much more the result of a very diverse membership."[133] The Swiss Union of Artisans, the Swiss Farmers' Union, the Swiss Union of Commerce and Industry, three of the other peak organizations, crosscut in general only with the bourgeois parties.[134] For example, the cantonal section of the Swiss Union of Artisans in Berne recommended the following candidates in the 1967 election: Swiss People's party, 5; Free Democrats, 4; Christian Democrats, 1.[135]

The Dutch term *verzuiling,* meaning reinforcing cleavages, can be used to describe the Swiss trade union movement.[136] The interests of organized labor are articulated by four organizations, all of which have close ties to a specific political party. The following unions, with membership figures as of 1971, represent the "pillars" of organized labor in Switzerland:[137]

Swiss Federation of Trade Unions (Social Democrats)	437,396
Swiss Federation of Christian National Trade Unions (Christian Democrats)	94,825
Union of Free Swiss Workers (Free Democrats)	18,207
Swiss Union of Protestant Employees (Protestant party)	13,790

It is obvious that the Swiss Federation of Trade Unions and the Social Democratic party represent the most important *verzuiling.* Masnata has studied the interrelations of these two groups, and has concluded that there are no formal obligations between party and trade union, nor do they have a common authority.[138] The only rule at the institutional level is that the Swiss Federation of Trade Unions can claim one seat in the political commission of the party. The real channel of communication between party and trade union is a multitude of role accumulations. The president of the Swiss Federation of Trade Unions is, as a rule, a member of the Executive Committee of the party. Further, of a total of fifty-one Social Democratic members in the 1959 National Council, fifteen were exponents of the Swiss Federation of Trade Unions, according to Masnata's investigations.[139] The Free Democrats also handle their communications with the economic interest groups primarily by role accumulation. The position of the president of the Swiss Farmers' Union in the Free Democratic Executive Committee is analogous to that of the president of the Swiss Federation of Trade Unions in the Social Democratic Executive Committee. The most important difference between the trade unions and the other economic interest groups is that each of the four trade union federations has role accumulations with only *one* party whereas the other economic interest groups extend this relationship to several parties.

The *verzuiling*, which may still be observed in the trade union movement, existed to a considerable degree in voluntary organizations at the beginning of this century. Particularly the gymnastic, rifle, and music associations showed a division between worker and bourgeois elements. This division has been increasingly overcome in recent years. In a community study in Belp I found that the worker music society and the bourgeois music society had been fused into a nonpolitical village music society.[140] In 1971 the Swiss associations of gymnastics and sports had 1,862,150 members. Of these only 5 percent were organized into separate worker associations: 48,666 in the Swiss Workers' Gymnastics and Sports Association, and 32,107 in the Swiss Workers' Cycle Association. In addition there was a slight "religious" *verzuiling* with 49,646 members in the Swiss Catholic Gymnastics and Sports Union, which represented 3 percent of the total membership of all the gymnastic and sports associations.[141] The overwhelming majority of voluntary associations crosscut with political parties, and evidence of this can be found primarily at election time. Gruner and Siegenthaler concluded, in their analysis of the 1963 election for the National Council, that "sports, motoring and travel associations mainly recommended candidates on different lists."[142] This phenomenon also occurred in the 1967 election. A typical example of this was the Sports Fishing Club of Berne, which recommended two Social Democrats, two candidates from the Swiss People's party, one Free Democrat, and one Independent.[143]

We have now seen the extent to which the boundaries of political parties crosscut with those of occupational groups, language groups, religious groups, cantons, regional groups, economic interest groups, and voluntary organizations. In spite of some exceptions, there is a clear general tendency for party lines not to coincide with those of the different groups, but rather to crosscut with them. This point is emphasized by the existence of the following interparty groups in the federal Parliament: the Group for Commerce and Industry; the Group of Artisans; the Group of Farmers; the Group of Clerical Employees; the Group for Traffic, Tourism, and Hotels; the Group for the Protection of the Interest of the Alpine Population; the Group for National Planning; the Group for the Protection of the Waters; the Group for Questions of the Press; the Group for Questions of the Film; the Group for Questions of Television; the Group for Inland Navigation; and the Group for Sports.[144]

In effect, then, the crosscutting of political parties with other groups seems to keep the parties from differing strongly in their demands on the political system. The similarity of the demands among Swiss parties may also be related to the fact that Switzerland is a small country. Stein Rokkan suggests that "the smaller the polity, the less the leeway for independent action and the greater the concern to maintain national unity across party lines," a hypothesis that seems to hold for Switzerland.[145] In matters of foreign policy the position of national unity is strongly emphasized. There is no party of any consequence that does not support the traditional Swiss policy of neutrality as the basic maxim in foreign policy. Even the Social Democrats, who originally viewed neutrality as an element of reaction, recognize neutrality as an axiom of Swiss foreign policy since the 1935 party program.[146]

Even if the parties articulate different demands with respect to the making of foreign policy, neutrality is the firm basis; it is challenged only by splinter parties. When the Social Democrats revised their program in 1959, they demanded that Switzerland apply for membership in the United Nations, but explicitly added that neutrality was to be retained.[147] My sample survey of eleven communities in 1962 confirmed the uncontroversial sentiment on the question of neutrality. The respondents were confronted with various proposals for Switzerland's behavior concerning attempts to unify Europe. Only 5 percent wanted to enter an integrated Europe if that meant the renunciation of Swiss neutrality.[148] Masnata has described the consensus on the neutrality issue as follows: "The quasi-mystical attachment to neutrality has had as its consequence the creation of a reflex of emotional self-defense. . . . With respect to the problem of neutrality the Swiss tend to 'react' and not to reason. The problem of Swiss neutrality does not seem to belong in the domain of politics, but rather in that of 'religion.' The whole country is subject to a diffuse pressure, which makes an objective examination of the problem difficult.[149]

The foreign policy consensus among the parties is not without some spillover effect on domestic politics. First, in contrast to many other systems, the Swiss political system has no domestic political conflicts reflecting controversies about international politics. Second, it must be taken into consideration that, according to the theory of cognitive dissonance, a pattern of conflict regulation used in one area tends to become used in others.[150] If the Swiss parties have "learned" to pursue similar policies in matters of foreign policy, this adaptation will also influence their behavior in domestic politics.

It may now be asked if the strong foreign policy consensus of the Swiss parties can be explained solely by Rokkan's small-state hypothesis. It seems to me that a second element that must be added in the case of Switzerland is the strong subcultural segmentation of the country. At the time of the religious wars in the sixteenth and seventeenth centuries the Swiss leeway for independent action in the international arena was limited by its being a small state, but a further limitation was its divisions on religious matters. In the nineteenth and twentieth centuries, when nationalism became a dominant factor in international politics, Swiss foreign policy was restricted because individual parts of the country distributed their sympathies in international affairs according to their language group. Thus, during World War I there developed the "trench" between the German- and French-speaking parts of Switzerland—the majority of the German Swiss and the majority of French Swiss sympathized with Germany and France, respectively.

The common denominator for Switzerland's activities in international affairs since the European wars of religion was the pursuit of a policy of neutrality. Jacques Freymond concludes: "Neutrality is not only the fundamental principle of our foreign policy, it is also one of the preconditions of internal stability of the Federation."[151] An extensive examination of the history and substance of Swiss neutrality is not necessary here.[152] The crucial point is that neutrality in the Swiss environment is a means toward strong consensus on foreign policy among the parties in spite of the extensive subcultural segmentation.

Up to now we have considered three principal characteristics of the input structure of the Swiss political system. First, it appears that relatively many parties exist and channel politically relevant demands into the system. Second, the parties are characterized by a frequent shift between demands in support of the government and demands in opposition to the government according to issues and the political constellation. Third, we have concluded that the demands generally do not vary greatly from party to party. Another characteristic of the structure is that there is generally no strong discipline in Swiss parties.[153] This was illustrated by Boeschenstein, an experienced observer of the Swiss Parliament, who has said that "whatever else may be found in the desk of a member of parliament, he has definitely neither the party program nor the proposals from the latest party convention before the election among his papers, nor does he have the statutes of the party or its most recent program of action."[154] According to table 14, the

TABLE 14. VOTING PATTERNS OF PARLIAMENTARY GROUPS IN THE NATIONAL COUNCIL IN 108 ROLL CALLS

Voting Patterns	Free Democrats	Christian Democrats	Social Democrats	Swiss People's Party
Unanimity without abstentions	13	32	86	52
Unanimity with abstentions	9	8	9	2
No Unanimity	86	68	13	54
Total	108	108	108	108

Source: Masnata, *Le parti socialiste*, p. 152.

Free Democrats, voting uniformly in only 12 percent of the cases, showed the least party discipline. The Social Democrats had the highest cohesion, with unanimity in 80 percent of the roll calls. But, as Masnata can demonstrate, a tendency to deviance may also be found among the Social Democrats. The parliamentary group has the formal authority to prescribe the vote to its members. But it happens more and more frequently that they refrain from such decisions: "Confronted with the impossibility of creating unanimity on numerous questions the group is reluctant to impose discipline at the final vote. In many cases the Social Democratic deputies are free to vote as their conscience demands."[155] Even when group discipline is called for, it may happen that individual representatives do not comply without the application of sanctions: "It happens, however, that a member votes against a project approved by the majority of the group. The chairman then notes this, but no sanction is considered. . . . In fact the group has never excluded a member because of noncompliance."[156] More recently it has even happened that the parliamentary group explicitly permitted some of its members to deviate from party discipline.[157] The main reason for the low level of party discipline in the federal Parliament may be that party lines crosscut other important cleavages. Thus the individual member of Parliament will sympathize with different reference groups whose role expectations do not always coincide. Which reference group then becomes the decisive one for the representative in such an inter-role conflict? The low party discipline shows that the representatives frequently choose other reference groups, such as economic interest groups, language groups, and so on, rather than the party itself. This can be illustrated by an example from the Free Democrats. When the decision to slow down construction was made in 1965 in order to curb the inflationary economy, the construction trade representatives in the Free Democratic parliamentary group experienced a role conflict because the party supported the decision and the Swiss Union of Artisans opposed it. The construction representatives voted against the decision, thereby making the union the decisive reference group.

The crosscutting hypothesis may help explain why party discipline is highest in the Social Democratic party. It is likely to be important that there is *verzuiling* in the trade union sector where the strength of the Social Democrats and the Swiss Federation of Trade Unions is by far the largest. Because of this *verzuiling* the Social Democratic deputies are less likely to experience inter-role conflicts and thus to violate party discipline.

Party discipline in Switzerland turns out to be even slighter if we consider not only the federal level, but the cantonal and local levels as well. As demonstrated by the case of the referendum concerning the decision to slow down the economy, the low-party echelons feel a very slight obligation to abide by the decision of the federal parties. This sense of independence decreases the cohesion of the parties even further. It is also important that the rank-and-file supporters of the parties are not at all committed to party decisions. The Swiss institution of direct democracy often leaves the final decision to the individual citizens. Proposals have been known to be rejected in a referendum even with the support of all parties, as in the case of a proposal concerning the civil defense of the canton of Aargau in 1967.[158]

2. THE DECISION-MAKING PROCESS IN THE INDIVIDUAL PARTIES

The Free Democratic Party

As I have already previously stated, I had an opportunity to observe the formation of the Free Democratic platform for the election of the National Council in 1967. I will now sketch the formal development of that platform. In the fall of 1965—two years before the election—the Executive Committee of the Free Democratic party appointed an ad hoc working group of nine members, which was commissioned to compose a platform with no further mandate from the Executive Committee. The general secretary, the highest full-time official of the party, presided over the group, which included an ambassador, a member of a cantonal government, a journalist, the full-time secretaries of three large cantonal parties, a sociologist, and a political scientist. All of the members of the group were concerned with politics as a main occupation in one form or another. The group proceeded with plenary sessions every three or four weeks on the average. No special subcommittees were formed.

At first the group made a thorough evaluation of the political situation with respect to the coming election, using a report by the journalist as a basis for discussion. Starting with this situation report, one of the social scientists prepared a first draft of the platform. This draft was then discussed in several sessions. When a second draft was to be written, the group instituted a division of labor by distributing various sections of the platform to individual members. For example, the ambassador assumed the reformulation of the foreign policy section. The second draft was again discussed in the group. After this a third, a fourth, and a fifth draft were prepared using a similar division of labor. The fifth proposal was presented to an ad hoc study conference, which met for two days in Spiez in the fall of 1966. The meeting was presided over by the chairman of the federal party. The participants were the members of the Executive Committee and two to four prominent members of each cantonal party, which brought the total number of participants to seventy-six. The Spiez meeting was ad hoc and not provided for in the party statutes; it could therefore make recommendations only, not authoritative decisions.

After introductory reports by the secretary general and two other members of the working group, the conference discussed the platform in plenum. It was then divided into seven groups, and each of these groups considered a specific part of the platform. Finally, the results of the group work were reported and discussed in plenum. The recommendations of the conference with respect to individual sections in some respects deviated considerably from the fifth draft of the original working group. Based on the criticisms articulated at the Spiez conference, the working group, with some new members, reworked its fifth draft of the platform during the winter of 1966–67. This revised version was approved without major changes in the spring of 1967 by the regular organs of the party—Executive Committee, Central Committee, and party convention. At the convention, which is open to the public, no changes were made, nor were any even proposed. This outline of the formal origin of the election platform gives the impression that only a tiny fraction of all party members exerted influence on its composition. Surely, an observer who sees only the publicly manifested events would not have evidence to believe otherwise. He would only know that the party convention accepted the platform submitted to it in the spring of 1967 without amendments. The conclusion could be drawn that only a small group within the party, perhaps only one person, has decided on the provisions contained in the platform. If, however, we are aware of more than the publicly visible occurrences and the formal aspects of the decision-making process, the picture becomes essentially different. Clearly no one person determined the actual content of the election platform. It was not the procedure of the working group for one and the same member to make all the proposals, which were then accepted by the other members in a more or less identical form. It was rather the result of team work; a comparison of the several drafts shows how the proposals and formulations of all group members became part of the final version.

With few exceptions the decisions of the group were not reached by formal votes. More often the discussion was carried on long enough to reach a compromise acceptable to all. In delicate matters the compromise consisted partly of a postponement of the actual decision. A clear example of this was the case of possible Swiss membership in the United Nations. There were contrary opinions in the working group, and neither wing could expect to convert the other. Instead of making the decision by formal vote, agreement was reached on the compromise that "the political authorities first should investigate the contingencies and modes of a possible membership." All the members of the group could agree to this suggestion because it deferred the actual decision, and neither supporters nor opponents would suffer a defeat. Both could hope to make their respective positions more effectively heard during the proposed investigations.

The analysis of the procedure in the working group has shown two phenomena characteristic of the political system of Switzerland, which will be found repeatedly in other contexts throughout this work. For one thing, group effort and not individual effort was the prominent feature in the preparation of the platform. Second, the decisions were not made by formal votes, which would have alienated the minority. On the contrary, there was a tendency to find compromise formulations acceptable to all, with a frequent postponement of the actual decisions in controversial matters. It might also be asked if the content of the election platform was determined solely by the working group, or if other individuals and groups had a decisive influence in determining it. The position of the higher regular party organs, the Executive Committee, the Central Committee, and the party convention, is of special interest here. Was the platform only allegedly decided by those agencies? Were the decisions really made by the working group? Is there then an oligarchy of full-time political experts in the party who exert actual power behind the facade of the regular party institutions? A superficial look at the origin of the platform could easily lead to this conclusion, since the proposals of the working group passed through the regular party organs without major changes. But such a conclusion would not be taking into consideration some essential elements in that decision-making process.

It should be considered that the majority of the members of the formal party organs attended the ad hoc conference in Spiez. On this occasion the proposed platform was subjected to rather severe criticism. The conference differed from the working group with respect to the issues they would give priority to in the platform. The criticisms articulated at Spiez turned out to be effective. By far the larger part of the recommendations made there were taken into consideration by the working group in the final version of the platform. Therefore, the Spiez conference was not at all a mere gesture of politeness to the members of the formal leading party organs.

The conference also illustrated a process that is characteristic of the political system of Switzerland. Important decisions are made frequently during a procedure prior to the framework provided for them by the existing institutions. In the present case the party convention was the agency authorized to deliberate and decide on the election platform. The actual decisions were made at the ad hoc conference in Spiez. Since the majority of the members of the party convention—and particularly the politically relevant members—also participated in the Spiez meeting, one might be led to believe that the decisions simply had been made half a year earlier than scheduled. A closer analysis does show, however, that there were structural changes during the course of the decision-making that were connected with the chronological change. Most of all, the decision assumed a provisional character. The working group made it explicit that its draft needed further scrutiny and was to be considered only a basis for discussion. In the invitation to the conference the secretary general wrote, among other things: "This is a working paper. . . . The working group is aware that the draft may provoke discussion in many respects, which is in conformity with the purpose of the conference, and that certain formulations need to be concretized." This view enabled the working group to avoid having to consider criticisms of the draft a disavowal of their own efforts. On the other hand, the conference participants typically prefaced their critical remarks with the following: "Since this is only a provisional draft, it is not possible to appraise it conclusively. I would, however, like to submit a few things for consideration in the further discussion."

The frequent reference to the provisionality of the discussion prevented the formation of barriers between the working group and the other participants in the conference. If the discussion had not taken place until the party convention, the working group would have been obliged to present a definitive draft. In such a situation it would have been much more likely for the working group to perceive critique as a loss of prestige so that they presumably would have reacted much more strongly to critical remarks than they did in Spiez. On the other hand, the critics would not have been content with giving polite recommendations, but they would have had to make concrete proposals, which would have had to be decided on in an immediate vote. Since the decision about the platform was already made at Spiez, conflicts had been concealed from the public because the conference had been held behind closed doors. It is evident that attacks made publicly appear more offensive than those made in a closed circle. In Spiez it could even be observed how many criticisms were communicated in personal conversations with members of the working group rather than in the formal meetings. If the discussion had not taken place until the party convention, all criticisms would have had to take place in plenum.

So far we have only judged the influence of the regular party authorities on the content of the platform by one criterion: those changes in the draft of the working group that were proposed by the regular party authorities in Spiez, and subsequently accepted. This one criterion would no doubt underestimate the influence of the regular party authorities. It is also important to note that the working group anticipated how the Spiez conference and later the Executive Committee, the Central Committee, and the party convention would react to their proposals. The anticipation of the working group was, to a large extent, the result of stored information based on old platforms. The Free Democrats have issued such platforms for a long time. During the sessions of the working group there were particularly frequent references to the 1963 platform. Such comparisons were relevant because the circumstances of the 1967 election were similar to those of earlier elections—a fact that points to the continuity of political developments in Switzerland. Information from past campaigns was available to the working group through documentation and also through the personal experiences of its members, most of whom had already assisted more than once in the preparation of election platforms. The secretary general, who presided over the group, had already experienced three other elections during his time in office. Because of the extended personal background of most group members the feedback effect was such that the drafters of the platform were able to take into account the earlier reactions of the regular party authorities.

To anticipate the reaction of the leading party members the working group did not rely solely on stored information, but also used current information. Role accumulation created a direct link to the most important organ of the federal party, the seventeen-member Executive Committee, three members of which were also members of the working group, which also included six of the eighty-two members of the Central Committee. Role accumulation also linked the working group with most of the standing committees of the party. Thanks to these channels information about the situation within the other party agencies flowed continuously into the working group. The information, both stored and topical, which was relayed to the working group, was so extensive that the group could anticipate fairly exactly the reactions in other parts of the party. Although the Executive Committee had not specified its mandate in great detail at the time the working group was formed, the group was well aware of what was expected from it. It was therefore in little danger of getting into a major role conflict by assuming a different role from the one the party authorities expected it to play. How the group anticipated these reactions and oriented its behavior accordingly can be shown by two examples. The first example has to do with the ideological character of the platform. Most members of the working group knew from personal experience and the results of scientific research that ideological formulations in an election manifesto do not have much appeal to the average voter. Although this position was presented with emphasis in many sessions, the final version contained ideological statements like the following: "Liberalism is based on the conviction that man is charged with the task of struggling again and again towards the right political decisions. It is a cultural and political orientation of critical openness on the basis of distinct liberal principles." The working group included such ideological statements in the platform because its past experience led it to anticipate that many members of the regular party authorities expected election platforms to repeat certain ideological tenets. The second example concerned the question of full-time parliamentary careers in Switzerland. Some members of the working group were supporters of such an innovation. But they did not even try to press their demand in the group, although it would not have been impossible to reach at least a compromise solution. They anticipated that their demand might have been rejected by the regular party organs because the idea that the members of Parliament should not be full time still had very strong roots at that level. Thus the conflict was regulated in such a way that the problem was not articulated at all.

It should now have become clear that the regular party organs helped to determine the nature of the platform in intricate ways. On the one hand, the working group made considerable changes in the manifesto on the basis of the Spiez recommendations, and on the other hand, it was quite able to anticipate the demands of the party authorities and to consider them during the preparation of the drafts. This does not mean, of course, that the working group had no influence on the program. The role assigned to the group allowed it influence within certain limits. An analysis of these limits could be made through the issues—the group's influence on foreign policy, for instance, might be different from its influence on agricultural policy. It would also be interesting to find out which members of the working group used what means to reach what ends and with what success. The same questions could be investigated for members of other party organs. Such an extended analysis would be necessary for the development of a theory of political parties.[159] In the present context it is not necessary to go that far. It is enough to state that the statutory agencies, i.e., the Executive Committee, the Central Committee, and the party convention, had considerable influence on the content of the election platform.

Within the party at large the members of the central organs at the federal level are but a negligible minority. The history of the origin of the platform demonstrates that besides the members of the central hierarchy, a large number of other party members, and even nonmembers, have also directly or indirectly influenced the election platform in one form or another. It is important in this case that the nine members of the working group all belonged to and were rather active in some local party organization. For example, the secretary general of the federal party was for a long time president of the party branch in a middle-sized Swiss town. This local role was more than merely symbolic in the sense of an honorary title, but it was actually a role he performed. The consequence of this was that the members of this local party organization perceived the secretary general as an exponent of the federal as well as of the local party. His local role reduced his social distance from the other members of his local organization, and he learned much that would not have reached him as a representative of the federal party. His dual role made for a direct channel of communication between local party members and the centralized party office. Other members of the working group had similar role accumulations that helped to establish direct communication between the local and the federal levels. The group was therefore kept continuously informed about demands articulated in the local party sections, and it believed strongly that those demands should be considered. A member would have been exposed to severe sanctions if he had declared that information from the local levels was irrelevant. This would have been a violation of a norm deeply adhered to in Switzerland, namely, that the political leadership must be accessible to demands from the grass roots.

The flow of communication to the working group by way of role accumulations at the local level went through a filtering process in that the members of the group often communicated demands in conformity with their own views. However, the group had developed a safeguard against information that was too strongly filtered. If a certain bit of information was produced by *one* member only, it was registered as a possibly atypical case, which took away its major influence. If several members conveyed the same information, the pressure on the group to consider it was much greater. Since role accumulation with the local level occurred in all the other party agencies as well, the total result was a rather complex configuration of communication lines through which the rank-and-file members of local party sections could exert their influence on the formulation of the election platform. However, not all local organizations had access to this communications structure because the number of local party sections far exceeded the number of members in the federal party organs.

A second channel through which the demands of the ordinary citizens reached the federal party hierarchy were elections and referenda. There is hardly a Sunday in Switzerland without an election or a referendum somewhere at the federal, cantonal, or local level. In the scholarly literature elections and referenda are primarily analyzed from the perspective of citizen participation in the processes that provide for the making of authoritative decisions. My case study of the Free Democratic election platform makes it clear that elections and referenda have a function not only for the output of decisions, but also for the input of demands.

During the two-year deliberations of the working group there were elections in several cantons and local communities. The Free Democratic strength after these elections was diminished; particularly painful was the loss of five seats each in the cantons of Berne and Geneva. Such losses caused the working group to discuss the following questions in detail: What demands do the voters who turn away from the Free Democratic party want to express? Do they think that the party is too progressive or on the contrary too conservative? Do they want to give the party a hint that it should be more oriented to social policy or less so? Has the party been too pragmatic or too ideological? In the discussion of these questions many diverse opinions could be found in the group. The different interpretations of these issues has to be connected with the fact that it is hardly possible to distinguish between government and opposition parties in the political system of Switzerland. Because of this diffuseness it was difficult for the group to deduce the real demands of the citizenry from the election results, since a loss of votes for the Free Democrats could not immediately be interpreted as a demonstration for or against government policy.

The demands of the voters were made clearer through the referenda. During the deliberations of the group the budget requests of several local communities were rejected by the voters, a phenomenon that had not occurred for a long time. If the budgets were cut, they were usually accepted by the people in a second or third referendum. The working group was in agreement that these referenda results could be interpreted as a demand by the public for more economy. This perception of public opinion had a considerable effect on the content of the election platform, which included the following provisions for fiscal stability:

1. fiscal planning at the federal, cantonal, and local levels by the creation of an inventory of the potential projects and a selection of priorities based on this inventory
2. increase in public expenditures only within the limits of the increase in national income
3. periodical review of all statutory expenditures, and approval of new subventions generally for limited time periods

In the period before the previous election in 1963 budgets were rejected much less frequently. The 1963 platform also contained no demands to restrict public expenditures, but only a vague allusion that measures to avoid an overload of taxation were overdue. This comparison of the two platforms supports my hypothesis that referenda constitute an effective channel for the communication of the demands from the citizen to the central party authorities. Of course it was possible that many voters intended their "no" to the budget to express demands other than the reduction of public expenditures. Specifically, citizen preferences with respect to *which* expenditures should be reduced reached the working group only in an oblique way. The group made comparisons with other referenda outcomes. It could see, for instance, that proposals in the health field (hospital construction, etc.) had usually received large majorities of "yes" votes. From this it concluded that the voters did not primarily want reductions in this area. Interpretations such as these are weakened, of course, by the fact that many voters perceive the connections between the individual referenda in a less conscious way than the working group did.

I have no data on which to base an appraisal of the validity of the group interpretation of the citizen demands as expressed on the ballot. It does seem probable, though, that referenda are more direct channels of communication than elections. The interpretations of the election outcomes by the working group did differ to the degree that no clear picture emerged that could have influenced the content of the platform. In contrast, the referenda enabled the members of the group to reach much more similar interpretations. Although these interpretations may not always have been quite correct, they were still able to influence the work of the group, and since it is not to be assumed that such interpretations were entirely unrelated to the actual demands of the citizens, the referenda thus constituted a channel of communication through which the citizens could influence the election platform rather strongly.

Intermediary groups constituted a third channel through which citizen demands were transmitted to the central party authorities. For example, the vice-president of the Federal Gymnastics Association at the time was a member of the working group. He frequently assumed the role of a representative of the gymnasts in presenting their demands to the group. This happened, for instance, in the following summary he made to the group:

> The promotion of gymnastics and sports is important not only with a view to the needs of the army and the defence of the country. Physical training is also a means of fighting and overcoming the negative consequences of the progress of civilization, including the general lassitude and the pamper-

> ing that have spiritual and psychological consequences as well. . . . The Free Democrats expect the state to contribute fundamentally to this by an active furtherance of projects aimed towards physical education where possibilities for direct public efforts appear in schools at all levels. Similarly subsidiary help (e.g., construction of and generous permission to use appropriate facilities) can be given to support gymnastics and sports clubs and all other organizations which serve the purpose of physical edification.

As will be shown below, the Federal Gymnastics Association has an extensive communications net from the individual local sections to the federal leadership. It can therefore be assumed that numerous bits of information from the local sections flowed to the vice-president who had the important task of relaying the demands of the gymnasts to the working group. By analogous role accumulations (the presidents of the Swiss Union of Artisans and the Swiss Farmers' Union both belonged to the Executive Committee of the party), the demands of many other intermediary groups found their way to the central party authorities. Demands of intermediary groups were frequently effective even though no representative was there to articulate them. For instance, there was no representative for the Swiss Farmers' Union in the working group. The demands of the union were manifest all the same, since they could be anticipated from recent reports, positions, press releases, etc.

A retrospective view of the results shows that there were many channels of communication through which ordinary party members as well as nonparty members could influence the content of the election platform. By role accumulation at the local and the federal level, by interpretation of election and referenda returns, and by giving an ear to the intermediary groups, the central party authorities gained access to the demands of the people.

One further fundamental factor that is characteristic of the political system of Switzerland in general is its federal structure. It is particularly relevant in this study of the Free Democratic party, in which the cantonal, regional, district, and local parties have a large measure of independence. In the present case the federal structure became important because of the reinterpretation at the lower levels of the election platform worked out by the federal party organization. I was able to observe this process in detail in the Bernese party.

In the early summer of 1967 the cantonal party of Berne held a two-day conference in Gstaad. The conference was devoted to a discussion of the election platform of the federal party, and it served basically the same function within the cantonal party that the Spiez conference had served at the federal level. It was also a nonstipulated ad hoc meeting, and most members of the regular party authorities participated in it. If the basis of the Gstaad conference was the election platform that had been approved by the federal party convention, one might imagine that the cantonal party meant to restrict itself to translating the content of the platform into a practical strategy for the campaign. In that case the cantonal party would have had only executive functions in relation to the federal party. But the Gstaad conference showed something quite different: the Berne party proceeded to reinterpret and to adapt the federal platform for local conditions. Practically, this came about through the development of a list of demands which, from Berne's point of view, deserved primacy in federal politics. The participants in the conference did not in the least perceive the federal platform as a mandate; rather, they viewed it as a recommendation and even occasionally only as an aid to their memory about the different possible categories of demands. The independence of the Berne party was illustrated by the fact that not only were the demands in the federal platform reconsidered, but additional demands were added.

Two members of the federal party working group also participated in the Gstaad meeting. However, they were not only representatives of the federal party, but also active members in the Berne party. One belonged to the Executive Committee and the other to the Committee for Press and Propaganda. It is characteristic of the Free Democratic party that this communication took place by role accumulation. Only rarely is the federal party represented at a cantonal party meeting by somebody who does not also belong to that cantonal party. This is particularly true for election campaigns in which it is uncommon for prominent national leaders to tour the cantons. The Free Democratic members of the Federal Council do not usually appear in the campaign. Other prominent representatives of the federal party, e.g., its president or the chairman of its parliamentary group, only rarely appear in cantonal parties to which they do not belong themselves. If the channels of communication between the federal and the cantonal parties consist primarily of persons with roles at both levels, this means a strengthening of the cantonal parties. In the present case both of the members of the working group who participated in the Gstaad meeting did not represent the federal party one-sidedly, but also let their cantonal roles become important. This was expressed by their use of the word "we" in a double meaning about both the federal and the cantonal party. They did not try to defend the federal platform at any cost, but presented it more as a basis for discussion, on which the Berne party could found its own proposals.

The relation between the federal party and the cantonal party was analogous to that between the latter and the Bernese Oberland regional party, which took the liberty to reinterpret once again the demands formulated by the Berne party and to adapt them to the conditions peculiar to the Bernese Oberland. Traffic proposals were much more salient to the regional than to the cantonal party and, with respect to the question of whether an airport should be constructed in Berne, there was even a certain amount of antagonism between the two party levels.

Finally, I was able to observe that the district party and the city party in Thun did not feel committed to the demands articulated at the higher party levels, but felt free to adapt them to local conditions. The independence of the lower echelons in the party expressed in this way caused the demands of the Free Democratic party for the 1967 National Council election to appear as a many-faceted whole.

The federalism expressed by these examples does not correspond to the widespread view that federalism is a process through which decisions are made in a stepwise movement from the bottom to the top. The federal platform did not start with the local sections articulating their demands, which were then gathered and condensed at each level. It was much more the case that each level worked more or less at the same time. The cantonal parties, for instance, did not delay their own work until the federal party had concluded its platform. Nor did the federal party wait for the cantonal parties before it started its own work. There was a feedback mechanism between individual party levels, and the channels of communication consisted primarily of people with roles at two or more levels. The feedback flowed in both directions—the intermediary levels trying to take the expectations of the levels above and below into consideration. It is because of this mechanism that the variation in the demands articulated by the party never became too blatant.

I have now presented the most important findings of my case study of the origin of the election platform of the Free Democratic party for the 1967 National Council election. I will summarize the results in some general descriptive propositions, abstracted from the concrete substance of the study:[160]

1* In the Free Democratic party the role of innovation on the federal level is basically restricted to a relatively small group of usually not more than twenty to thirty members.

2* These groups consist primarily of persons who are perceived to be experts in the issues related to the innovation. (They will therefore be called "expert groups" from now on.)

3* The expert groups include persons in leading positions in the formal party hierarchy and persons in subordinate positions in the formal organization of the party.

4* The amount of influence among the individual members of the expert groups tends not to be too different.

5* The expert groups tend to regulate conflicts not by the majority principle but by the principle of amicable agreement.

6* If the expert groups cannot regulate a conflict by the principle of amicable agreement, they tend to defer the decision.

7* The individual expert groups are in a relatively close feedback relationship to a relatively large group varying in size from fifty to two hundred.

8* This reference group consists primarily of persons who, with respect to the topic of a certain expert group, are perceived not as experts, but as generalists. (This group will be called a "generalist group" from now on.)

9* A member of a generalist group on one topic may belong to an expert group on another topic.

10* A generalist group may include generalists in a narrower sense, that is, persons who are not experts in any particular topic, but who, to some extent, are specialists in synthesizing the individual topics.

11* The leaders in the formal party hierarchy usually belong to the generalist group.

12* On the other hand, many of the members of the generalist group are not in leading positions in the formal organization of the party.

13* The expert groups tend to anticipate the reactions of the generalist group relatively precisely and to make their decisions according to these anticipated reactions.

14* The expert groups anticipate the reactions of the generalist group on the basis of stored as well as current information. The stored information, which originates mainly in the personal experience of the group members, is a relatively reliable basis for the anticipation process, because the membership of the expert as well as the generalist groups changes relatively infrequently, and the political process in Switzerland is relatively continuous. The current information is usually transmitted to the expert group by persons with many role accumulations.

15* There is a tendency to reduce conflicts between the expert and the generalist groups by moving important decisions from the statutorily provided institutions to prior meetings in an ad hoc environment not visible to the public.

16* Both the expert group and the generalist group are in a feedback relationship with the majority of the party members, a relationship which is looser than the one referred to in Proposition 7* between the expert group and the generalist group.

17* The most reliable information from the ordinary party members reach the generalist and expert groups primarily through the following channels: (a) role accumulations at the local and the federal party levels, (b) other intermediary groups, and (c) referenda results. In contrast, the ordinary party members have little opportunity in elections to articulate their demands unambiguously since the political system of Switzerland makes a vague distinction between government and opposition parties.

18* At the lower party levels there are expert and generalist groups similar to those in the federal party. The interlevel communication consists primarily of persons with role accumulations.

Since the above propositions have been formulated from a single case, it might be useful to determine whether they can be applied to other decision-making processes in the Free Democratic party. I am in the fortunate position of being able to test them in another rather different situation, namely, by examining the history of the origin of a letter from the Free Democratic party to the Federal Department of the Interior on June 29, 1967, in which the party articulated several demands with respect to federal university policy. This case is different from the election platform situation primarily in the following respects:

1. The letter was restricted to one topic, i.e., university policy, whereas the platform contained demands from all policy areas.
2. The demands of the letter were based on the text of a concrete law, whereas the platform formulated its demands in more general terms.
3. The demands of the letter were reviewed and resolved by the Executive Committee, those of the platform, by the party convention.
4. There were only two months available for the formulation of the letter, which was an answer to a letter from the Federal Department of the Interior of April 24 of the same year. The preparation of the platform took almost two years.
5. The letter was not published, whereas the platform was distributed in large numbers.

The overview shows that the two cases differ in many respects. In order to generalize from one to the other, the propositions would have to apply in both cases. I will now proceed by comparing each of the eighteen propositions to my second case.

*Proposition 1**:

> In the Free Democratic party the role of innovation on the federal level is basically restricted to a relatively small group of usually not more than twenty to thirty members.

*Proposition 2**:

> These groups consist primarily of persons who are perceived to be experts in the issues related to the innovation.

The content of the letter was proposed not by the Executive Committee itself, but by the Committee for Politics and Culture. Was this committee a relatively small group as dictated by Propositions 1* and 2*? It had twenty-nine members of whom only approximately one-third were perceived as experts on university affairs. The rest of the members were experts in some of the other areas that the committee had to concern itself with, the protection of the environment, for example. It seems, then, that Proposition 2* is not valid in this case since only a minority of the committee members were experts in the relevant policy area. A closer look does show, however, that, on one hand, most of the nonexperts did not participate in the deliberations at all, and, on the other, that the committee was supplemented ad hoc for the university policy discussion by six definite experts in the field. Because of these two circumstances, the deliberations were carried out mainly by experts on university policy. Some of the experts were (1) the president of the Swiss Council of Science, (2) an administrator of a university, (3) the university affairs editor from a large newspaper, (4) a former board member of the Union of Swiss Student Groups, and (5) a former member of a cantonal government responsible for educational affairs. Propositions 1* and 2* may thus be considered confirmed. Within the institutional framework of the Committee for Politics and Culture there had actually been formed a relatively small ad hoc group that consisted mainly of experts in university affairs.

*Proposition 3**:

> The expert groups include persons in leading positions in the formal party hierarchy and persons in subordinate positions in the formal organization of the party.

On the basis of the study of the election platform I formulated the proposition that the members of the expert group are neither all represented in, nor all excluded from, the top of the formal party hierarchy. This proposition could not be confirmed for the Executive Committee. One member of the Committee for Politics and Culture did belong to the Executive Committee, but he was not an expert in university policy and did not participate in the discussions relevant to our present concern. One of the university experts, however, belonged to the Central Committee of the party. Of the expert group preparing the election platform, one-third belonged to the Executive Committee and two-thirds belonged to the Central Committee. The difference between the two cases can hypothetically be explained by the fact that the party perceived university policy as less central—at least at that time—than the preparation of an electoral campaign. The party therefore found it more important to have experts in campaign management among its formal leaders than experts in university policy. In a more general way, the hypothesis states that role accumulation between formal leadership and expert groups increases as the specialty of the relevant expert group is seen as more central to the party.

*Proposition 4**:

The amount of influence among the individual members of the expert group tends not to be too different.

*Proposition 5**:

The expert groups tend to regulate conflicts not by the majority principle but by the principle of amicable agreement.

The university affairs expert group limited its deliberations to one session of a little more than two hours. The basis of the discussion was laid out by the president of the Council of Science in a fifteen-minute introductory report. The discussion concentrated almost exclusively on the problem of the extent and the manner in which the federation should attach conditions to its financial support of cantonal universities. With respect to the direction of inquiries for information and opinions, and the giving of information and opinions, it was clear that the president of the Council of Science was the center of the group. Such a centering of communication on one person had hardly ever occurred in the working group that had prepared the election platform. The president of the Council of Science held this prominent position because the other members perceived him as particularly knowledgeable in the subject; his position as a former university president and member of the National Council also contributed to the respect he received.[161] However, this exceptional position did not give him a monopoly of influence and the other members did not content themselves with mere approval of his views. The president of the Council of Science did not aim at such a monopoly of influence, either, because he was well aware that it would have been contrary to the accepted social norms of such expert groups. His efforts to present his statements as provisional and in need of criticism clearly showed his relationship to the group. A comparison of the decisions of the expert group and the stated opinions of the president also demonstrates that many decisions followed the proposals of other members of the group.

Furthermore, there was a clear tendency to strive for compromises. No supporter or opponent of strong federal influence on the cantonal universities used the negotiation strategy to present his views in an extreme form. It appeared to me that many of the speakers put forth their opinions in a more moderate form than had often been the case in personal conversations. In some questions the will to compromise was extended so far that agreement in the sense of Proposition 5* was reached without a formal vote. The tendency to avoid formal votes was, however, less prominent than in the expert group that had prepared the election platform.[162] In spite of the above reservations it may be concluded that Propositions 4* and 5* can be considered confirmed, at least in general.

*Proposition 6**:

> If the expert groups cannot regulate a conflict by the principle of amicable agreement, they tend to defer the decision.

The tendency to defer the actual decisions in case of excessively large differences of opinion could also be found in this group. In the strongly controversial matter of the composition of an anticipated coordination agency at the federal level, a compromise in the sense of Proposition 6* was reached, since the letter to the Department of the Interior says: "We do not consider it our task to submit detailed proposals. However, we urge that the respective article of the bill be reconsidered." This formulation corresponds closely to the one in the election platform calling for a review by the federal authorities of the possibilities and modes of Swiss admission to the United Nations.

*Proposition 7**:

> The individual expert groups are in a relatively close feedback relationship to a relatively large group varying in size from fifty to two hundred.

*Proposition 8**:

This reference group consists primarily of persons who, with respect to the topic of a certain expert group, are perceived not as experts, but as generalists.

*Proposition 9**:

A member of a generalist group on one topic may belong to an expert group on another topic.

*Proposition 10**:

A generalist group may include generalists in a narrower sense, that is, persons who are not experts in any particular topic, but who, to some extent, are specialists in synthesizing the individual topics.

*Proposition 11**:

The leaders in the formal party hierarchy usually belong to the generalist group.

*Proposition 12**:

On the other hand, many of the members of the generalist group are not in leading positions in the formal organization of the party.

These propositions deal with the question of whether there was feedback contact between the expert group on university policy and a generalist group. My observations during the deliberations and particularly in informal conversations outside the sessions showed that the expert group had a reference group to which its decisions were at least partially oriented. The communication channels connecting expert group and reference group will be investigated in connection with the Propositions 13* through 16*.

At the moment the problem is to delineate the reference group more closely. First, we could see that its members were perceived by the expert group to be not competing experts, but generalists who were expected to bring university policy into a more general political context. This confirms Proposition 8*. Whom did the expert group perceive to be the members of this generalist group? In the forefront were the eighteen members of the Executive Committee, who were the formal respondents to the letter from the Department of the Interior. In the second rank, but still clearly visible, were the sixty-four members of the parliamentary group. This is explainable by the fact that the issue was related to a draft of a bill, which in a later phase had to be considered by Parliament. A third subgroup within the generalist group was perceived differently by the individual members of the expert groups. In principle it comprised individuals who were generalists in the present context but experts in other areas. Members of the committees for financial and youth affairs belonged to it since the university policy had important financial aspects on one hand, and was, on the other hand, of particular interest to the young. Furthermore, some members of the expert group also counted the members of the committees for agricultural and artisan affairs among the generalist group because they anticipated that an excessive support for university education could be perceived by these committees as directed against the interests of farmers and artisans. Finally, some journalists were perceived as the fourth subgroup of the generalist group. On the whole, we can conclude that the generalist group could not be defined unambiguously. Certain persons, particularly the members of the Executive Committee and the parliamentary group, were perceived by almost all members of the expert group to belong to the generalist group. This was not the case for most of the experts from other fields and for most journalists.

We might also ask whether the expert group perceived the generalist group as a whole or as individual subgroups. That is, were the relevant reference groups the individual subgroups, such as the Executive Committee, the parliamentary group, and so on, or was the generalist group seen as a whole? My observations showed that the generalist group was perceived as a whole. Whether a person belonged to the Finance Committee or to the parliamentary group was far less important than whether he belonged to the generalist group. The same was true for the self-perception of the generalists. The "we feelings" were much more prominent within the total generalist group than within the individual subgroups. The generalist group considered itself the inner circle of the party, and, as such, responsible for the political line of the party. That the individual subgroups of the generalist group did not display much group consciousness is probably primarily related to the many role accumulations among the subgroups. What was the size of the generalist group? The answer to this question depends on who is answering it—the expert group or the generalist group. I have not undertaken any elaborate attempts at counting, but I estimate that the generalist group comprised 90 to 150 members. It is at least within the limits of Proposition 7*, which requires 50 to 200 members.

Proposition 13:*

> The expert groups tend to anticipate the reactions of the generalist group relatively precisely and to make their decisions according to these anticipated reactions.

*Proposition 14**:

> The expert groups anticipate the reactions of the generalist group on the basis of stored as well as current information. The stored information, which originates mainly in the personal experience of the group members, is a relatively reliable basis for the anticipation process, because the membership of the expert as well as the generalist group changes relatively infrequently, and the political process in Switzerland is relatively continuous. The current information is usually transmitted to the expert group by persons with many role accumulations.

Before we can determine to what extent and how precisely the expert groups anticipated the reactions of the generalist group, we should investigate what kind of stored information was available to the expert group, and how relevant it turned out to be. According to Proposition 14* the relevance of stored information is increased by the fact that the political development in Switzerland is relatively continuous. Since the total revision of the Federal Constitution in 1874, the federal government has had the authority to subsidize the cantonal universities (Article 27). On several occasions and particularly in 1888, 1906, and 1946, unsuccessful attempts were made to put this article into practice. It was only in 1966 that the federal Parliament decided provisionally to give two hundred million Swiss francs in federal aid to the cantonal universities for the years 1966–68. When in 1967 the Free Democrats had to formulate their demands for the definite regulation of the federal contributions, that theme had been salient in Swiss politics for almost a hundred years. Furthermore, the arguments for and against federal aid had not changed substantially. In 1888, for instance, the university cantons, Basel-City, Berne, Geneva, Neuchâtel, Vaud, and Zurich gave as the reason for their requests for federal aid the increasing costs of the natural sciences, an argument that recurred in the 1960s. This slow and continuous evolution permits information gathered over decades to have a certain relevance for the present situation. Even information about what had happened in the last century was of actual importance to the Free Democratic party. Since the Federal Council at that time consisted almost exclusively of Free Democrats, the present-day party's freedom to suggest changes was somewhat restricted. It could not criticize the federation too strongly for not having acted earlier on financial assistance for the cantonal universities. Such criticism would very probably have caused the opponents to attack the historical contribution of the Free Democrats.

Even more relevant were the events leading to the positive decision of the Parliament in 1966. The behavior of the party during that time kept its present latitude of maneuvering relatively narrow. A political change of mind could be even less justified with a change in circumstances than a deviation from the policy of the past century. My observations show that the information about the past stand of the party was of great importance in the expert group. On the basis of this stored information, the expert group anticipated the reactions of the generalist group. The expert group did not expect the generalists to oppose federal aid in principle after the party had approved the provisional regulation. On the other hand, the experts anticipated that the generalist group would not accept a federal take-over of the cantonal universities because that would have contradicted the cultural policy of the party for the past century. An extrapolation of the past into the future was made easier for the expert group not only by the continuous development of university policy, but also by the fact that the members of both the expert and the generalist groups typically had had these roles for a relatively long time. It is evident that it is simpler to anticipate specific role expectations if the role players remain the same.

Finally Proposition 14* was also confirmed insofar as there were many role accumulations connecting generalists and experts. Two members of the expert group were members of the parliamentary group. There were also role accumulations with expert groups from other fields; one member of the university expert group, for example, was also an expert on financial affairs. He said explicitly in one of his statements that he wanted to speak as a representative for the Committee for Finance and Taxation. The multitude of role accumulations between the expert and the generalist group allowed many pieces of information to flow to the former and facilitated its anticipations of the reactions of the latter. Combined with the previously mentioned information about the earlier stands of the party, the expert group had a broad basis for a relatively precise prognosis about the behavior of the generalist group. That the experts oriented their decisions strongly to the anticipated reactions of the generalists, and that these reactions were anticipated relatively correctly, can be seen from the fact that the Executive Committee on the whole conceived the letter to the Federal Department of the Interior in accordance with the proposals made by the expert group. Occasional negative comments were made in quite different directions; some thought that the expert group gave too much authority to the federation, and others that it gave too little. The expert group was able to manipulate its proposal in such a way that it assumed a middle position on the spectrum of opinion.

*Proposition 15**:

> There is a tendency to reduce conflicts between the expert and the generalist group by moving important decisions from the statutorily provided institutions to prior meetings in an ad hoc environment not visible to the public.

Between the session of the expert group and that of the Executive Committee there were no ad hoc deliberations between the two groups. Does this mean that Proposition 15* does not hold since it states that conflicts between expert and generalist groups are reduced by the fact that important decisions are made outside of and prior to the forum provided by the institutional framework? It should be noted that the expert group had anticipated and taken into account the reactions of the generalist group so precisely that there were no conflicts to reduce, which means that Proposition 15* cannot be applied to this specific case.

*Proposition 16**:

> Both the expert group and the generalist group are in a feedback relationship with the majority of the party members, a relationship which is looser than the one referred to in Proposition 7* between the expert group and the generalist group.

*Proposition 17**:

> The most reliable information from the ordinary party members reach the generalist and expert groups primarily through the following channels: (a) role accumulations at the local and federal levels, (b) other intermediary groups, and (c) referenda results. In contrast, the ordinary party members have little opportunity in elections to articulate their demands unambiguously since the political system of Switzerland makes a vague distinction between government and opposition parties.

Was there a feedback loop between the expert group and the generalist group on one hand and the majority of the party members on the other? My observations allow for an answer to this question only with respect to the expert group. Proposition 17* refers to referenda as one possible channel of communication between the rank-and-file party members and the expert group. This channel was active in the present case: the experts tried to interpret several referenda concerning educational affairs. The referenda had taken place within recent months at the cantonal and the local levels and had had negative outcomes in higher proportion than referenda in earlier years. In particular, expensive projects for construction of school buildings had generally barely been accepted and sometimes had even been rejected. The expert group concluded from this that excessively generous federal grants-in-aid to the cantonal universities would produce a negative response from the man in the street. These reactions could have great political relevance, since the federal law for the development of universities was subject to optional referendum.[163] Because the referendum was hanging over the proposal like the sword of Damocles the expert group could not ignore the anticipated reactions of the citizens.

In conformity with Proposition 17* the expert group also received information about the electorate through intermediary groups. The clearest example of this channel of communication was one member of the group who combined the roles of university expert and full-time official for an economic interest group. That member informed the other experts that his interest group believed that federal university expenditures should not be fixed at such a high level that it would endanger the position of vocational education at the lower levels. A representative of another intermediary group articulated the same view in a somewhat less extreme form. The referenda and intermediary groups reinforced each other's influence. This can be understood if we recall the meaning of the optional referendum: 30,000 signatures are required to call for a referendum against a law at the federal level, and to accomplish this, it is necessary to have an organization of a size, which, as a rule, only major groups have. The intermediary groups represented in the expert group had extensive experience in the organization of referenda. It therefore had to be taken into account that failure to honor their demands for a certain limit to the federal expenditures in support of cantonal universities would lead them to call for a referendum. Their influence was great because the members of the expert group knew that educational proposals recently had run a higher risk of being defeated in a referendum. On the other hand, the influence of past referenda outcomes was increased because the expert group was aware of the existence of groups that were prepared to call for a referendum if their demands were given insufficient consideration. The expert group learned that many citizens were against large federal subsidies to the cantonal universities not only from referenda and intermediary groups, but also through role accumulations at the federal and the local level, i.e., the third channel of communication mentioned in

Proposition 17*. In summary it has been shown that the expert group, in conformity with Proposition 16*, was in a feedback connection with the majority of the party members and even with many nonparty members, and that the channels of communication were, in conformity with Proposition 17*, primarily constituted by role accumulations at the local and the federal levels, by intermediary groups, and by referenda.

Proposition 18:*

> At the lower party levels there are expert and generalist groups similar to those in the federal party. The interlevel communication consists primarily of persons with role accumulations.

As was the case with the election platform, the lower party echelons articulated some demands concerning university policy that were not in agreement with the position of the federal party in every respect. Again, I was able to observe this primarily in the cantonal party in Berne. Whereas with the election platform, the cantonal party of Berne had articulated its demands only after the decision of the federal party, it had by the winter of 1966–67 worked out proposals for a definitive regulation of federal support for the cantonal universities. This indicates that there are no fixed rules as to which party level has chronological priority in the articulation of demands.

The Berne cantonal party primarily considered the university problem with a view toward the University of Berne, which is administered by the canton of Berne. But beyond that it also directed its attention to university affairs at the federal level and articulated demands on that level without prior consultation with the federal party. That the independently made decisions of the cantonal party of Berne and the federal party finally did not deviate too strongly from each other was due to the fact that there were three role accumulations connecting the expert groups in university matters at the two levels, which confirms one further aspect of Proposition 18*. In accordance with Proposition 18* it was also possible to distinguish an expert and a generalist group in the Berne party, which had a mutual feedback loop and also one to the majority of party members. These two feedback systems functioned in much the same way as they did at the federal level.

In conclusion, it may be said that the eighteen propositions that developed from the case study about the origin of the election platform were confirmed more or less by the study concerning decision-making in university policy. The important thing about the comparison is that two feedback systems are operative when party demands are articulated, and that these two systems overlap. One system connects a group of experts with a group of generalists, and the other connects both of these groups with the majority of party members. These two feedback systems do not exist only at the federal level, but at all party levels down to the local sections.

I will now turn to the question of whether these feedback systems are goal-seeking or goal-changing. Let us first consider the feedback system between the experts and the generalists. As shown by the case studies the feedback system is operative here in the sense that the expert group tried to orient its behavior to the goals of the generalist group. If this had been a goal-seeking feedback, the expert group would have taken the generalists' goals as given and would have aimed only at adjusting their own proposals to these goals. In that case the expert group would have had only an auxiliary function in making its expertise available to the generalists. Neither of the expert groups that we have studied restricted themselves to such an auxiliary function. On the contrary, they tried to change the goals of the generalist group.

We cannot judge the extent to which this intention was realized in our two case studies. For one thing, the goals of the experts and the generalists were very similar from the beginning. Consequently, any success on the part of the expert group in changing the goals of the generalist group could have only taken place in such small dimensions that an observation of it would have required very sensitive methods of measurement. Second, our two case studies dealt with only small sections of long processes. Thus, concerning the question of whether the federation should give subsidies to the cantonal universities, the feedback process between experts and generalists had not started with the preparation of the letter to the Federal Department of the Interior, but had already been in existence for almost one hundred years. Therefore, more sequences of the process would have to be studied to determine whether the expert group actually could change the goals of the generalist group. Third, it must be noted that the feedback process between one particular expert group and the generalist group cannot be studied in isolation from all the other expert groups, which also constantly attempt to change the goals of the generalist group. For example, the problem of whether the high proportion of foreigners at Swiss universities should be reduced interests not only university experts, but also—to mention only the most obvious groups—the financial and foreign policy experts. It is possible, and maybe even likely, that the three groups of experts would reach different conclusions from their specific points of view. It is not a question, then, of uniting the total influence of all expert groups into one measure because the influence of individual expert groups may cancel one another out. To reach conclusive results all expert groups that try to change a certain goal of the generalists should be studied during a particular interval. It would then no longer be the general question of whether expert groups change the goals of the generalist group, but rather more specifically which expert groups exert what influence. Finally, another complex factor that has to be considered is that the goals of the generalist group can be changed independently of the expert groups by the rank-and-file party members, by other parties, by economic interest groups, by voluntary associations, by the mass media, and so on. This list points to a wide field for promising individual studies.[164] For the moment, suffice it to say that the expert groups try to change the goals of the generalist group. The feedback system connecting the generalists and the experts with the majority of the ordinary party members is likewise a goal-changing feedback. According to my observations, neither group was content to adjust its proposals to the goals of the rank and file, but tried to change these goals.

It is important to understand the consequences of a blocked feedback system. Let us first look at the system connecting the expert and the generalist groups. A blocking of this system could happen if the experts were not informed sufficiently well and sufficiently early about the reactions of the generalists. The other possible blocking could come about if the experts were informed well enough and early enough about the reactions of the generalists, but did not take that information into consideration when making their decisions. In this case the experts would think themselves powerful enough to ignore the goals of the generalists.

The first of these possibilities is not important in the present context. For one thing, neither of the case studies showed major signs of such a blocking. Both expert groups were connected to the generalist group with such a multitude of narrow connections that information flowed abundantly. Second, such a blocking would more likely constitute a technical problem, the solution of which would be an improvement of the relevant channels of communication. Such a task would be interesting, but not fundamentally important in this study.

Of great relevance, on the contrary, is the question of what happens when the expert group consciously neglects to adapt its decisions to the goals of the generalist group. What sanctions does the generalist group use to exercise control over the expert group in such a situation? Neither of the case studies offers an adequate illustration of this because the analyzed expert groups had strongly internalized the norm that expected experts to be guided by the goals of the generalist group. Further observations of the Free Democratic party do, however, supply some cases, though not very blatant ones, in which the experts broke this norm. Reasons of discretion prohibit me from describing these violations in detail. More important are the sanctions that the generalist group resorted to in such cases. It turned out that there was a strong tendency to use informal sanctions that were scarcely visible externally. I am not aware of a single instance in recent years of an expert who was expelled from the party or suspended from his office. Even at the reelections by the party convention it has not happened that such experts were subjected to sanctions in that they either were not nominated or were voted off the ballot. The procedure in such elections is that the members of the various expert groups are asked to indicate on questionnaires whether they are available for reelection. If they answer yes, they can be quite certain that they will be reelected by the party convention. The absence of formal sanctions does not mean—as might appear to be the case to outside observers—that the generalist group has no control at all over the expert group. The sanctions usually consist in putting the norm-violating experts "on ice" without taking their functions away. This practice is manifested, for instance, by the lack of attention they are given when they speak. Their reports are treated very sparsely in the minutes, and they are not invited to attend informal predeliberations. These experts are, in short, no longer taken seriously. They become only figureheads.

The sanctions require no formal decision by any party authority. An almost tacit consensus is usually formed as to who shall be punished in this manner. Most of the time those sanctioned perceive that their positions have become untenable and retire voluntarily from their posts. Occasionally it happens, however, that someone does not understand the writing on the wall or does not want to understand it. He can then still participate in the sessions—not as an outcast, but as somebody laughed at or maybe only ignored. It seems to me that this sanction mechanism has proved very effective. It is probably because of it that the generalist group and the various expert groups constitute a largely homogeneous whole. This type of sanction is characteristic not only of the Free Democratic party, but of the entire political system of Switzerland. As described above, unpopular members of the Federal Council are usually not forced to resign by a vote, but rather made to hand in a "voluntary" resignation through subtle informal mechanisms.

There is a much greater chance of a technical blocking of the feedback system connecting the expert and the generalist groups with the rank-and-file party members than of the one connecting the two kinds of elite groups (the experts and the generalists). The most important channels of communication connecting the elite group with the nonelite group are, as have been shown above, role accumulations at the local and federal party levels, the intermediary groups, and the referenda. Role accumulations constitute a direct channel of communication with no extra relay stations where the information could be filtered. However, this advantage must be contrasted with the disadvantage that many local party sections do not have connections with this channel, since the number of members of the elite groups is considerably smaller than that of the local sections. The communication flow via intermediary groups has many relays where the information flow from the nonelite group is filtered before it finally reaches the elite group. Furthermore, not all party members have access to this channel as they either belong to no other intermediary group besides the party, or they are members of intermediary groups with no access to the elite group of the federal party. In the case of the referenda, finally, the information transmitted by the votes of the nonelite group has to be interpreted before it can be used. This process of interpretation usually results in some distortion of the information. The communication system between the elite group and the nonelite group is further reduced by the fact that many party members do not use the channels of communication available to them. Political passivity is a widespread phenomenon among the nonelite party members. For example, the local Free Democratic section in Thun has a traditional informal meeting in a local café every Friday night which all party members are invited to attend. The mayor, who for some time had been a member of the federal Executive Committee and who has even been chairman of the parliamentary group, participated regularly in these meetings. His role accumulations were utilized by local rank-and-file members to communicate information to the federal party elite. However, relatively few party members actually took advantage of this opportunity. Of the approximately eight hundred local members only ten to twenty attended these meetings at a time, and these groups always consisted of roughly the same people.

Because of the structural shortcomings of the communication system and the lack of interest of many party members in making full use of the available channels of communication, the federal elite group is rather incompletely informed about the preferences of the rank and file. This situation produces, according to my observations, a certain tendency on the part of some elite members to reject the received information as unrepresentative and to make the decisions without considering the goals of the nonelite group. What set of sanctions are open to the nonelite group to control such members of the elite group? The feedback system between elite and nonelite also tends to avoid formal and strongly visible sanctions. The most immediate formal sanction would arise if the ordinary party members instructed the delegates to the party convention to reprehend or even not to reelect those elite members who ignored the goals of the masses of the party. However, this has not happened at the recent party conventions which I could observe either directly or indirectly.

This absence of formal sanctions does not mean that no sanctions are applied at all. The basis for sanctions is the already frequently mentioned fact that the members of the party elite group combine that role with other roles. The sanction mechanism consists then in withdrawing these other roles from the members who are to be sanctioned. In this way their position in the party elite group usually becomes untenable sooner or later so that they "voluntarily" resign. Particularly effective are the sanctions that the nonelite party members can apply to those members of the elite group who are also members of the federal Parliament. In actual practice the parliamentary candidates are usually nominated by the local party sections or by the district parties. This practice can be illustrated by an example from the cantonal party of Berne. At the elections for the National Council in 1967 the five regional party organizations within the canton presented their own lists. Formally speaking, these lists were approved by the cantonal convention, but the decisions were actually made in the regions, the districts, and the local sections. In the Bernese Oberland, powers were divided so that the regional party distributed the number of candidates on the list among the individual district parties, which in turn undertook a distribution among the local sections. The local section in Thun, for example, had three assigned candidates, which it nominated at its own discretion. District, regional, and cantonal party gave formal approval later; the federal party did not even have a formal right of approval.

Through this delegation of the actual authority of nomination to the local sections the members of Parliament are to a large extent dependent upon their local party friends. If they give too little attention to the goals of the rank and file, they run the risk of being denied nomination by the local section at the next election. It does not usually happen that they are voted down at the local party convention, but rather that they are made to renounce another term "voluntarily" by informal means. In principle, this is the same method of sanctioning used by the generalist group against experts. If a member of Parliament loses his mandate in this way, the news will spread fairly soon. This usually weakens his position in the party elite to such an extent that he also resigns "voluntarily" there. It is of primary importance to our argument that this mechanism of sanctions can be managed by ordinary members in the local sections. Yet the idealistic view of democracy that sees all members of the local section participating equally in the operation of these sanction mechanisms is inappropriate. A leading group always carries more weight in the application of sanctions than do ordinary party members. It is usually more difficult for ordinary party members to sanction members of the party elite who do not belong to Parliament. Those most susceptible to sanctions are individuals whose elite positions on the federal level depend on a leading position at a lower-party level. Prominent in this group are the presidents of the cantonal parties, who are ex officio members of the federal Central Committee. They are closer to the ordinary members in their cantonal role than in their federal role. Because they are less distant, geographically and socially, from the ordinary party members, they run a greater risk of being sanctioned in their cantonal role rather than in their federal role. If a cantonal party president retires from his office, he usually also leaves the Central Committee.

Members of the federal elite group who are neither members of Parliament nor have important office in a cantonal party are not very numerous. They include some, but clearly not all, officials of interest groups. Indeed the more influential interest group officials are members of Parliament, and, as such, are exposed to the above-mentioned sanctions from the rank and file. In 1967, for example, the presidents of the Swiss Union of Artisans and of the Swiss Farmers' Union were both members of the Executive Committee and the National Council. At the same time, other interest group officials were aiming at a seat in Parliament, which subjected them even more to the control of the ordinary party members, since they had to be initially nominated by a local section. The interest group officials in the Free Democratic leadership who neither have a seat in Parliament nor an important role in a cantonal party are not politically influential persons. They are relatively unimportant experts, who in general content themselves with illuminating the technical aspects of a problem. They are, however, practically removed from the control of the rank and file. The most effective sanction that could be utilized against them is a withdrawal of their interest group role. Without that role they would probably also disappear from the Free Democratic leadership. It is, however, very difficult for the ordinary party members to cause an interest group official to lose his position.

Finally, a small residual group within the elite is made up of some so-called independent experts, who belong neither to Parliament nor to an interest group, nor do they have important functions in a cantonal party. These experts, mainly scientists, are exempt from any control by the ordinary party members, since their roles in the elite group are not combined with other roles that could be withheld from them by the rank and file. But they usually do not exert great political influence, since they generally restrict themselves to treating particular technical problems. If such experts gain more influence, they usually become members of Parliament or take over functions in an interest group or a cantonal party, and are thus no longer in the residual group. In conclusion, we can say that the members of the elite group are subject to different degrees of control by the ordinary party members. I believe that the influential members, generally speaking, are subject to stricter control than the less influential ones. This is due to the fact that in the political system of Switzerland the most influential persons have accumulated leading roles in several intermediary groups and are thus subject to control from a variety of constituencies.

The Social Democratic Party

I had no opportunity to follow the making of decisions in the Social Democratic party by participant observation, but I can refer to a monograph by Masnata on this party. However, Masnata does not base his study on participant observation of individual decisions, but primarily on surveys of the party elite, which makes a comparison with my two case studies of the Free Democrats difficult.[165] His study nevertheless gives enough information so that we can determine the extent to which the main propositions developed from the Free Democratic study would also hold for the Social Democrats. First, we can see that the ordinary party members choose to participate as little in the decision-making process of the Social Democratic party as do the ordinary members of the Free Democratic party. The institutional opportunities for such participation in the Social Democratic party are, however, considerable. Every local party has the right to send one delegate to the federal party convention for a membership up to 50; for each additional 150 members it can send another delegate.[166] Then, too, a referendum can be called against the decisions of the party convention; such a referendum requires two-fifths of the delegates at the party convention or a quarter of the local sections with at least 10 percent of the party members.[167]

Masnata's study shows that little use was made of the institutional opportunities. Usually almost two-thirds of the local party sections refrain from sending delegates to the convention.[168] The participating sections send party leaders almost exclusively, although ordinary members can be delegates according to the party statutes.[169] To a strong degree the party convention's function is one of acclamation: "Most people attend the conventions to listen rather than to speak, to approve rather than to criticize."[170] This function of acclamation is manifested in the way the convention usually receives the report of the Executive Committee: "In practice, for almost forty years, no serious critique has been formulated and as a whole the reports of the party bureaucracy has been accepted either unanimously or quasi-unanimously. Often there were not even any debates."[171]

A further method of articulating a demand at the party convention is the presentation of a motion. All local party sections have this right. It gives the ordinary party members an opportunity to influence the policy of the party as a whole, since "it is in this manner that the member can affect the direction of the party if his proposition gets through the local section, and is adopted by the convention."[172] This right is used far more frequently than the right to discuss the report of the Executive Committee. An average of thirty to forty motions are discussed at a party convention.[173] Gruner considers this a "genuine dialogue between the party leadership and the rank-and-file, which is in some sense a refutation of the sociologist Robert Michels's thesis of oligarchy that is acclaimed by many skeptics."[174] As one of these skeptics, Masnata thinks the importance of these motions is slight, for they are never discussed until the final phase of the party convention—frequently under time pressure. "The main part does not consist, as one might be led to believe, of the discussion of the motions, but rather of the presentation and the discussion of the reports which often takes more than two hours. There is thus usually not much time left to discuss the proposals of the local sections. . . . In fact they are often submitted to a vote without previous expositions; the president gives his opinion and the convention usually follows his recommendations."[175] Even if the delegates vote for a proposal against the recommendation of the president of the party, the effect is slight according to Masnata's investigation. "The motions demanding a parliamentary intervention are transmitted to the Social Democratic parliamentary group; they have no imperative character. The members of the National Council assess them themselves according to their competence and are at complete liberty to decide about their opportunities and their chances of success. Here once more one notices that the representative does not perceive himself as depending on the delegate. The motions not envisaging parliamentary intervention are transmitted to the appropriate party organs. If it is possible at all to account for the attention given to some precise proposals by the party leadership, it is difficult to disentangle a general tendency. One single fact is indisputable: Those responsible frequently seem to forget the motions in the files of the general secretariat."[176] Masnata reaches the conclusion that the ordinary party member "does not participate effectively in governing" through the medium of the motions at the party convention.[177]

As further evidence of this widespread nonparticipation Masnata records that only 15 to 30 percent of the ordinary party members regularly attend the party activities of the local sections.[178] Because of their passivity ordinary party members rarely present their demands directly to the Social Democratic members of Parliament: "The habit of writing to a member of the National Council is not common, they receive a maximum of ten or so letters a year . . . [and] oral demands are no more numerous."[179] The low participation of the rank and file in the formation of the political line of the party is probably most strikingly expressed in the fact that the internal party referendum has not been used since 1920: "This system of 'direct democracy' thus seems to be completely abandoned, and the article providing for it only appears in the statutes as a testimony to a bygone epoch."[180] As a whole Masnata's study shows that the demands of the Social Democrats are hardly ever worked out in steps from the bottom up even though provisions have been made for these steps. Evidently there is in the Social Democratic party as in the Free Democratic party an elite group whose function it is to articulate the demands of the party.[181]

On the basis of Masnata's investigations it seems that the Social Democratic elite group has a structure similar to that of the Free Democratic elite group. It too has little identity with any party organ. "The real power is in the hands of a certain number of persons and does not belong to this or that organ."[182] Those who hold leadership roles seem primarily to be persons who accumulate a certain number of roles. "The accumulation of roles has as its effect that one finds the same persons everywhere. Consequently, the transfer of authority does not favor this or that organ but rather is profitable for certain persons."[183] Particularly important is the accumulation of a party role with a role as a member of Parliament: "The Social Democratic members of parliament are, in various capacities, members of numerous committees of the party whether at the local, the cantonal or the federal level. The parliamentary group has its 'antennas' in the majority of the party organs."[184] Important, too, is the role accumulation between the party and the Federation of Trade Unions. The communication between these two organizations "is assured by certain persons who accumulate roles of responsibility in the trade union as well as in the party."[185] Finally, most members of the Social Democratic elite hold roles in other intermediary groups such as the Federation of Swiss Consumer Associations, employees' associations, sports clubs, and so on.

Masnata was not able to investigate in detail the nature of the relevant decision and control mechanisms within the Social Democratic elite because it was not possible for him to observe the elite group at work. He concludes that "it is always difficult to evaluate the influence of this or that person in a committee in sessions which it was not possible to attend."[186] From the few references by Masnata it nevertheless can be assumed that the decision and control mechanisms in the Social Democratic elite group are similar to those used by the Free Democratic elite groups. It seems that the function of innovation in the Social Democratic party also belongs to small expert groups. Masnata here restricts himself to the statement that there are in the parliamentary group "several small study committees with the task of giving the whole group their opinion on a specific problem."[187] It remains unclear by which channels of communication such expert groups are connected with the other parts of the elite group, which feedback processes exist, and what happens if the feedback is blocked.

As in the Free Democratic party many conflicts among Social Democrats seem to be regulated by compromise. Masnata concludes that the Social Democrats "seem to have adopted the dominant doctrine which holds that compromise serves as the principal director of all politics."[188] This pattern of conflict regulation is used, for example, in conflicts with the trade-union wing of the party: "Under the penalty of alienating the trade unions, the parliamentary group must in certain cases accept what it would not have accepted otherwise."[189] How such compromises are made Masnata does not tell us in detail. Nor does Masnata's study fully discuss the questions of whether and to what degree the elite group orients its decisions according to the anticipated or effective reactions of the rank and file. Masnata merely asks what formal sanctions the ordinary party members use against the elite group. The situation here is analogous to that in the Free Democratic party, since the members of the Social Democratic elite group hardly run the risk of being sanctioned by formal votes. "Not voting for somebody is a personal insult to him—it is to break the most elementary rules of 'socialist comradeship.' To consider voting against somebody because one does not share his opinions is an idea which does not agree with the spirit of the delegates to the convention of the Social Democratic Party."[190]

Masnata thinks that a consequence of the ordinary party members' failure to sanction the elite is "to leave those in leading positions completely independent of the will of the underlying base and to dig a trench between it and the leadership."[191] My investigations of the Free Democratic party showed, however, that in spite of the failure of formal sanctions, the Free Democratic elite group did to a certain extent make decisions that took into account the anticipated or effective sanctions of the ordinary party members. Such reactions were primarily communicated by role accumulations at the local and federal party levels, by intermediary groups, and by referenda results. If this feedback mechanism is blocked in the Free Democratic party, the members of the elite group can be sanctioned informally. Feedback processes connected with informal sanctions are also probably at work in the Social Democratic party, but could not be perceived by Masnata because of methodological reasons. His statement that the members of the Social Democratic elite group are "completely independent of the will of the underlying base" therefore seems to be too extreme a conclusion.

In one further respect Masnata's investigation of the Social Democratic party largely confirms my findings about the Free Democratic party. He shows that the Social Democratic party also has politically relevant elite groups not only at the federal level, but also at the lower levels: "Each cantonal party has a tendency to consider itself a whole and not a part of an aggregate. . . . The Social Democratic party has tried and tries to create a Swiss political mentality without otherwise wanting to unify the country, but its attempts run up against a force of inertia which is opposed to every movement by federal call, and which is characterized by a quasi-pathological fear that a mortal blow will be struck at the federal structure of the country."[192]

In summary, Masnata's study gives the impression that in general there are decision and control mechanisms in the Social Democratic party similar to those in the Free Democratic party. To what extent the details differ cannot be inferred with reliability from Masnata.

The Other Parties

There are no reliable investigations about the two other large parties represented in the Federal Council—the Christian Democrats and the Swiss People's party—that concentrate on aspects of the decision and control mechanisms of concern to us. The following three factors, however, lead us to believe that the Christian Democratic party and the Swiss People's party are not any more different from the Free Democratic party than the Social Democratic party:

1. Historically the Social Democrats had a national leadership from the beginning; in contrast, the Christian Democratic party and the Swiss People's party were originally organized on a cantonal basis similar to that of the Free Democratic party.[193] These historical conditions lead us to believe that the structure of the Christian Democratic party and the Swiss People's party is more like the Free Democratic party than the Social Democratic party.

2. Studies of the participation of ordinary party members have shown that the members of the Christian Democratic party and the Swiss People's party participate as little as do those of the Free Democratic and the Social Democratic parties. This similarity makes it feasible to assume that the Christian Democrats and the Swiss People's party are not fundamentally different from the Social Democrats and the Free Democrats in other aspects as well.

3. In a later context we will see that patterns of conflict regulation used in the output process of the Swiss system are similar to those used by the Free Democratic and Social Democratic parties. According to the hypotheses of Harry Eckstein and others, this congruence between input and output processes leads to a greater role security for those who are politically active. Since the members of the Christian Democratic party and the Swiss People's party show role security as great as that of the Free Democratic and the Social Democratic members, we can deduce in reverse that the Christian Democrats and the Swiss People's party also have patterns of conflict regulation that, to a large extent, are congruent with those applied to the output process. Thus, according to this congruence hypothesis, the Christian Democrats and the Swiss People's party do not differ fundamentally from the Free Democrats and the Social Democrats.

Any statements about the relevant decision-making and control mechanisms of the small parties without representation in the Federal Council will have to await further analysis.

The Size of the Elite Groups in the Parties

Now that we have investigated which parties articulate demands to the political system of Switzerland and how these demands originate in the individual parties, we can attempt to determine how many people actively participate in articulating these demands. My analysis of the Free Democratic party reveals that the task of articulating demands on the federal level essentially falls to an elite group, which, depending upon the issue and the method of counting, includes 50 to 200 members. Masnata's investigations indicate that the elite group in the Social Democratic party is of a similar size. Certain factors indicate that the situation is similar with the Christian Democrats and the Swiss People's party. It should be noted that the Swiss People's party is only half the size of the three other Federal Council parties with respect to the number of seats in Parliament so that its elite group may be correspondingly smaller. If these assumptions are correct, the elite groups of the four Federal Council parties would include a maximum of 700 members (200 + 200 + 200 + 100) and a minimum of 175 (50 + 50 + 50 + 25). If the extreme values are evened out, we get a mean in the range of 400 to 500 persons. In the case of the smaller parties for which we have no firm bases, we must proceed almost arbitrarily. We assume that the elite groups in the Federal Council parties are approximately double the size of their representation in Parliament. If this is also assumed to be the case with the smaller parties, the sum of the elite groups of these parties is about 100 persons.

These computations would lead us to conclude that there may be 500 to 600 persons in Switzerland who participate significantly in the articulation of party demands at the federal level. The bases of these computations are so uncertain in many places that they can only be considered an approximation. Research in this direction would be fruitful if it attempted to determine the individual members of these elite groups.[194]

In Switzerland, parties may articulate relevant demands not only at the federal but also at the cantonal and the local levels. Consequently, there are elite groups at the lower echelons whose function it is to articulate demands. These elite groups are partially identical with those at the federal level because of the role accumulations. As shown in my study of the Free Democratic party and Masnata's study of the Social Democrats, the lower elite groups also include a large number of persons who are not members of the federal elite. In order to determine how many persons belong to the leadership at one level or the other, we should first attempt to determine the total number of party members. The Federal Bureau of Statistics estimates that 15 to 20 percent of all persons with voting rights are members of a political party.[195] A study I did of the 20- to 35-year-old voters in an urban area showed that 10 percent were members of a party, a somewhat lower figure than the estimate of the bureau.[196] In a random sample I found that 40 percent of the total electorate of the community of Belp were party members,[197] 50 percent of the electorate in the rural district of Seftigen were party members, and of the electorate in the city of Berne, 13 percent were party members.[198] Jaeggi concluded from a study that one person out of two in Blumenstein, one out of three in Guggisberg, and one out of four in Lenk were members of a party.[199] A survey done by Gruner in the canton of Aargau showed that 24 percent of the population belonged to a political party.[200] There is obviously considerable variation with regard to the number of party members. For Switzerland as a whole it seems that the estimate of the Federal Bureau of Statistics is relatively accurate.

The percentage of party members who belong to the leadership at one level or the other could only be determined conclusively if concrete cases of decision-making were investigated at the different levels. Since there are no such case studies available, we must temporarily rely on survey results.[201] Surveys show that quite a large number of party members do not participate at all in the life of the party. For example, three out of ten party members among the 20- to 35-year-old voters in urban areas declared that they had participated in no party activity within the previous year.[202]

In order to distinguish the party members who belong to elite groups from those who in one form or another participate in party life, several criteria can be used. In my community study in Belp I asked each party member whether he had already held formal party positions, and whether he had often spoken at party meetings. If he said yes to both questions I assumed that he belonged to the leadership of the local party section. According to this criterion, 12 percent of the party members belonged to the leadership group. This group constituted about 5 percent of the total electorate. If we assume, as a working hypothesis, that the suburban community of Belp is to some extent representative of all of Switzerland, we reach the conclusion that about 5 percent of all persons qualified to vote participate actively at one level or another in articulating the demands of the parties. In absolute number this results in a group of approximately 180,000 persons (5 percent of the

3,600,000 persons entitled to vote). It goes without saying that this figure should also only be considered a rough approximation.

In conclusion, we have the following picture of the elite groups of the parties. About 500 to 600 party members participate actively in the articulation of demands channeled into the political system at the federal level. Approximately an additional 180,000 persons, 5 percent of the electorate, participate in articulating demands channeled into the system at the cantonal and the local levels. The elite groups of the parties are in a feedback connection with the ordinary citizens whose anticipated or effective reactions direct the decision-making of the elite groups to some extent at least.

However, all citizens do not participate to an equal degree in this feedback process. The resident aliens, a group of considerable numerical importance in Switzerland (about 15 percent of the population at the end of 1971), are in practice excluded from participation. Almost as limited for a long time were the political rights of women. Through a referendum in February, 1971, however, equal political rights were given to women at the federal level. But there are even today a few cantons and local communities where women do not yet have the right to vote. For Swiss citizens participation in referenda, active membership in political parties, and membership in other intermediary groups are the most effective ways of entering the feedback process with the party elite groups. My sample surveys show that these channels of communication are used at below average rates by young and very old voters, the lower social classes, those who are geographically and socially mobile, and socially poorly integrated persons.[203]

CHAPTER III

The Input of Demands from Other Intermediary Groups

1. THE ECONOMIC INTEREST GROUPS

The economic interest groups in Switzerland are not mere satellites of political parties. Their considerable influence derives primarily from five factors:[1]

1. The boundaries of most economic interest groups do not coincide with those of a particular political party. This lack of identification with any political party gives the economic interest groups a greater opportunity to function independently.

2. The economic interest groups can articulate demands to the system through channels of communication other than the political parties. Article 32 of the Federal Constitution includes the following statement concerning economic legislation: "The appropriate economic organizations are to be heard before the laws are made." In Switzerland this "hearing" is called the *notification procedure (Vernehmlassungsverfahren)*. It is a channel of communication to the decision-makers of the system that bypasses the political parties. In addition, the economic interest groups can also call for, or at least threaten to call for, a referendum or a popular initiative.

3. The independent influence of the economic interest groups is strengthened by the fact that their total membership is far larger than that of the political parties. Whereas only 15 to 20 percent of the electorate are party members, 68 percent of eleven communities responding to a recent survey claimed membership in an occupational organization, 15 percent did not belong to an occupational organization, and there was no information for 17 percent.[2]

4. Partly because of their larger membership the economic interest groups also have more money available than the political parties. Masnata investigated these differences as they applied to the Social Democrats and the Swiss Federation of Trade Unions. In 1959 the income of the federation was 914,000 francs whereas that of the party was only 255,000 francs.[3] There are no comparative figures available from other parties and interest groups. According to some confidential explorations which I undertook, it seems, however, that the financial differences between other economic interest groups and parties are in

general at least as great as they are between the Swiss Federation of Trade Unions and the Social Democratic party.

5. Finally, it should be mentioned that the economic interest groups have much more strongly developed secretariats than the parties.

As with the parties we must determine what characterizes the input of demands from the economic interest groups. First, the number of organizations is relatively high. On the employers' side there are four leading organizations: the Swiss Union of Commerce and Industry, the Swiss Federation of Employers' Organizations, the Swiss Union of Artisans, and the Swiss Farmers' Union. Besides these four "big powers" there are other smaller employers' organizations such as the Swiss Bankers' Association and the Swiss Association of Hotel-Keepers. On the employees' side, the Swiss Federation of Trade Unions is the strongest organization with about 440,000 members.[4] There are many other organizations such as the Swiss Federation of Clerical Employees' Unions, the Swiss National Federation of Christian Trade Unions, the Swiss Union of Protestant Employees, the Union of Free Swiss Workers, the Swiss Teachers' Union, and so on. The fragmentation among the economic interest groups seems even greater when we consider that the individual groups constituting the head organizations carry out relatively independent policies. We will see an example of this in the case study of the Aargau university question in which several sections of the Swiss Federation of Clerical Employees' Unions were in direct contact with the authorities of Aargau. A fragmentation also exists by virtue of the fact that the federal element in the economic interest groups is so strong that the lower organizational levels enjoy a high degree of independence with respect to the higher ones. This phenomenon could be observed in the recommendations of the Swiss Union of Artisans for the 1967 National Council elections in the canton of Berne. The cantonal branch of this organization recommended a total of ten candidates for election.[5] The branch in the city of Berne did not feel restricted by the decision of the cantonal organization; in its election recommendation it only considered six of the ten approved by its cantonal organization and added six additional candidates to those.[6] This was not just revision of the cantonal recommendations from a local point of view—the city organization had simply taken the liberty to decide for itself who the candidates from the canton should be. The head organization at the federal level intervened in the cantonal campaign only through the president who, in a personal letter, recommended a particular candidate for election. Interestingly enough, many representatives of the artisans in Berne held this move against him, which shows how the lower echelons in an economic interest group feel about an infringement on their independence. The structure of the economic interest groups in Switzerland, then, is characterized by a definite pluralism which ensures that the demands of the economic interest groups flow to the political system through many separate channels.

A second characteristic is that the substance of the demands of the economic interest groups differs relatively little from one to the other. The trade unions do not in general articulate any extreme class struggle position. Their moderate stand was expressed in the following statement made by the president of the Swiss Metal and Clock Workers' Union: "Labor politics as I see it is only possible in a regime of liberty. It excludes any intention of nationalizing the machine, metal and watch industries. It is not the system of property, the legal status of the factory or the branch which are the determinants of the conditions of the workers, but the level of productivity and an equitable redistribution of the fruits of everybody's work. . . . Is the participation of the workers and their organizations in decision-making (at the factory level) desirable? I do not think so."[7]

Like the trade unions, the employers' organizations also generally strive to pursue moderate policies. Since the demands of the employers and the workers do not differ too strongly, it has become more and more possible to resolve conflicts between the two groups in a peaceful way. Masnata characterizes the relations between employers and workers as follows: "The owner is no longer looked upon as an exploiter; he is a partner with whom one negotiates on equal terms."[8]

Third, the input of demands from the economic interest groups is characterized by an ambivalent attitude toward government policies. None of the economic interest groups opposes the latter in principle, but neither is there a group that supports government policy as a matter of principle. In the 1965 decision to slow down the economy, for example, the Swiss Federation of Trade Unions supported the government, whereas the Swiss Union of Artisans opposed it.[9] In the referendum about the land ownership question in 1967 the opposite situation was the case—the Swiss Union of Artisans supported the government and the Swiss Federation of Trade Unions opposed it.[10]

In conclusion, it appears that the manner in which the economic interest groups convey their demands is similar to that of the political parties. Are the demands of the parties and those of the economic interest groups sharply opposed? Or are they more or less identical? Neither of these two extremes is the case. As a matter of fact the demands of the parties and the economic interest groups are intertwined in a very complicated way. The relay stations between parties and interest groups are usually persons with roles in both organizations. Often these persons do not indicate which role they are playing at any particular moment. This is illustrated by the following statement of a Social Democratic party secretary: "We are happy to see how many trade union officials declare themselves to be 'Social Democrats' when it is a matter of being on the Social Democratic list for the National Council. We wish they would remain Social Democratic after the campaign, not only in the National Council and in the party, but also in the trade union movement."[11]

2. THE VOLUNTARY ASSOCIATIONS

The input of demands becomes even more diffuse when we note that voluntary associations may also articulate demands to the system along with parties and economic interest groups. Voluntary associations, too, can call for referenda and initiatives, and furthermore they frequently participate in the notification procedure. For example, the demands of the automobile clubs are regularly heard in matters concerning traffic questions. The automobile clubs also use the referendum and the initiative and with their large number of members they never have much trouble in gathering the necessary signatures. The conservationist associations make their demands in matters related to the protection of nature, and the sports clubs do the same with respect to the construction of public sport facilities. Even such apparently unpolitical associations as those for fishermen may articulate politically relevant demands. Thus, a circular of the Sports Fishing Club of Berne at the time of the National Council election in 1967 states the following: "The Executive Committee in the most recent session unanimously agreed about the necessity, even the urgency, of nominating candidates who for a long time have stood up for the importance of the protection of waters and fishing."[12]

Most voluntary associations have close ties with political parties and economic interest groups. An exception is the Swiss Movement against Nuclear Armament, whose composition was studied by Roger Girod. This movement consists primarily of "a fraction of the intellectual subculture. This fraction is no doubt small compared to the size of the subculture as a whole. . . . Some of these intellectuals—very few numerically—have as their 'base of subsistence' a function in the service of a workers' organization, a pacifist movement, etc.; others work in the service of a church, a university or some other cultural institution."[13] That the antinuclear armament group has only few ties with the political parties can be seen from the results of the two popular initiatives about nuclear armament in 1962 and 1963: at the federal level the initiatives were supported only by the Communist party and a few Social Democratic cantonal parties.[14]

The conscientious objectors and their supporters form another group whose goals lie almost completely outside the scope of the big parties and economic interest groups. There are, however, strong ties between the conscientious objectors and the opponents of nuclear armament.[15] It has become customary to label the members of these outsider groups as nonconformists. This denotation is appropriate in that these groups usually articulate demands that do not conform to those of the larger parties and interest groups. Kurt Marti, a typical representative of the nonconformists, is explicitly opposed to the principle of amicable agreement as it is practiced among the big parties; he insists that "the parties have been unified to much too strong a degree. When agreement is considered the highest value even by members of the Federal Council, then democracy itself is suspect."[16]

The nuclear armament opponents, the conscientious objectors, and other nonconformist groups constitute a small minority among the voluntary organizations. The large membership bodies are found in the traditional associations of marksmen, gymnasts, singers, etc. Out of Switzerland's total population of six million, the Swiss Association of Marksmen, founded in 1924, can count 533,000 members, and the Federal Association of Gymnasts, founded in 1832, claim 305,000 members.[17] The demands articulated to the political system by these large associations are intertwined with those of the political parties and the economic interest groups whose concerns are similar and with whom there is a large mutual overlap in membership. Furthermore, the demands of the marksmen, gymnasts, singers, etc., are frequently articulated by persons who at the same time have important roles in political parties and economic interest groups. (I have noted elsewhere that the vice-president of the Federal Association of Gymnasts belonged to the Executive Committee of the Free Democratic party.)

In order to study the decision-making processes in the voluntary associations, I have analyzed the decision-making and control mechanisms in the Federal Association of Gymnasts. I have had to limit myself methodologically to intensive interviews with members and analyses of meeting minutes.[18] Therefore, my results cannot be as valid and reliable as they might have been if I had been able to use participant observation. Bearing in mind the need for closer studies, I have concluded that the decision-making processes in the association of gymnasts seem to run parallel to those in the political parties. It seems, too, that the institutional structure of the association is very similar to that of the political parties. Three examples may illustrate this. First, the association has cantonal, district, and local sections analogous to the subdivisions of the parties. Second, the formal leadership is constituted at each level as in the parties so that the president is only *primus inter pares*. Third, the ordinary members have a very extensive right of codetermination in the general assembly of the local sections and they can also choose the delegates for the higher levels.

The institutional framework is filled out in a way that is quite similar to the parties. The members of the association also make relatively little use of their right of codetermination. Participation by the gymnasts in the general assemblies of the local sections usually is never more than between 10 and 30 percent of the total membership. It is noteworthy too, that many local sections do not utilize their rights to send delegates to the decision-making bodies at the upper levels of the association. The elite group of the association is not identical with the members of a specific committee. The elite group consists primarily of persons who accumulate various roles inside and outside the association. The vice-president in the cantonal section of Berne can be cited as an example of a person with many role accumulations inside the association. He has been at one time (1) a delegate at the federal level, (2) a member of the cantonal Press and Propaganda Committee, (3) a cantonal course leader for sectional gymnastics, (4) the president of the Technical Committee of the district section of Seeland, and (5) an honorary member of the local section in Lengnau. At the Federal Gymnastics Festival in Berne in 1967 the president of the organizational committee was both a member of the cantonal Parliament and of the executive of the city of Berne. At the cantonal gymnastics festival in Biel in 1967 the organizational president was also a member of the cantonal Parliament, the secretary general of the federal Free Democratic party, and a member of the executive of the city of Biel. It is customary in the gymnasts' association, as it is in the political parties, to begin one's rise to the federal elite group at the local level. A typical example of a man who moved up from the lower levels is the president of the cantonal section in Berne in 1967. In 1930 he became the leader of a youth section on the local level. In 1936 he rose to assistant treasurer of the local section and secretary of the district section. In

1945 he became president of the local section, in 1952, president of the district section, and in 1954, honorary member of the local section and treasurer of the cantonal section. In 1956 he became honorary member of the district section, and finally, in 1962 he was named president of the cantonal section.

The gymnasts' association is also similar to the parties in that its elite groups show a strong tendency to divide themselves into expert groups for the consideration of special matters. In the cantonal section of Berne there are, for example, the following standing committees: the Press and Propaganda Committee, the Auditing Committee, the Committee for Youth Sections, the Committee for Skiing, the Committee for Sports Medical Service, the Committee for Section Presentations, and the Play Committee. Like the parties, the association solves conflicts primarily by amicable agreement. The cantonal section of the association in Berne is allotted money each year from the sports lottery; it then has the delicate task of distributing this money to the suborganizations. Although the responsible body usually has rather divergent opinions concerning this distribution, it has never been necessary in recent years to make the decision by vote; a compromise has always been found that everybody could accept. Another analogy with the parties is that the leaders of the gymnasts' association are hardly ever sanctioned in a formal way. I have not been able to find a case in recent years in which somebody was rejected in a formal vote. To withdraw one's vote from somebody in a renewal election seems to be just as alien to the gymnasts as it is, according to Masnata, to the socialists. However, there are also informal mechanisms in the association by means of which those who hold leadership roles can be forced to resign "voluntarily." Those means, as described to me, are rather exactly like those found in the political parties. Finally, the refusal to be dictated to by the federal element is as prominent in the association as it is in the political parties. This point is manifested most clearly by the fact that the finances of the association are not administered centrally; each level of the association has its own budget without further control by a higher level.

That the decision-making and control mechanisms in the gymnasts' association are more or less comparable to those in the political parties is not a chance occurrence. It should be remembered that the progressive forces in the nineteenth century did not organize primarily into political parties, but into gymnastics associations—and associations of marksmen, singers, and students.[19] The Free Democratic party grew out of these associations and played a leading role in the first decades of the federation. Since its party structure served as a model for the other parties to a large extent, we can see why the structure of the present gymnasts' association is very similar not only to the Free Democrats, but also to the other parties. In addition to these historical reasons, the many intertwining role accumulations between the gymnasts' association and the political parties are accountable for the similarity of their views. On the basis of unsystematic observations of the artisans', teachers', and marksmen's associations, I would conclude that other voluntary associations and economic interest groups make their decisions in a way similar to that of the political parties. If this congruence among the various intermediary groups is confirmed, it means that a person who had learned a role pattern as president of a sports club could expect to be confronted with a similar role pattern if he were to be elected president of an economic interest group or of a party.

3. THE MASS MEDIA

The Press

According to Andreas Thommen, Switzerland is the country with the highest number of newspapers relative to the size of the population. "In Switzerland 490 newspapers are published in 280 places with a total circulation of 4.72 million copies. In addition, there are some 88 entertainment magazines and 1,036 periodicals and professional journals of various sorts with an estimated total circulation of 14 million copies in 1965. Consequently—from a statistical point of view—there are roughly 12,000 inhabitants (children included) for every newspaper and 5,300 inhabitants for every professional or entertainment journal."[20] Closely connected with the high newspaper density is the fact that the circulations of Swiss newspapers usually are relatively low: "Real mass circulations do not exist in Switzerland as they do abroad."[21] Of 490 newspapers in 1966 only 16, or 3.3 percent, had a circulation of more than 50,000. The highest circulation for any Swiss newspaper was only 180,000.[22] Table 15 gives a survey of the Swiss newspapers according to the size of their circulation.

The head newspaper system is a cooperative development described by Thommen as follows: "The so-called newspaper shell—the pages with general national content (foreign, domestic, economic, sports, cultural, technical news, etc.)—remains unchanged with the exception of the title of the newspaper, and a local or regional page and regional advertisements."[23] This system is still relatively uncom-

TABLE 15. NEWSPAPER CIRCULATION IN SWITZERLAND IN 1966

Number of Copies	Number of Newspapers Absolute	Percentages
Below 2,500	160	32.7
2,501–5,000	128	26.1
5,001–10,000	83	16.9
10,001–15,000	43	10.8
15,001–20,000	17	3.5
20,001–50,000	33	6.7
Over 50,000	16	3.3
Total	490	100.0

Source: Thommen, *Die Schweizer Presse*, p. 37.

mon in Switzerland although it is widespread in the Federal Republic of Germany. "In the past decade about a dozen such head newspaper systems have been set up in Switzerland, and they connect more than two dozen papers."[24] Until now more limited forms of cooperation were the production of common topical pages, the pooling of employees, the common use of printing machines, and common distribution.[25]

The trends toward concentration of resources have become considerably stronger in very recent times, although, as Thommen puts it, there are not yet "newspaper lords" in Switzerland.[26] The Swiss Cartel Committee confirms these conclusions in its newest investigation: "In the newspaper market one can observe a general concentration process, which in the last years has gained momentum above all in the French- and German-speaking parts of Switzerland."[27]

What is the relationship between the demands of the newspapers and those of the political parties? Thommen has found that 53 percent of all newspapers represent the political views of a distinct party.[28] In most cases, however, they are not party newspapers in the sense that they are directly connected with a party. The linkage between party and newspaper is usually a matter of role accumulation in that important journalists assume leading roles in the party. These dual role holders, then, dictate to what extent a newspaper will represent the official party line. If the parties do not pay attention to a journalist's views, the journalist will usually take the liberty of presenting his opinions in his paper. In 1965, for instance, the *National Zeitung* in Basel, primarily Free Democratic at the time, was among the most vociferous opponents of the slow-down-the-economy decisions, although the Free Democratic party had recommended them at least on the federal level.[29] Even in the case of party-oriented newspapers the demands of the parties and those of the newspapers may vary.

According to Thommen's investigation, 47 percent of Swiss papers cannot be assigned to a particular political party. Only a few of these newspapers, however, are opposed in principle to the ruling parties. Most nonaligned papers are in the middle of the party spectrum and support various parties at different times. Thommen concludes that "the real political party press is on the decline."[30] This trend was also noted by the Swiss Cartel Committee: "For some time now it can be seen that an increasing number of newspapers are forced to loosen their traditional ties to a specific political party by the economic need to increase the readership."[31]

Radio and Television

In Switzerland there are neither purely public nor purely private radio and television stations. The only broadcast license is held by the Swiss Radio and Television Corporation, a semipublic, semiprivate, nonprofit organization. Special radio and television programs are beamed to each of the three main language areas. On the basis of unsystematic observations, it seems to me that the corporation attempts to be neutral with respect to the political parties. The radio and television stations collaborate with all political parties rather than with one or another; furthermore, they often allow commentary on domestic political events to be presented by representatives of the various parties, economic interest groups, voluntary associations, and newspapers rather than by the staffs of radio and television stations. Consequently, the corporation articulates its own demands only to a very low degree. In Switzerland, radio and television serve primarily as amplifiers of the the views of other groups.

4. THE JURA SEPARATISTS

Of the demands described so far only those of the Communist party were clearly not in conformity with the system. This party is so small that it has little relevance. Of great political importance, however, are the demands of the Jura separatists, which also oppose the system.

The separatists demand that the districts of the Jura be separated from the canton of Berne to form an independent canton. This goal does not conform to the Swiss system because it would prevent crosscutting among the various groups. The preservation of crosscutting seems to be of great importance for peaceful coexistence in Switzerland (for a theoretical development of this argument see pp. 265–68). The separatists claim that in the area of the present Berne canton cantonal and linguistic boundaries coincide rather than crosscut. At present the predominantly German-speaking canton of Berne has a French-speaking minority of 15 percent. More than two-thirds of this minority live in the Jura districts, which have a German-speaking minority of 23 percent.[32] These figures show that there are no sharp linguistic boundaries in the canton of Berne. The separatists want the Jura to become completely French-speaking and to form an independent canton. The stated goal of the separatists is that the German-speaking people in the Jura should either leave the area or become assimilated into the French culture. If Berne accepted this demand, it would lose its function as mediator between the two linguistic groups. Instead of maintaining a flexible language line, Berne would become a single-language canton that allowed the language interests to coincide with cantonal interests. The success of the Jura separatists may cause attempts in the two other mixed French- and German-speaking cantons, Freiburg and Wallis, to affect a similar division along language lines. Then French-speaking Switzerland would constitute a closed group of cantons, a consequence that could seriously affect the continued existence of Switzerland as a unified political system. The Jura problem has a religious component in addition to the linguistic one. In the canton of Berne as a whole, 19 percent of the population is Catholic, whereas 59 percent of the population is Catholic in the Jura districts. Thus the creation of an independent Jura canton would also lead to a decrease in crosscutting between cantonal and religious boundaries.[33]

Nor do the Jura separatists conform to the present system with respect to the means by which they wish to achieve their ends. Most of them are not prepared to deviate from their extreme demands and to agree to a compromise according to the principle of amicable agreement. The authorities in Berne have for some years tried in vain to use the pattern of conflict regulation so characteristic of the Swiss political system. A constitutional revision in 1950 made various concessions to the separatists, and it was hoped that these might be the basis for a compromise solution. The Jura was given the constitutional right to have two seats in the nine-member cantonal government, which is greater than their proportional share. Whether the Jura should form a distinct electoral district for the National Council elections is now being debated.[34] All compromise proposals have so far been rejected by the separatists, who for the time being even refuse to talk to representatives of the Berne government. To realize their demands, some separatists have resorted to violence by interrupting a railway line and by setting the houses of their opponents on fire. In the context of the present political system of Switzerland, the expression of demands by such terroristic actions is clearly exceptional.[35]

CHAPTER IV

The Channels of Communication between the Intermediary Groups and the Formal Decision-makers

1. NONPUBLIC CHANNELS OF COMMUNICATION

Many channels of communication from intermediary groups to the formal decision-makers are characterized by a low public visibility. This is the case if there are role accumulations between the formal decision-makers and the intermediary groups. In a study of these relationships in the canton of Berne I found that 90 percent of the members of the Bernese Parliament play a role in their party, and it has already been shown that there are frequent role accumulations between the elite groups of the parties and the Parliament on the federal level.[1] The economic interest groups are also strongly represented in Parliament. The Berne study showed that 79 percent of the members of the cantonal Parliament had a leading position in an interest group.[2] Peter Gilg has estimated that 96 of the 200 members of the National Council elected in 1967 can be considered spokesmen of economic interest groups; these 96 members of the National Council are distributed among the individual economic sectors as follows: agriculture, 25; industry, wholesalers, big banks, 22; workers and clerical employees, 21; artisans, retailers, small banks, 21; traffic and tourism, 4; health insurance societies, 2; and house owners, 2.[3] The voluntary associations and the newspapers have a strong representation in Parliament. I found that two-thirds of the members of the Bernese Parliament belonged to the leadership of a voluntary association,[4] and Gilg's study revealed that fourteen members of the National Council are journalists who were elected in 1967.[5]

One of the reasons that role accumulations between intermediary groups and Parliament is so feasible is that Switzerland does not have a full-time parliament. Therefore, a full-time office in an interest group or party may be combined with a role as a member of Parliament. Some occupational groups—medical doctors, for example—often find it more difficult to combine occupational and political activities. The problem attracted some attention in the fall of 1967 when a reputable member of the federal Parliament refrained from seeking reelection for the reason that, as an independent practicing attorney, he could not maintain his parliamentary activity.[6]

Whereas the intermediary groups frequently have direct access to Parliament through role accumulations, there are no such role connections to the Federal Council. Interestingly enough, the Federal Council is outside the far-ranging system of role accumulations in Switzerland. Article 96 of the Federal Constitution specifies that "the members of the Federal Council may not hold other offices whether in the service of the federal government or in a canton, nor practice any occupation or craft." This article is interpreted very broadly since the members of the Federal Council have no functions in either intermediary groups or in their parties. Switzerland is thus fundamentally different from those political systems in which the members of the government have top positions in their parties.

There is a second channel of communication between the intermediary groups and the formal decision-makers that is not very visible to the public. The decision-makers let the intermediary groups participate in the making of decisions in a multitude of ways. This participation is probably most developed in the field of foreign-trade policy. Dusan Sidjanski has shown that Swiss delegations at international negotiations about trade treaties regularly include representatives of economic interest groups: "They are considered government delegates: their travel and other expenses are paid by the Federal government."[7] The participation of the economic interest groups in foreign-trade policy-making is manifested perhaps most clearly by the fact that the federal government has made an office available in the Federal Building for the secretariat of the Swiss Union of Commerce and Industry which has its main offices in Zurich.[8] The close cooperation between bureaucracy and economic interest groups in the field of foreign trade policy, "which has acquired the value of an institution, is a phenomenon peculiar to Switzerland. It is true that examples exist in other countries. But they are more exceptions to the rule that the bureaucracy alone negotiates in the name of the government."[9]

Intermediary groups participate not only in the making of foreign trade policy, but also in the decision-making process in other political areas. The expert committees include almost without exception representatives from intermediary groups. In its composition the Federal Committee for Labor Market Affairs can be considered a typical expert committee. It was presided over by a civil servant, the director of the Federal Bureau for Industry, Crafts and Labor, for the term 1965–68. The members were, in addition to four cantonal representatives and two university professors, five representatives each for employers and employees:[10]

Employer Representatives:

- The general secretary of the Swiss Contractors' Organization.
- The vice-director of the Swiss Farmers' Union.
- The assistant director of the Swiss Union of Artisans.
- A secretary of the Swiss Federation of Employers' Organizations.
- A secretary of the Swiss Union of Commerce and Industry.

Employee Representatives:

- A member of the federal board of the Swiss Federation of Trade Unions.
- The general secretary of the Swiss Construction and Wood Workers' Union.
- A member of the federal board of the Swiss National Federation of Christian Trade Unions.
- A secretary of the Swiss Federation of Trade Unions.
- A member of the Executive Committee of the Swiss Federation of Clerical Employees' Unions.

As an additional intermediary group the women's organizations were represented with one seat on the committee.

Sending members to expert committees is not the only possibility for participation in the decision-making process by intermediary groups. If the draft for a decision is ready, it is usually communicated to the groups involved in the so-called notification procedure so that they can express their position. It may even happen that individual functions in the decision-making process are transferred completely to intermediary groups. In 1966, when debate focused on the extent to which the federal government should support industrial research, it was not the Swiss Council of Science, the federal authority in charge of this area, that procured the information about the trends in the development of industrial research, it was the secretariat of the Swiss Union of Industry and Commerce that took over this function on "the invitation" of the Council of Science.[11] Even when the law is being carried out, intermediary groups are called in, since, according to Article 32 of the Federal Constitution, "the relevant economic organizations" are not only "to be heard before the issuance of the executing laws," they may also "be called in to aid in the implementation of the regulations." To illustrate the point, it is the Swiss Farmers' Union, not the federal administration, that computes the average agricultural income, a figure that has central importance for the determination of the federal subsidies according to the Agricultural Law.[12]

2. PUBLIC CHANNELS OF COMMUNICATION

A third possibility for bringing demands to the attention of the decision-makers is the introduction of a referendum or an initiative. Primarily this instrument of direct democracy gives the necessary emphasis to demands put forward through other channels. Kurt Mueller describes it in this way: "An explicit or even only an implicit 'threat of referendum,' i.e., the threat to call for a referendum if a proposal does not take the desired form, plays a considerable role in all phases of the legislative process; it is a trump card readily used by parties and interest groups in the political game."[13] Gruner argues in a similar way: "It is necessary to realize that in most cases the mere threat of a referendum will influence the contents of the laws considerably."[14] The threat of a referendum was made explicit in the *Neue Zuercher Zeitung* during the parliamentary deliberation on a bill concerning the tobacco tax: "And if all strings should break in Berne contrary to expectation, the people are still there in the background. The final word will then belong to them, since the Free Democratic Party of the canton of Zurich, as is well known, already has decided to make use of the referendum against a tobacco bill containing state price protection."[15] According to Gruner, a total of 871 laws have been subjected to the optional referendum at the federal level between 1874 and 1967. It was used only in sixty-one cases, i.e., 7.5 percent of all cases, which confirms that the right of referendum is used with moderation.[16]

A fourth avenue open to intermediary groups for getting demands through to the formal decision-makers is public expression—whether in mass media, in pamphlets, on posters, or in speeches. The public manifestation of demands has a different function for the *outsider groups* than for the *concordance groups*. By role accumulations, by participation in the decision-making process, and by threats of referenda, the concordance groups make their demands so visible to the formal decision-makers that public proclamation of the demands is actually redundant. In spite of this the concordance groups do not refrain from making their demands in public. But the function of such public statements by the concordance groups is less to communicate with the formal decision-makers than it is to show their own members that they represent their interests. The publicly articulated demands of the concordance groups frequently differ from those they express in expert committees. According to my observations the publicly articulated demands tend to be much more diffuse than those put forward behind closed doors. The demands manifested publicly by the concordance groups can almost be compared to a smokescreen that covers the real input process. Girod suggests that "in a general way politics more and more becomes like a game of chess, where the important things take place in technical committees and in meetings of strategists. In sum it becomes internal diplomacy."[17]

The outsider groups have only a few role accumulations with the formal decision-makers; they also have relatively few opportunities to participate in the decision-making process in expert committees, and so on. Finally, their use of the threat of referendum is less effective because they have less chance of success in a popular vote than the concordance groups, and often do not have the necessary financial means to stage a successful referendum campaign. When the outsider groups articulate their demands publicly their primary purpose is to protest against the concordance groups. To make this protest as visible as possible the outsider groups sometimes use methods that are atypical in Switzerland: the Easter marches of the nuclear armament opponents and the hunger strikes of the conscientious objectors are examples of these methods. The Jura separatists have even gone so far as to introduce their demands with violent actions.

In conclusion it may be said that the input and output processes overlap strongly with respect to the concordance groups, and far less strongly with respect to the outsider groups. There is no exact line of demarcation at which the input processes end and the output processes begin. The transition from input to output processes becomes even more diffuse because the different levels of the system can articulate reciprocal demands. We will see in the two case studies concerning university policy-making how the federal government makes demands on the cantons and the cantons make demands on the federal government. The same relationships exist between cantons and local communities, and occasionally between the federal government and the local communities. Because of the increasing importance of horizontal federalism there is a growing number of reciprocal demands among the cantons and among the local communities.

There are channels of communication similar to those between the intermediary groups and the formal decision-makers that connect the different levels of the system. For instance, cantons and local communities are connected to the federal level by many role accumulations: among the two hundred members of the National Council elected in 1967, twenty-six were members of cantonal governments, and seventeen were full-time members of local executives.[18] This does not exhaust the number of role accumulations between the National Council and the cantonal and the local levels because it does not include the cantonal and local legislators and those members of local executives who do not work full time. In a recent study of all role accumulations between the cantonal Parliament in Berne and the local levels, I found that only 10 percent of the cantonal legislators held no office in their communities.[19] The three levels of the system are also interconnected by their mutual participation in the decision-making process. In the federal Committee for Labor Market Affairs, a typical expert committee, there are also four representatives of cantonal governments. On the other hand, we will see in one of our case studies that federal representatives participated in a cantonal expert committee.

In summary, then, the demands of the ordinary members of the system are communicated to the formal decision-makers through a multitude of intermediary groups. Thus Switzerland is far from being a mass society, as William Kornhauser defines it, in which "both elites and non-elites are directly accessible to one another by virtue of the weakness of groups capable of mediating between them."[20]

CHAPTER V

The Output of Authoritative Decisions

In this chapter I intend to show how the input of demands is transformed into the output of authoritative decisions in the Swiss political system. To clarify the process, I will illustrate it with two case studies that concern university policy-making, and in order to facilitate the understanding of the case studies, I will preface them by a few general remarks on the uinversity system of Switzerland.

At the beginning of the period of my observations in 1960 Switzerland administered nine institutions at the university level: the universities of Basel, Berne, Freiburg, Geneva, Lausanne, Neuchâtel, and Zurich, the Federal Technical University, and the University of St. Gallen for Business Administration and Social Sciences. The Federal Technical University belonged to the federation, the University of St. Gallen to the canton and the city of St. Gallen, the other seven universities to the cantons in which they were located. At the creation of the federation in 1848 the federal government was empowered by Article 22 of the Constitution "to found a (regular) and a technical university." Based on this article the Federal Technical University was founded in 1854, but the plans for a regular federal university fell through. With the total revision of the Federal Constitution in 1874 the influence of the federal government in the field of higher education was extended to its present limits. The federal government was authorized by Article 27 of the Constitution "to create a regular university in addition to the existing technical university and to support other institutions of higher learning."

The federal government did not found a federal university after 1874, nor did it make any use of its authority to support the cantonal universities financially. In response to two parliamentary initiatives in 1947, the head of the Federal Department of the Interior referred to "the decision made in 1854 on the occasion of the founding of the Federal Technical University: The Federation has the Technical University and the cantons the regular universities. This arrangement has the appearance of unwritten constitutional law. The university cantons have always rightly been proud of their sovereignty in university affairs. Their autonomy in educational affairs constitutes an essential foundation of and a crucial guarantee for the cultural, political, and federal structure of the country."[1] The arrangement referred to as "unwritten constitutional law" in the 1947 parliamentary debate had something arbitrary about it. It was not logical for the federation to support one university while one-third of the cantons supported the other eight. This arrangement constituted a very unequal distribution of the burdens of higher education among the individual parts of the country.

When the university costs skyrocketed in the 1950s and especially in the 1960s, the demand was made that university expenditures be distributed more equitably. The increase in expenditures was caused for one thing by the rapidly increasing number of students. From the winter semester 1956–57 to the winter semester 1966–67 the number of students increased from 16,465 to 34,131—that is, it more than doubled in ten years. By the winter semester 1971–72 an additional increase brought the total to 44,624.[2] Besides the increasing number of students new research and instructional needs also contributed to the increase of university expenditures.[3] Consequently, university expenditures went up from 162 million francs in 1960 to 736 million francs in 1970.[4] The Swiss political system reacted in two directions to the demand for a more equitable distribution of the costs of higher education. First, the federation made use of its authority, according to Article 27 of the Federal Constitution, to support the cantonal universities; on June 16, 1966, the federal Parliament made the decision to give 200 million francs in federal support to the eight university cantons from 1966 to 1968 as a provisional solution.[5] Second, efforts were begun by Aargau and Lucerne, i.e., two cantons without a university, to found universities of their own.[6]

1. FEDERAL SUBSIDIES TO THE UNIVERSITY CANTONS

The demand for federal financial support to cantonal universities was articulated early in the history of the federation. The federal government had already received constitutional authority to support the universities in 1874. In the years 1888, 1912, and 1946–47, three unsuccessful attempts were made to put this authority to use.[7] The fourth attempt, which is to be considered here, was introduced by a motion in the federal Parliament in March, 1960. The author of the motion, Rainer Weibel from the canton of Berne, was a member of the Christian Democratic parliamentary group. The motion reads as follows: "The pleasing as well as necessary increase in the number of university students in addition to the enormous development of various disciplines, primarily in the natural sciences, call for a further consolidation of our cantonal universities. The rapidly increasing size of this urgent task begins to surpass the capacities of the university cantons. In spite of this, the further development of the universities must be accelerated in the cultural and economic interest of the country as a whole. The Federal Council is therefore instructed to submit a proposal to Parliament to make federal subsidies for the costs of expanding the cantonal universities possible."[8] Weibel's motion was signed by nineteen members of all the major groups in the National Council. On December 21, 1960, it was accepted by the National Council without debate or dissenting votes. The arguments of Weibel's motion were similar to the ones used in the three earlier attempts. In the first attempt in 1888 reference had already been made to the great progress of the natural sciences, and it was noted that "they require an increase in and an improvement of the scientific equipment of the universities, which leads to large additional expenditures."[9]

Since the attempt in 1960 used the same arguments and had the same goals as the three earlier attempts, it would be interesting to know what conditions made the 1960 attempt successful. It was, no doubt, of decisive importance that the insufficiency of the existing university structure was becoming much more apparent. Because of the large increases in the number of students many lecture rooms and laboratories were overfilled; there was a marked failure of recruitment in many academic disciplines; in international competition, research in Switzerland was lagging behind in many areas; and quite a few young scientists were leaving Switzerland for other countries, especially for the United States. In view of this situation, many groups had already articulated the demand for federal support of the cantonal universities before the submission of the Weibel motion. The legislature had only to register and express this consensus. It was therefore relatively insignificant who authored the motion. We know that other members of Parliament were about to do so, but they were just too late. It should be remembered that there is no opposition in the classical sense in the Federal Assembly. In Switzerland criticism of the government can be made by any parliamentary group; this often leads to competition—as was the case here—about which parliamentary group is the first to stage the proper advance.

Only when Parliament had intervened in 1960 did government and administration begin to look more closely at the matter. They had not themselves set the decision-making process moving by beginning to collect information or even by working out alternative proposals. Before the Weibel motion was submitted, the federal bureaucracy did not have any statistics about total university expenditures in Switzerland. Neither had it made a prognosis concerning student population growth. We may now ask if the decision-making process at the institutional level was started with a lead or a lag.[10] We could assume that the structure of higher education established during the founding of the federation was arbitrary and unsuitable even at that time. Or we could assume that the deficiencies of that structure only became apparent during the mid-1950s when the number of students began to increase rapidly. If we assume the latter, the Weibel motion was submitted with a lag of about five years. When the decision-making process reached its conclusion in 1966 with the passing of the subsidy law, the lag had increased to more than ten years.

Since the increase in the number of students did not come about with the unpredictability of a natural disaster, it would have been possible in principle to start the decision-making process with a time lead. It would have been relatively easy to make a prognosis of the increase in the number of students that would be brought about by demographic factors. When the number of births rose rapidly in the early forties, it could have been predicted that the number of students would go up correspondingly in the early sixties. If all the information, including comparisons with similar experiences from abroad, had been evaluated systematically, it should also have been possible to predict that the percentage of university students would increase sharply. The rapid growth of research expenditures should have been predictable without too much difficulty. Looking back at the 1946–47 debate about the university issue, the Federal Council stated laconically in a message in 1965: "Today it cannot be questioned that the two members of Parliament from Geneva made the right prediction of future developments. But the time was not ripe then for the ideas they developed."[11] "Not ripe" evidently meant that sufficient consensus had not yet been formed. This consensus was not created until the negative consequences of the existing university structure became clear to everybody. This means that the political system of Switzerland had an insufficient intake of information about the future and that the existing future-oriented information was underestimated in comparison with the information from the past and the present. Therefore the system responded to the stress caused by the skyrocketing costs of higher education with a lag of about ten years rather than with a lead of ten years which would have been possible in view of the information that was actually available.

With its acceptance of the Weibel motion, Parliament had not only authorized general clarifications measures, but, to a large extent, had already anticipated a decision about fundamentals. The Federal

Council was instructed "to submit a proposal . . . which made federal support of the costs of expanding the cantonal universities possible," and this had led the investigations in a specific direction. It should be considered that federal subsidies did not constitute the only possibility for creating a broader financial basis for Swiss higher education. The federal government could have taken over all the universities, the cantons could have found a solution without the help of the federation, or the private sector could have been given incentives (like tax exemptions) to increase their financial support of the universities. Such alternatives were discussed somewhat in the later stages of the decision-making process, but they were never considered seriously. The main reason for this was that Parliament had already shown its preference for a specific solution at the beginning of the decision-making process.

It seems that the functional contents of different phases of the decision-making process had begun to overlap. Before the systematic gathering of information had started at all, Parliament had made an important decision of principle. The information available to Parliament at that time was only that which the individual member happened to supply. According to Deutsch, a system has to receive three types of information: "first, information about the world outside; second, information from the past with a wide range of recall and combination; and third, information about itself and its own parts."[12] Information about "the world outside" of the political system of Switzerland in this case concerned the state of and the trends in Swiss higher education which were the sources of the stress put on the system. In 1960, not a single member of Parliament could have had systematic information about higher education in Switzerland because there were neither statistics about the total expenditures for higher education nor any prognosis of trends in the number of students. Systematic information about the political system itself would have assumed an investigation of the general forms of relationships between the federation and the cantons, and how the payment of federal subsidies for the cantonal universities would affect these relationships. Such an investigation had not been made in 1960. In contrast to the information about the universities and the political system, information about the past was plentiful. Since the founding of the federation in 1848, the cantons had frequently not been able to continue supporting a program on their own. More often than not in such cases the federation would give direct or indirect financial support to the cantons. The federation had already given subventions to primary education, vocational education, commercial education, and training in home economics. Federal subsidies had also become so common in other fields that one-quarter of all federal expenditures in 1960 consisted of subsidies.[13] In the debate about the Weibel motion information from the past was so dominant that it appeared self-evident to the members of Parliament that the university problem should also be solved by subsidies.

Parliament did not define in more detail which criteria were to be used in drafting the law. For instance, whether federal subsidies were to be used only for expansions or also for costs of operations was left an open question. In such "how" questions Parliament gave the Federal Council a free hand to draft a bill according to its own judgment. The Federal Council became as active after the parliamentary authorization as it had been passive before the Weibel motion. The phase of the Federal Council as a collegiate body was more or less by-passed, since the relevant actions were not taken by the collegium, but by Hans-Peter Tschudi, who headed the Federal Department of the Interior during the whole period of my observations. Before he did anything else he conferred with those directly involved. Immediately after the submission of the Weibel motion, even before the parliamentary debate on it, Tschudi asked the following persons for a written statement of their opinions: the government members responsible for education in the eight university cantons, the president of the Federal Technical University, and the president of the Swiss National Science Foundation. The same persons were also invited to a meeting on January 24, 1961, one month after the acceptance of the Weibel motion by Parliament; in addition, all university presidents received an invitation to the meeting.[14]

The conference was presided over by Tschudi; with an exception in each category all those responsible for educational affairs in the cantonal governments and all university presidents participated in the meeting. This conference thus brought together at the same table those with the highest responsibility for Swiss university education. The participants had dual roles. On one hand, they perceived themselves to be university experts and were in general also looked upon as such by outsiders. On the other hand, members of the cantonal governments and the university presidents made demands on the federation, and were thus directly interested in the outcome. It is important to stress this role accumulation between experts and directly interested persons. One further characteristic of the conference was that it was not open to the public, and only a short, vague statement was released about its subject matter. The decision-making process had thus been withdrawn from the public view. Had the decision-making process also been removed from Parliament's view? Although it may seem so at first glance, it was not the case. Three of the eight members of cantonal governments were also members of the federal Parliament so that, through role accumulations, Parliament was able to participate in the decision-making process.

It was agreed at the January conference to propose a bill requesting federal subsidies. One of the participants suggested that there were other solutions; as an example he mentioned the possibility that the university cantons might be given a reduction in taxes by the federation. However, he did not insist that the limits of the mandate be extended to investigate the possibility of other solutions besides the subsidies. He rather stressed that he would not oppose federal subsidies for the cantonal universities. At this point in time, opinions about the basic principle had become so widely accepted that it appeared hopeless to oppose it. The system no longer had the capacity to let fundamentally different solutions enter the decision-making process: in Deutsch's words it lacked the "ability to combine items of information into new patterns, so as to find new solutions that may be improbable in terms of their likelihood of being discovered."[15]

Was it by chance that the conference on January 24 reached a consensus similar to the one reached a month earlier in Parliament? Was it not to be expected that the experts gathered at the January conference would use a perspective different from the politicians in Parliament? A closer look shows that this contraposition of politicians and experts is problematic. First, it should be noted that there also were university experts in Parliament; three of them participated in the January conference in their roles as members of cantonal governments. The other five members of cantonal governments at the January conference were university experts but they were seen primarily as politicians in their cantons. The university presidents were most clearly bona fide university experts, but their role as experts was combined with their role as directly interested persons who were making demands on the political system. There was thus no polarization between experts and politicians, but rather many transitions with different degrees of dominance of one or the other role. This role structure was perhaps the reason that there was no strong difference of opinion about the solution of the problem between the Parliament and the members of the conference. In addition, it should be remembered that Parliament more or less registered and articulated a consensus that had been formed in intermediary groups prior to the parliamentary debate. As has been shown earlier, opinions are formed in intermediary groups—in political parties, economic interest groups, etc.—through feedback processes between expert and generalist groups. The participants in the January conference had already taken part in such feedback processes in intermediary groups in one form or another. This factor, too, may have caused the January conference to reach the same results as Parliament had reached. In conclusion, I believe I am justified in postulating that the consensus of the two bodies was more than a random occurrence.

Whereas Parliament had restricted itself to register and articulate the basic consensus, the January conference discussed the details of a possible solution. In contrast to the agreement about the basic need, greatly divergent opinions were expressed concerning the best ways of satisfying that need. Controversy centered about whether the humanities as well as the natural sciences and medicine should be subsidized, whether operations were to be supported in addition to expansions and improvements, how high the rates of the subsidies were to be set, and what conditions were to be attached to payment of federal subsidies. Since the conference met behind closed doors, the divergencies of opinion were not communicated to the public. Therefore, the public discussion—in the press, radio, and television, and among the political parties, economic interest groups, etc.—did not parallel the discussion among the experts, but lagged behind it. The lag was almost four years in duration because the public discussion did not really start until an expert report was published in the fall of 1964.

In view of the differences of opinion at the January conference, it was decided that systematic information should be gathered about the universities. The old and well-established channel of communication between the cantonal departments of education and the Federal Department of the Interior was to be used. Six days after the conference the Federal Department of the Interior submitted the following three questions to the departments of education of the eight university cantons:

1. What buildings and other facilities do you plan for the next five years and what are the estimated costs of the individual objects?
2. Which of these buildings and facilities are possible only with federal help?
3. How high should federal contributions be?

It was thus the conference of directly interested persons that planned further procedures. It is important to stress this fact because the conference was to have been only consultative. But its function appeared to become more than just consultative, since the head of the

Federal Department of the Interior chose to communicate with the cantonal departments of education as a result of the conference. Furthermore, it was one of the members of a cantonal government rather than Tschudi himself who made the proposal that was finally accepted by the conference.

The survey of the cantonal departments of education did not yield a systematic picture of the trends in the development of Swiss universities. Because there had been no prognosis of student population growth for Switzerland prior to the survey and because the assumptions underlying the answers to be given were not specified, the survey results were hardly significant. When the participants of the January conference met again on October 26, they agreed that the results of the survey were insufficient. In the second session it was decided to procure the necessary information through other channels of communication. It seemed that the participants first had to learn that the traditional channel of communication from the cantonal departments of education to the Federal Department of the Interior was insufficient before they were ready to contemplate the use of other channels of communication. This is one further example of an overestimation of information from the past compared to information about the future. Information from abroad, for example, would have made it easy to predict that many more differentiated channels of communication were needed to bring systematic data to the university question. The failure in the steering capacity of the system caused the decision-making process to be drawn out for almost a year; instead of becoming active at the January session, the appropriate channels of communication did not begin to work until the October meeting.

At the second session a special expert committee was appointed to collect the information needed. There was a lively discussion about the composition of this committee. The head of the Federal Department of the Interior, Tschudi, proposed that the committee be composed as follows: four representatives from the departments of education in the university cantons, four members from the faculties of the cantonal universities, two representatives from industry, and one each from the Federal Technical University, the Federal Department of the Interior, the Swiss National Science Foundation, the Swiss Society for Research in Natural Sciences, the Swiss Society of the Humanities, and the Academy of the Medical Sciences. The proposal was criticized, on one hand, because it did not give representation to all departments of education of the university cantons and to all universities, and, on the other, because the committee was already too big to be able to work.

After the articulation of several proposals that alluded to a division of the committee into subcommittees, it was finally agreed that the committee should include a representative from each of the nine universities with due consideration of all faculties. Thus the conference had not accepted a proposal from the head of the Department of the Interior without debate, nor had the department head been forced to accept a solution. A compromise was reached in this case with which all the participants could agree—as it is so often in the political system of Switzerland. Which individuals were to be members of the expert committee was largely fixed by the head of the Department of the Interior in cooperation with a prominent university professor. The procedure did not follow the delegation principle as the committee members were not nominated by the universities. The universities were not even asked to make proposals. Afterward in its message of November 29, 1965, the Federal Council gave the reasons for this procedure: "In order to procure as independent a study as possible the members of the committee were not named as official representatives of their universities, but as experts nominated by the Department of the Interior."[16]

Since certain individuals, such as the president of the Swiss Conference of University Presidents, had to be nominated more or less a priori, and since all universities and important academic disciplines were to be represented, the composition of the expert committee was complicated. On February 8, 1962, the Federal Department of the Interior finally appointed the following committee of experts: a professor of zoology (University of Basel); an associate professor of business administration (University of Berne); a professor of civil law (University of Freiburg); a professor of church history (University of Geneva); a professor of anatomy (University of Lausanne); a professor of classical philology (University of Neuchâtel); a professor of zoology (University of Zurich); a professor of economics (University of St. Gallen); and a professor of mathematics (Federal Technical University).

Professor André Labhardt from the University of Neuchâtel was appointed president, and the committee was then commonly referred to as the Labhardt Committee. Of the nine members, two were at the time of their appointment presidents of their universities, three were former university presidents, and one member became president during the active period of the committee.[17] There was thus a strong trend for the universities to be represented by their formal leaders. To be able to work, the Labhardt Committee also had to have a full-time academic secretary. The position was filled, at the proposal of a committee member, by a sociologist who took on the job after the second session of the committee in March, 1962.

Were the members of the Labhardt Committee solely experts in their fields or did they combine their role of expert with that of representative of interests? As university professors the committee members were associated with university interests in general and with certain universities and academic disciplines in particular. During the course of this study I will show how these interests were articulated and what importance they had for the decisions of the committee. Two years had lapsed between the time the Weibel motion was made in Parliament in March, 1960, and the constitution of the Labhardt Committee. The first major sequence had thus terminated.

The Labhardt Committee began its work by collecting information about the state of and the trends in the Swiss university system. I will attempt to show the channels of communication through which the information reached the committee, how it was filtered there, and which channels the committee used to pass the information on.

The committee procured information by taking a written survey of the Swiss universities, the aim of which was to open as many channels of communication as possible. The committee did not restrict itself to sending a questionnaire only to all the universities, or even just to the Swiss Conference of University Presidents as the representative of the universities; instead, it sent one type of questionnaire to the universities, one to the faculties, one to the academic disciplines, and one to the individual professors. In order to prevent the answers of the individual professors from being filtered by the disciplines, the faculties, or the universities as a whole, the professors were invited to return their personal questionnaire directly to the committee. In contrast, the questionnaires of the disciplines had to pass the faculties and the universities before reaching the committee, and the questionnaire of the faculties had to go to the committee by way of the universities.

The committee decided to collect the information in the following way. First, the president drafted a list of the information to be obtained; the list was discussed by the full committee and approved with minor modifications. The secretary then made up the detailed questionnaire, which he first discussed with all the committee members one at a time and then with the committee as a whole. No major changes were made. At the beginning of the winter semester 1962–63 the questionnaires were distributed, and they were returned to the committee toward the end of the semester. The returns were unusually complete. All the questionnaires from the universities, the faculties, and the academic disciplines were returned, and only 16 out of 2,059 from the individual faculty members were missing. The survey yielded mixed results. For example, the question as to whether the future supply of university professors would be adequate was answered positively by 55 percent of the disciplines and negatively by 45 percent. The principle of a coordination of the universities for all of Switzerland was welcomed without reservation by 51 percent of the disciplines, with 49 percent indicating reservations on various accounts.

The results of the survey were evaluated by the secretary of the committee. He was assisted by an official from the Federal Bureau of Statistics and two Ph.D. candidates from the University of Berne who worked half time. The evaluation consisted of a summary and a categorization of the answers. The members of the committee received the results of the survey only in this processed form; although any member would have been free to look at the original data, none of them took advantage of the opportunity.

The results of the written survey were not the only units of information received by the committee. Another unit of information was the result of an inquiry about total Swiss expenditures for higher education. The inquiry was made by the Federal Tax Administration at the request of the committee. The questionnaire was drafted by the professor of business administration in the committee, the secretary of the committee, and an official of the Federal Finance Administration. In contrast to the method used in the university survey, the committee as a whole was not consulted this time. The conduct of the inquiry was carried out by three officials from the Federal Tax Administration who went through the books "on location" in the university cantons. The Federal Bureau of Statistics supplied demographic data to the committee about the increase in the population of persons of university age. Conferences with the appropriate officials from the Federal Bureau of Statistics were carried out by the committee secretary who did not call in other committee members. The secretary also conferred alone with an architect who supplied the committee with information about the average construction costs per student in different disciplines. Some committee members were familiar with university systems abroad as a result of their own experience. The representative from the University of Geneva, for example, had held office as president of the European Conference of University Presidents. The secretary of the committee had been on three study tours abroad, and had been brought into contact with such relevant international organizations as UNESCO, OECD, and the Council of Europe.

Seen as a whole the process of gathering information did not follow a predetermined scheme, but rather originated ad hoc from the activity of the committee, which was free to determine the extent of cooperation it wanted from the federal administration. At its discretion the committee sought the service of the federal administration in some cases, and it proceeded independently in others. The same pragmatic course could also be found with respect to the division of labor within the committee. It was decided from case to case who was to conduct the information gathering. As a rule the secretary took the initiative and conferred with the president to decide whether other committee members were to be called in.

To a certain extent the president and the secretary performed the function of gatekeepers in that they largely determined what information flowed to the committee. However, the gatekeeper function was exercised very broadly because the president and the secretary perceived that their role was to make a wide variety of information available to the committee. Furthermore, they anticipated sanctions from the committee if they exercised their gatekeeper role restrictively. In order to avoid such sanctions they decided in cases of doubt to make the information flow to the committee broad rather than narrow. A comparison of the information that came to the president and to the secretary and that which reached the committee shows that the loss of information in this sequence was relatively low.

The committee itself constituted a filter so strong that the information flow away from the committee was substantially reduced. The committee did not think its task was to forward the received information in all its heterogeneity; it rather aimed at homogenizing the information. This can be illustrated by two examples: the planned increase in the number of professors and the student prognosis.

The committee had received many contradictory answers in the survey concerning the projected faculty increase from 1962 to 1975. The committee took pains to find a common denominator for these divergent opinions. In the first phase the committee split into six subcommittees according to academic disciplines. Three committee members considered law, economics, and the social sciences, two, the natural sciences, and one each, the rest of the disciplines. In a full session the results from the individual subcommittees were compared with one another. It turned out that the necessary increase in the number of professorial positions was estimated to be far above average by one discipline and far below average by another. The committee members responsible for these two disciplines were asked to correct their estimates in the direction of the average in order to achieve a better balanced picture. Now a process of bargaining began in the committee. Through this process, which proceeded partly informally outside of the session, the increase in the number of professorial positions in the individual disciplines was finally agreed upon. It was not necessary to resort to formal votes. Through mutual persuasion—particularly during breaks—it was possible to reach a compromise that was acceptable to all members.

The universities, faculties, and academic disciplines had stated in the survey what increase they expected in the number of students in their field. There were two prognoses of the growth in student population published outside the committee that showed very different results. The lower prognosis came from the Federal Bureau of Statistics, the higher from an economist at the University of St. Gallen. The committee invited both the director of the Federal Bureau of Statistics and the St. Gallen economist to participate in the work of the committee to produce a student prognosis. In this case, too, a compromise was successfully reached.

The committee managed to treat other information similarly. It was always possible to negotiate a compromise without making it necessary to divide a minority from a majority by a formal vote. The results of the work of the committee were summarized in a report. The committee chose to publish only homogeneous information. It chose not to forward the heterogeneous information it had received. The report did not contain any information about what increases in the number of professorial positions were considered necessary by the individual universities, faculties, and disciplines; only the conclusions that the committee had drawn on the basis of the information it had received were stated.

Although the information flow to the committee was characterized by many channels and heterogeneous content, only a single channel of communication—the committee report with a very homogeneous content—was sent from the committee to the public. The report was made public at a press conference in September, 1964, after the committee had been working for two-and-a-half years. One university lecturer was not satisfied with this *one* channel of communication and submitted a request to the committee for access to the original data of the survey so that he could scrutinize the final conclusions of the committee. His request was turned down, which shows how selective an information filter the committee was.[18] The committee let more information through only for the Federal Department of the Interior. The chief official in charge of university affairs in the department attended the sessions of the committee regularly and was just as well-informed as the members of the committee. The department secretary, the highest-ranking official in the department, also took part in some sessions. The head of the department himself was only present at the opening session; he was, however, informed continuously by his officials about the activity of the committee. Presumably the other members of the Federal Council as well as the members of Parliament were able to get access to the original data, but they did not take that option, so that in fact only the Federal Department of the Interior possessed information beyond the content of the committee report.

The report was printed in an edition of three thousand copies, which were distributed to the Federal Council, the Federal Assembly, the cantons, and the universities, and were available for purchase by other interested persons as well. The majority of Swiss citizens were informed through the mass media about the content of the report. The mass media thus constituted another important information filter. I have compared the information about the committee report in the mass media with the content of the report itself. Quantitative information passed through the mass media filter far better than qualitative information. Primarily, the press, radio, and television gave figures for the number of places that would be needed for students, the number of additional professorial positions that would be needed, etc., and described particularly broadly the expenditures that would be connected with the fulfillment of these needs. In contrast, the media gave only very sparse information about qualitative problems such as the revision of teaching methods.

A further screening probably took place among the consumers of the mass media. I was not able to perform a systematic sample survey of public awareness in this context. However, unsystematic observations revealed that many citizens, even members of parliaments, did not know much more about the committee report than that Swiss university expenditures were to increase to approximately one billion francs annually. Surveys that I have made concerning the level of information in the citizenry about other political issues confirm the results of these unsystematic observations (see pp. 228–33).

The information gathered by the Labhardt Committee about the Swiss university system was not subjected to a systematic evaluation during the rest of the decision-making process. For one thing, several potential competent critics had already worked with the committee and thus could not be expected to make independent evaluations. Furthermore, in a country as small as Switzerland the number of potential competent critics is relatively low. For instance, the architect called in by the committee was evidently the only expert with the necessary theoretical knowledge to calculate the average construction expenditures per student in the different disciplines. It was finally decisive that no other official agency was institutionally equipped to offer a serious evaluation of the information in the report. In the Federal Department of the Interior there were only three officials working with university affairs. Their working load would have made them unable to seriously evaluate the information of the committee. Furthermore, they had taken part in the work of the committee to such an extent that they were largely included in the consensus of the committee and thus could not be considered as independent critics.

In many countries the chief of government has a bureaucracy of his own that can check the information from the specialized departments. In Switzerland the office of federal president rotates among the seven members of the Federal Council for a year at a time, and each federal president is still head of his regular department. Neither the federal president nor the Federal Council as a collegiate body has a competent staff to assist in evaluating the information that comes from the individual departments.[19] Therefore, the information from the Labhardt Committee could not be checked at the level of the Federal Council. Nor could the information be checked in Parliament, either, because Parliament has no assistance for other than administrative matters.[20] Neither were the political parties equipped to scrutinize the report. The Free Democratic party, for instance, had at that time only two full-time employees in addition to a clerical staff, a general secretary, and an assistant, and the situation in the other parties was similar.

Because the information gathered by the Labhardt Committee was not systematically scrutinized, the committee had an actual information monopoly. This did not mean that the information part of the report was completely protected from criticism. After the publication of the report a discussion arose in the public about the quality of the information produced by the committee. Criticism in general centered implicitly or explicitly on the composition of the committee. For instance, among young scientists reference was made to the high average age of the committee, and it was deduced from this that the interests of the younger generation had not been taken into consideration sufficiently. On the other hand, the prominent individuals represented in the committee guaranteed the political authorities that the selection of information had not been made by extremists. It was also important that all universities and academic disciplines were represented in the committee. If, for instance, the French-speaking universities had been underrepresented, it would have been easy to predict that criticisms would have been greater in the French-speaking areas.

When one considers that the quality of the report was judged by the composition of the committee, it becomes clear that the Federal Department of the Interior was not so free in its appointment of the committee as might appear at first glance. The department had to foresee a committee whose credibility would make its information seem altogether trustworthy to the different groups. The department had succeeded to a high degree in anticipating the expectations of the most relevant groups, and because all criticisms of the committee were approximately equal in intensity, the report was finally able to take a strategically favorable middle position.

According to Karl W. Deutsch a political system needs information about itself, about its environment, and about the past to steer itself (see p. 132). The information collected by the committee primarily concerned the universities—the environment of the political system. With respect to information about the past, a report by an official of the Federal Department of the Interior about earlier attempts to get federal support for the cantonal universities was available to the committee. But the information about the past came mainly from the personal experiences of the committee members themselves. In this context the relatively high age of most members was important: five were more than sixty, three were between fifty and sixty, and only one was below fifty. With this age structure it was possible for the committee to mobilize information that went quite far back in time. This stored information from personal experiences was usually not articulated during the formal sessions, but rather on informal occasions—especially at the meals the committee had together. The professor of anatomy, for instance, told more than once how, at the beginning of his teaching career, students had a whole cadaver available for dissection, whereas today several students had to share a single cadaver. Such information, frequently told as anecdotes on informal occasions, had a considerable influence on the activity of the committee. The age of the committee members was not irrelevant because it helped to provide a great deal of information from personal experience.

With respect to the political system itself it would have been important to have had information about the relationship between the federation and the cantons, since a law about subsidies was bound to influence these relationships. It would have been valuable to know, for example, what the general influence of the federation was compared with that of the cantons, and how the payment of federal subsidies to the cantonal universities would affect these spheres of influence. The Labhardt Committee considered the collection of information on this subject outside its mandate; nor was there another agency that had assumed responsibility for this task in any systematic way.

During the work of the committee the *process of innovation* began long before the gathering of the information had been concluded. There was thus an overlap of these two functions in the same sequence. The Federal Assembly and the conferences on January 24 and October 26, 1961, had already restricted the scope of innovation substantially, since federal subsidies had been cited as the only possible solution. The Labhardt Committee did not consider itself obliged to go beyond its mandate and study alternative solutions, although its report mentions that direct contributions from the nonuniversity cantons or the founding of a federal university could bring about financial relief for the university cantons. These alternatives were included in the report for the sake of completeness without being worked out in detail. The committee restricted itself to putting forth some negative arguments. It was argued, for example, that a system of intercantonal contributions would present "too many legal and practical difficulties."[21] But these difficulties were neither mentioned nor investigated, and no mention was made of how they could be overcome. The committee also argued that "the contributions which could be obtained presumably would not be nearly sufficient."[22] This presupposition was based on the personal experiences of the committee members, but not on a study of the nonuniversity cantons. The committee's argument against the founding of a federal university was that the development of cantonal universities corresponded better to "the federal structure of our state," a position presented in the absence of a detailed examination of the form a federal university might take.[23] Although the committee report presented alternative solutions at the verbal level, the scope of innovation of the committee was actually restricted to the question of federal subsidies. The committee thus stayed within the limits of the mandate given it by the Federal Department of the Interior.

In the fall of 1962 the committee appointed a subcommittee to come up with a concrete proposal for the structure of the federal subsidies. At that time the committee had been working for half a year and the survey of the universities was just about to start. The subcommittee thus became active when there still were no results from the gathering of information. Although it was not difficult to predict that the subcommittee would have considerable importance, there were no contests in the election of its members. In a formal plenary session the president of the committee asked who would be willing to participate in the work of the subcommittee. There were no spontaneous volunteers; in subsequent discussions general agreement was reached that those members who could add most experience to the deliberation through their academic disciplines should make themselves available. Persuaded by the committee, the two economists, the lawyer, and the mathematician finally declared themselves willing to form the subcommittee; the secretary also agreed to attend the sessions. Before the first session of the subcommittee one of its members made a catalogue of the alternative ways in which the federal subsidies could be utilized. The following criteria were used to define construction expenditures:

A. Subsidies for any construction costs, even for buildings completed, but not yet paid for.
B. Subsidies only for specific expenditures:
   1. for new buildings, but not for alterations
   2. for buildings expanding the capacity, but not for replacements
   3. for buildings with certain functions (e.g., for natural science research, for dormitories), but not for general buildings with lecture rooms
   4. for the building itself, but not for the equipment, or for the equipment, but not for the building
   5. for buildings whose costs exceed a certain amount
   6. for buildings considered urgently needed and appropriate by the federation
C. Subsidies for all buildings basically, but with certain restrictions:
   1. not for books (even when they are equipment expenditures)
   2. not for the construction of university clinics (since these do not serve purely university functions)
   3. not for the construction of institutes that are only loosely connected with the university or perform paid functions for third persons

In the committee report that was published two years later a specific recommendation concerning the subsidies had been deduced from seven basic principles. How had the committee managed to make one choice among the variety of alternatives in less than two years? Above all, it stressed the following four aspects of the decision-making process:

1. The committee did not proceed deductively by first developing the basic principles from which the structure of the subsidies were drawn. It proceeded much more by trial and error: possible concrete solutions that seemed to be somehow promising were examined to see what effect they would produce for each university. If the solution led to a distribution of the federal funds that was perceived to be disproportional, it was dropped. For example, when the federal subsidies were calculated according to the financial capacity of the cantons, the results led the committee to believe that the university cantons with a relatively low population would be at a disadvantage. Further calculations were then undertaken in which the index of the financial capacity of the cantons was multiplied by the number of inhabitants in the cantons, a process that produced more satisfactory results.

2. The process of trial and error was characterized by its predominantly informal character. The full committee or the subcommittee did not decide beforehand who should calculate which alternative solutions in what time order. On their own some members did compute solutions that looked particularly promising to them. Informal conversations among the committee members, mainly by telephone, were important in this context: such conversations often led to new possible solutions that had to be computed. An analogous situation existed with respect to the evaluation of the outcomes of the different calculations. Informal phone conversations among the members of the committee were also of great importance here. The function of the formal sessions was primarily to register the informally achieved consensus. This method of working made it possible to restrict the number of sessions of the subcommittee to four; the committee as a whole did not need more than seventeen sessions to complete its total workload.

3. The expectation of the committee was to aim at a solution with which all members could agree. Nobody at any time seriously considered the possibility that a majority decision could bring about an effective solution; the important point at all times was to achieve a unanimous solution. To a large extent, this attitude determined the interactions in the committee. The most frequently approached members were those who seemed to endanger unanimity. The resulting pattern of interaction did not lead to factions in the committee, but rather to its integration. With one exception unanimity was finally reached on all points of the committee report. The exception concerned the agency that was to be created in connection with the federal subsidies. Was it to be an independent body or only a consulting body? Five members were in favor of the former solution and four of the latter. The aversion for majority decisions was now shown by the fact that the committee

merely cited the vote ratio and explicitly refrained from "recommending one or the other solution specifically."[24] Even in this case the principle of unanimity was stressed in the following statement: "But the committee agrees on the demand that a particular agency has to be created for the subsidies and that it has to be constituted such as to further cooperation among the university cantons and to pay due regard to the idea of the autonomy of the universities."[25]

4. Before the publication of the report, the committee had tried to attract the support of other agencies such as the Swiss Conference of University Presidents and the Swiss National Science Foundation. The channels of communication to these institutions consisted—as so often is the case in the political system of Switzerland—of role accumulations. The president of the Labhardt Committee was also the president of a branch of the National Science Foundation and a member of the Conference of University Presidents; the president of the Conference of University Presidents was vice-president of the Labhardt Committee.

Even after the publication of the Labhardt Report in September, 1964, the innovation process was limited largely to federal subsidies in one way or another. The Labhardt Committee proposal was not accepted unseen; in contrast to the informative part of the report which, as we have seen, was not evaluated systematically, the modalities of the federal subsidies proposed by the committee were examined very closely.

Now discussion began to take place in public more often. So far the acceptance of the Weibel motion by the National Council in 1960 was the only part of the decision-making process that had been fully available to the public. The public had only been informed about what had happened in the following four years by some vague press releases and a few indefinite allusions in speeches by the head of the Federal Department of the Interior. Not until the publication of the Labhardt Report did the public begin to participate more broadly in the decision-making process. It turned out that a large information deficiency had to be filled first. After the publication of the Labhardt Report the mass media and the organizers of meetings began to concentrate on interpreting the information part of the report. Only very gradually did the public start participating in the innovation process, which, in the meantime, had begun to gain momentum behind closed doors.

The first important meeting behind closed doors took place on November 9, 1964, at the invitation of the head of the Federal Department of the Interior. Invited to this meeting were the participants of both 1961 conferences—the government members of the university cantons responsible for educational affairs, the university presidents, and the representatives of the Swiss National Science Foundation. Additional persons invited at this time were the members of the Labhardt Committee, government members from the cantons interested in founding new universities, i.e., Aargau and Lucerne, and two high officials from the Federal Department of Finance and Customs. The inclusion of the Department of Finance and Customs needs a further comment. When Parliament had voted for the Weibel motion in 1960, the responsibility for the drafting of the bill was given directly to the Federal Department of the Interior without the intervention of the Federal Council as a whole or of other departments in any essential respect. Subsequently, Finance and Customs contributed to the study of total university expenditures that had been undertaken by the Labhardt Committee; the Department of Foreign Affairs and the Department of Economic Affairs assisted the committee in gathering certain types of information. Apart from these purely technical contacts the Department of the Interior acted independently of the other departments until the fall of 1964 when the Labhardt Report was published.

The composition of the November, 1964, conference was not much different from the first conference in January, 1960. Tschudi was still head of the Federal Department of the Interior. There had been only one change in the eight government members of the university cantons. The president of the National Science Foundation was still the same person. None of the university presidents from the first conference still held office, but two of them participated in the meeting as members of the Labhardt Committee. This strong continuity in the composition of the conference caused a narrowing of the scope of innovation. The points about which a consensus had been reached at the first conference were no longer questioned by the participants, especially with regard to the idea that the solution to the problem would be federal subsidies. The aspect of continuity was referred to by one of the participants when he said explicitly that since the principle of subsidies had been accepted at the first conference he would not refer to it again.

Within the scope of innovation left open by the acceptance of the principle of federal subsidies, the conference in November, 1964, produced a great variation in proposals. There were controversies concerning the ratio of distribution, the amount of the subsidies, and the question of whether a definitive or a provisional solution should be considered. The decision-making process had not been narrowed down so much that it was only a question of voting for or against the Labhardt Committee proposal. On the contrary, the participants felt free to articulate new proposals as they saw fit; opinions had not yet become so fixed that it had come to a formation of fronts. Various speakers said that they reserved their right to take a definitive position at a later time. It is noteworthy that a representative of the Federal Department of Finance and Customs took on the job of putting the idea of subsidies for the universities into a general political context. In other political systems this role would most likely have been assumed by the chief of government. As there is no chief of government in Switzerland, the Department of Finance and Customs at least partly performed this role in this case.

Negotiations concerning further developments were made at the conference itself, just as had been done at the earlier conferences. The university cantons were requested to state their position with respect to the Labhardt Report in writing; at the same time the Federal Department of the Interior, in cooperation with the Federal Department of Finance and Customs was asked to make a preliminary draft of a federal bill. As soon as the opinions of the university cantons and the draft of the bill were in, a new conference was to be called. The opinions of the university cantons, which were all in by April, 1965, essentially confirmed the positions taken by the government members of these cantons at the November, 1964, conference. Again, there was a great variation in the proposals for the modalities of the federal subsidies. The Conference of Swiss University Presidents sent an unsolicited opinion to the Federal Department of the Interior. The opinion was drafted in a session on February 13, 1965. In it the university presidents came out in favor of a transitional solution, and they presented the first concrete proposal for such a solution.

The universities, which had already been allowed full expression in the Labhardt Committee, made their presence felt in this sequence, too. In addition to being heard through the conference of their presidents, they were active in influencing the opinions of their cantonal governments. The Parliament also participated in this sequence of the innovation process. As we have seen, it had opened the whole decision-making process in 1960 with the acceptance of the Weibel motion. From the end of 1960 to the end of 1964 Parliament did not actively appear as a body in the decision-making process. Yet those individual members who combined the role of member of Parliament with that of government member responsible for educational affairs of a university canton were also active in the decision-making process in the meantime. In December, 1964, Parliament reappeared as a body in the decision-making process. In a new motion, Weibel, the initiator of the first motion, demanded that a transitional solution be found in the interest of an acceleration of the project. Another member of the National Council made a similar move in the same direction in March, 1965. The debate in Parliament on these two motions did not take place until September, 1965, i.e., at a time when the decision-making process had already entered the phase at which the actual decision was taken. It will be shown below how these two motions influenced this phase. At the moment, it is important to note that Parliament participated not only informally, particularly through role accumulations, but also formally, as a legislative body, in the innovation process about the modalities of the subsidies.

Of the economic interest groups and the political parties, only the Swiss Union of Commerce and Industry had intervened in the innovation process. It had developed its position on the basis of a survey of its members. The necessity of an opinion was expressed in a circular to the members: "The questions submitted for discussion by the Labhardt Committee are important to commerce and industry from various perspectives. The universities are educating a considerable part of the top and middle level leaders for Swiss private enterprise. But they are also places of scientific research; the pure research in the universities and the applied research in industry are mutually dependent. If private enterprise thus is to a large extent a beneficiary of the furtherance of the universities, it also finances them to a large extent by being the most important tax payer to the Federation and the cantons and by voluntary contributions."[26]

It is evident that the Union of Commerce and Industry saw itself as a representative of specific interests. Its opinion, which it gave to the Federal Department of the Interior in June, 1965, was written by a group representing specific interests, as had been the case with those of the university cantons and the universities themselves. The union still considered many substantive problems unsolved and concluded that a provisional solution had to be found.

What part did the head of the Federal Department of the Interior take in the innovation process? On September 17, 1964, when he presented the Labhardt Report at a press conference, Tschudi imposed a conscious limitation on himself by saying: "The Federal authorities and the university cantons will have to examine the report closely. It is not my intention to anticipate the results of this examination." Tschudi showed the same reservation at the conference on October 9,

1964; but on that occasion he participated in the innovation process in the sense that he expressed doubt whether a provisional solution would be appropriate.

The evaluation of the written opinions concerning the Labhardt Report was entrusted by the head of the Federal Department of the Interior to the Swiss Council of Science, which, in March, 1965, was named the highest consultative organ of the Federal Council in matters of science policy. It included thirteen members—representatives for the university cantons, the universities, private business, and the federal administration. What was the relationship of the Council of Science to the Labhardt Committee and to the three conferences that had advised the head of the Federal Department of the Interior up to now? Three of the six university representatives in the Council of Science had taken part in the Labhardt Committee. The three other university representatives had participated in the different conferences, either as university presidents or as representatives of the National Science Foundation. The representative of the cantonal governments had also participated in the different conferences. Thus, those members of the Council of Science not connected with the decision-making process were the four representatives of private business and the two federal officials, one from the Department of Economic Affairs, the other from the Department of Transportation and Energy.

The composition of the Council of Science shows that it was not a completely new element added to the decision-making process. The majority of its members had already participated directly in the previous decision-making process. The only important difference between the Council of Science and the Labhardt Committee and the former conferences was that the council had a somewhat broader basis. It included representatives from private business and it had stronger connections with other departments within the federal administration.

If we survey the innovation process to this point, we see that the participants were always more or less the same people. This pattern made any distinct alternative solutions impossible. Only different agencies working without role accumulations independently of one another could have realistically raised alternative solutions. The method that was used actually predestined the innovation process to end with a compromise solution. It was arranged in such a way that differences between alternatives were covered up rather than stressed. For example, since the majority of the Council of Science's members had already participated decisively in the innovation process in other roles, it did not have the necessary impartiality to come up with very different solutions. It believed its task was not to propose alternative solutions, but to find a common denominator for the already articulated proposals so that they might receive the broadest possible support. In its recommendations, which were submitted to the head of the Federal Department of the Interior on July 6, 1965, it supported a provisional solution. The council was thus in agreement with the unanimous opinion of the Conference of University Presidents, the Swiss Union of Commerce and Industry, and half of the university cantons. With respect to the distribution ratio, the Council of Science essentially relied on a proposal of the Conference of University Presidents. It is important to know that the president of the Council of Science belonged to the committee of the Conference of University Presidents, which had worked out the distribution ratio. That is another illustration of the far-reaching importance of role accumulation in the political system of Switzerland.

After the submission of the recommendations of the Council of Science, the head of the Federal Department of the Interior, who until now had more or less withheld his opinion, was expected to make up his own mind. Because of the course the innovation process had taken he had not been confronted with the task of deciding among various alternative solutions. The only option open to him was to accept or to refuse the compromise that had been reached in the decision-making process so far. He accepted the proposal of the Council of Science with few modifications. Late in the summer of 1965 the innovation process had essentially come to an end. The phase of the actual decision-finding began in the fall of 1965 with three additional conferences presided over by the head of the Federal Department of the Interior. The head of the department had invited the most politically relevant interested persons to these conferences. Those invited included the government members responsible for educational affairs of the university cantons and of the cantons interested in founding new universities, and the presidents of the Council of Science, the National Science Foundation, and the Federal Technical University; occasionally government members responsible for the finances of the university cantons also attended the discussions.

The university presidents and the members of the Labhardt Committee, participants in the earlier conferences, were not invited to the conferences in 1965. If the making of the actual decisions rather than information gathering and innovation was now the business at hand, then the members of the cantonal governments were to be the principal role players. This does not necessarily mean that they influenced the making of the actual decisions conclusively; the decisions could have already been made elsewhere. But that was not the case here. The proposal of the Council of Science, which the Federal Department of the Interior had approved, was not accepted by the conferences in its most important point. The objection was to a clause that stated that a part of the federal subsidies should be put aside as an available contingent which the federal government could put to use for specific purposes at its own discretion. The conferences demanded that all subsidies be distributed completely for free use by the university cantons. This question was generally thought to be the most important point in the bill, because the federation's influence on the use of the subsidies depended on the answer. This conflict between the head of the Federal Department of the Interior and the members of the cantonal governments responsible for educational affairs was solved with the following compromise. Tschudi gave up all claim to a separate available contingent; in return, the members of the cantonal governments promised that they would themselves see to a proper distribution of the federal funds by the creation of an intercantonal coordinating agency. With these two assumptions a consensus was finally achieved during the last of the three conferences.

On September 29, 1965, between the second and the third conference, Parliament discussed the two parliamentary motions made in December, 1964, and March, 1965. These two motions had suggested that a provisional solution be found in the interest of the acceleration of the project. When Parliament now debated these motions, the question of a provisional solution had already been decided positively by the conferences between the Federal Department of the Interior and the directly interested parties. The unanimous decision of Parliament to accept these motions only amounted to a confirmation of decisions already made elsewhere. Therefore, it cannot be said that in this sequence Parliament had led the decision in a specific direction. By the end of September, 1965, the controversial question was not whether to look for a final or a provisional solution, but whether to allow the federal government to withhold a part of the subsidies. Parliament would have had the opportunity to lead the decision-making process in a specific direction by expressing its opinion early. But it refrained from doing so and left the initiative to the Federal Department of the Interior and the directly interested parties. Previous negotiations about this question had taken place behind closed doors and that may have contributed to Parliament's inaction, since it did not have the necessary information for a well-reasoned position at that time.

The head of the Federal Department of the Interior submitted the compromise reached between him and the government members of the university cantons to the Federal Council in November, 1965. For the first time the latter considered the whole set of problems in detail. It expressed reluctance to accept a solution that gave the federation no opportunity to influence the way its subsidies were spent. In its message to Parliament on November 29, 1965, the Federal Council expressed its concern as follows: "It has not been easy for us to consider a solution which is limited exclusively to fixed, freely available amounts and robs the Federation of any opportunity to influence the way they are spent."[27] Nevertheless, the Federal Council accepted the solution submitted to it and gave the following reasons for doing so: "The establishment of a separate contingent at the disposal of the Federation has run into violent opposition on the part of the government members of the university cantons responsible for educational affairs. They advocated the position that the investigation and regulation of the problem of coordination be left to the cantons. In order to study this question they are willing to proceed without delay with the creation of an intercantonal coordinating agency."[28] These quotations from the Federal Council show how it accepted the conclusiveness of the compromise between the Federal Department of the Interior and the directly interested parties. In fact the Federal Council could not possibly work out an alternative of its own because it lacked the necessary facilities. In Switzerland there is no chief of government who can put his own staff to work checking the proposals that come from the departments. The federal president, who is changed every year and who also heads a department during his term as president, is only *primus inter pares*. The Federal Council could have expressed its dissent only by returning the report to the Department of the Interior for revision. A strong argument against such a move was that the decision-making process had already caused a considerable time lag. Above all, the time pressure led the Federal Council to pass on the proposal to Parliament practically without changes. The Federal Council found some comfort in the fact that it was only a provisional solution. With respect to a permanent regulation of the federal subsidies it stated: "Without a satisfactory solution to the coordination problem a continuation and an expansion of the Federal support can hardly be defended."[29]

Almost five years had elapsed since Parliament had accepted the Weibel motion in December, 1960. Not until November, 1965, did the Federal Council give detailed attention to the problem as a collegiate body. The rest of the time had been used by the Department of the Interior to reach a compromise with the directly interested parties.

When the Federal Council had to act, its decision-making situation was characterized by time pressure and by the absence of personnel that could have helped it to check the proposal appropriately. That this was only a provisional solution made it easier for the Federal Council to agree to the achieved consensus, since the answer to the central question of coordination could be put off to the final solution.

Only after the publication of the message of the Federal Council did the intermediary groups and the mass media enter the decision-making process on a broader basis. The proposal had been almost completely out of the public eye before the publication of the Labhardt Report in September, 1964. From the fall of 1964 to the end of 1965 the public began to be aware of the Labhardt Report. The television station of the German-speaking part of Switzerland began to discuss the subject of federal support for the cantonal universities for the first time in September, 1965. The moderator of the program informed the participants that for the time being the discussion was to be mainly informative. That is, at the same time as the head of the Federal Department of the Interior and the government members of the university cantons negotiated their final compromise behind closed doors, television started the first informative program about the set of problems. The controversial question at that time—the question of the federal influence on the use of the subsidies—was not mentioned at all, although the discussant representing the educational affairs of a big university canton would have been up to date on the available information. The other mass media and the political parties lagged behind the actual decision-making process in a similar manner.

When the Federal Council finally published the compromise solution, there had not been much time for public discussion because the law was passed in the National Council in March, 1966, and in the Council of States in June, 1966. I was able to observe the discussion that took place in the Free Democratic party. The issue was delegated to the standing Committee for Political and Cultural Affairs, which made its final decision regarding the matter in a single half-day on January 21, 1966. The secretary of the Labhardt Committee, an important participant in the earlier parts of the decision-making process, made the introductory report. In addition to the report, the committee had no sources of information other than the official documents of the federal authorities. At that time there were only two full-time officials in the party at the federal level—the general secretary and his assistant. Neither of them had the time nor the professional competence to procure information about university problems for the committee. The committee had no full-time secretary who could have been responsible for the collection of information. In view of both the absence of information and the time pressure, it would have been impossible for the Committee for Political and Cultural Affairs to prepare an alternative solution. Considerable uneasiness was expressed in the committee that the federation would not be able to influence the manner in which its subsidies were to be spent. The only possible way for the committee to articulate its dissent effectively would have been to suggest that the bill be sent back to the Federal Council for revision. It was reluctant to do this, however, because it reasoned that a further delay would be irresponsible. Yet at the session the committee tried to make a certain improvement in the bill. An attorney, who otherwise did not occupy himself with university matters, made an ad hoc proposal to take out of the total amount of federal support a contingent fund that could be at the disposal of the federal authorities for special purposes. This proposal was accepted unanimously by the committee with a few modifications. Since the National Council committee in charge of the matter was to meet in February, 1966, the pressure of time was so great that the Free Democratic party had no opportunity to have the proposal of the Committee for Political and Cultural Affairs considered by the Executive Committee. To shorten the procedure somewhat, the Free Democratic members of the National Council committee were informed about the proposal from the committee by letter. One of the Free Democratic members then made a corresponding proposal in the committee of the National Council. Because the head of the Federal Department of the Interior and the president of the Swiss Council of Science both participated in the meeting of the National Council committee, they had no difficulty in pointing to the weak spots in the Free Democratic proposal. The proposal was turned down in the committee and in the plenum of the National Council. It was evident that the party had not had the necessary time and facilities to prepare the proposal properly. In one sense the party was in the same position as the Federal Council: both agencies had had only little time and expertise to put together an alternative to the compromise that had been reached by the Department of the Interior and the university cantons. Other parties were in a situation similar to that of the Free Democratic party.

The two houses of the Federal Assembly alternate in having priority. As already mentioned, the National Council was the first to consider the present matter. The only information available to it was the report of the Labhardt Committee, the message from the Federal Council, and oral reports by the head of the Federal Department of the Interior. The National Council did not do anything to counterbalance this information, all of which originated within the executive. Neither the National Council as a whole, its commissions, its parliamentary groups, nor its individual members, had at their disposal the expertise of anyone in university affairs. Assistance of this kind was almost completely missing in other areas as well. One exception was the Finance Commission, which, at the time of the present case study, had acquired an academic secretary. However, some progress has been made in recent years. Parliamentary commissions now have academic secretaries, arrangements are being made for the setting up of a legislative reference service, and the parliamentary groups are also being given secretaries.[30] Though provisions for technical assistance have been made in Switzerland only recently, they have been taken for granted by the parliaments of most other Western democracies for many years.

It has to be stressed that the National Council in the spring of 1966 did not have the facilities to systematically check the information about the university problem it received from the executive. It also has to be remembered that the individual members of Parliament do not have much time available, since they do not have full-time positions. Yet the National Council was not at all totally uninformed. It did include, among others, the president of the Swiss Council of Science and three government members responsible for educational affairs from university cantons, that is, persons who had participated directly in the decision-making process up to that time. There was no opposition to the bill from these members of the National Council, since they had helped to prepare the solution that was now being submitted to Parliament. With the head of the Department of the Interior, they formed a common front in defense of the bill. As far as party affiliation was concerned this was a very heterogeneous group. The Social Democratic head of the Department of the Interior, the Free Democratic president of the Council of Science, and the government member responsible for educational affairs from the canton of Zurich who belonged to the Independent party were the most vehement defenders of the bill. It should be remembered that these three persons had not at all been of the same opinion concerning the central question of federal influence in an earlier phase of the decision-making process that was not visible to the public. Now in the public debate they did not try to articulate the previous divergencies following party lines. This occurrence confirms how hard it is to differentiate between government and opposition parties. In the present case, a representative from the Independent party, a party that formally is in opposition at the federal level, had contributed significantly to the formation of the proposal of the Federal Council.

A Free Democrat who, as the personnel director of a big firm, had not participated in the decision-making process up to this time, made a motion to oppose that part of the bill that had to do with the question of an available contingent at the disposal of the federal government. It has already been mentioned that his motion had been made at the Free Democratic Committee for Political and Cultural Affairs, and that it had not been prepared in great detail, as neither he nor the party committee had had the necessary time or information. In the debate about this motion, interests were not gathered along party lines at all. For one thing, even members of the Free Democratic parliamentary group—in particular the president of the Council of Science—fought the motion. Since the matter could not be considered further within the party because of lack of time, it reached Parliament without attempts to win over the president of the Council of Science and the other members of the parliamentary group who had not participated in the session of the Committee for Political and Cultural Affairs. At first the attempt was made to settle the controversy in the parliamentary commission that was preparing the bill and in parliamentary groups behind closed doors, but it was unsuccessful, and so the controversy finally reached the full session and thus the public at large. Since the conflict could not be settled in the full session according to the principle of amicable agreement, a majority decision had to be made. In this case, the majority decision led to the defeat of the proposed change.

Did this type of parliamentary procedure contradict the proposition according to which conflicts in the political system of Switzerland are usually regulated by the principle of amicable agreement? First, it may be said that the formulation of the proposition does not reject the possibility that majority decisions are made to a limited extent. Second, it should be noted that the question of a separate contingent at the disposal of the federation was an important point, but it was not the only one in the bill; the acceptance of the principle of federal subsidies as well as the size of the contribution and the distribution ratios remained undisputed in the National Council. Finally, it should also be considered that the bill was only a provisional solution for a period of three years. According to the intentions of the Federal Department of the Interior and the directly interested parties, the delicate question of the extent of the federal government's directive powers was to stay unresolved during this time. It was suggested that the contingent that was to be at the disposal of the federal government hardly allowed any influence worth mentioning, since three years were too short a time to use it properly. In response to this, the proponents of the amendment said that their greatest concern was that the later definitive solution not be prejudiced in a wrong direction. The amendment was thus primarily a symbolic act expressing a demand for a later definitive regulation. This feedback information was also taken into consideration by the Federal Department of the Interior and the directly interested parties when they set out to prepare a definitive regulation of the federal subsidies.

It becomes evident, then, how a conflict situation may be eased by putting off the solution of a controversial problem. In spite of their defeat in the vote, the proponents of the amendment had more or less reached their goal; they had succeeded in making it clear that a later definitive solution had to give more influence to the federal government. On the other hand, the Department of the Interior and the directly interested parties were also among the victors, since they had guided their proposal past the parliamentary obstructions. It will be seen in a later context that putting off decisions may not only ease conflict situations, but it may also contribute to the reduction of the learning capacity of the system. The Council of States reviewed the matter in June, 1966. It accepted the proposal of the Federal Council as the National Council had done, making the procedure to solve differences between the two chambers unnecessary.

The people would have been able to call for a referendum within ninety days after the decision of the Council of States by submitting thirty thousand signatures. But nobody attempted to resort to a referendum, so that that phase of the decision-making process was left out. However, the reactions of the people in a possible referendum were anticipated all through the decision-making process, not on the basis of scientific public opinion polls, but primarily on the basis of stored information. Particular reference was made to a referendum in 1882, by which the position of a school secretary would have been instituted in the Federal Department of the Interior. The referendum was rejected with a considerable majority because of the strong feeling that no "Federal overseer of the schools" should come into existence. Although that event took place almost one hundred years ago, the mere mention of a "Federal overseer of the schools" was enough to give the participants in the decision-making process an awareness of the public sentiment. Since it was anticipated that a proposal giving the federation greater authority in school affairs could easily be made to fail in a referendum, the scope of innovation was very limited from the beginning. Thus a federal take-over of the cantonal universities was not given serious consideration, because it was anticipated that such a solution would be rejected by the people. Since the experiment was not made, it is hard to judge if the popular reactions were correctly predicted. It is still conceivable that the reference to the conservative stand of the people served as a rationalization for those participants who chose to keep the scope of innovation on a small scale.

The head of the Department of the Interior and the directly interested parties tried to avoid a referendum by leaving out the controversial question of direct federal influence, and proposing a temporary arrangement for three years. They assumed that no group would go to the expense of a referendum if it had the opportunity in the near future to articulate its demands once again. This assumption was proved to be correct in 1968 when the attempt was made to transform the provisional solution into a definitive one. The groups who had already called for a stronger federal influence in the provisional solution could no longer be kept quiet by the statement that it only was a temporary arrangement. They therefore used the referendum threat liberally, as the following example of a newspaper advertisement shows: "If the present bill is not improved fundamentally, it runs the risk of having to go through a referendum campaign."[31] Such threats were avoided by the 1966 bill, since the most controversial matter of federal influence had been postponed for the first three years. In conclusion it may be said that in this case study the institution of the referendum influenced the decision-making process decisively, although it was never put to actual use. On the one hand, the fear of the referendum caused a restriction of the scope of innovation, and on the other, it caused a postponement of the confrontation about the central problem of federal influence.

The carrying out of the federal decision to give the university cantons a total of two hundred million francs in federal support for the years 1966–68 was relatively simple for the federal authorities, since the distribution followed a fixed predetermined ratio. The monies were at the free disposal of the university cantons; the only reservation was that a closer cooperation among the Swiss universities be achieved. However, the execution of this was not entrusted to the federal authorities, but to a coordinating agency constituted by the university cantons. Again, it was the directly interested parties to whom important functions were transferred in this last phase—the administering phase—

after they had already been active in a decisive manner in all the earlier phases of the decision-making process.

Preparations to substitute the final arrangement for the provisional one had already begun in 1966. The provisional arrangement was the beginning of a new decision-making process, which was closely connected to the previous one. The provisional arrangement had produced reactions in the universities, in the economic interest groups, etc., which were returned to the political system as feedback information. A circuit was formed connecting the input and output of the system. It is not the task of this study to describe how the new demands were articulated and aggregated, how the information gathering and the innovation process proceeded, and how in 1969, a definitive arrangement was implemented.

I will now attempt to summarize the results of this case study in some general descriptive propositions, which I will abstract from the concrete substance of the case.[32]

19* Parliament tends to start the formal decision-making process.

20* The formal decision-making process tends to start with a time lag rather than a time lead with respect to the stress situation in question.

21* When Parliament has started the formal decision-making process, the initiative tends to be transferred from Parliament to the government.

22* At the government level, only the department in charge tends to become active at that point, not the government as a whole.

23* The department in charge tends to negotiate further procedures with the directly interested persons.

24* Many of the directly interested persons who participate in the preparliamentary decision-making process also tend to be members of Parliament.

25* Negotiations about further procedures between the department in charge and the directly interested persons tend to take place away from the public view.

26* Even at the beginning of the decision-making process alternatives that are based on new and unusual combinations of information tend to be ignored.

27* The department in charge tends to entrust experts from outside the administration with the gathering of information.

28* The nonadministration experts also tend to be directly interested persons.

29* The directly interested persons tend to have an authoritative voice in the selection of the nonadministration experts whom the department in charge entrusts with the gathering of information.

30* The department in charge also tends to entrust nonadministration experts with the task of innovation.

31* The innovation experts from outside the administration also tend to be directly interested persons.

32* The directly interested persons tend to have an authoritative voice in the selection of nonadministration experts whom the department in charge entrusts with the innovation function.

33* Role accumulations tend to exist between information and innovation experts.

34* Information experts tend to receive an abundant and heterogeneous flow of information through many channels of communication.

35* The information experts tend to homogenize the heterogeneous information that they receive.

36* The information experts tend to regulate conflict by the principle of amicable agreement and not by the majority principle.

37* The decision-making process among the information experts tends to be strongly informal.

38* The information experts tend to include all potential information experts in their consensus.

39* The information experts tend to forward only the homogenized information.

40* An exception to Proposition 39* is made for the department head in charge and his officials who usually also have access to the nonhomogenized information.

41* Information emanating from the information experts tends not to be subject to a systematic examination.

42* The quantitative information emanating from the information experts tends to be communicated more precisely than the qualitative information.

43* The point of reference for judging the credibility of the information collected by the information experts tends to be the composition of the expert groups.

44* The innovation process tends to start long before the information gathering has been completed.

45* The innovation experts tend to work out their proposals by the trial-and-error method.

46* The innovation experts tend to proceed in a predominantly informal way in working out their proposals.

47* Different groups of innovation experts do not tend to work out alternatives independently of one another.

48* Proposition 47* also tends to obtain if the institutional environment of the innovation process changes because, due to frequent role accumulations, roughly the same persons participate in the decision-making.

49* The major part of the innovation process tends not to become manifest to the public.

50* Representatives of the Department of Finance tend to be called in toward the end of the innovation process.

51* The innovation process tends to develop in a way such that the scope of innovation decreases gradually.

52* The department in charge, the directly interested persons, and the Department of Finance finally tend to agree on a common solution.

53* If it is not possible to find a common solution for all points according to Proposition 52*, the controversial points tend to be left out and their solutions put off to a later time.

54* The reactions of the government members who do not participate directly are anticipated relatively precisely and are taken into consideration to a large extent throughout the process leading to a compromise in the sense of Proposition 52*.

55* The decision-making process usually has such a big time lag with respect to the existing stress that the government members who are not directly interested feel constrained not to delay the decision any longer.

56* The members of government who are not directly interested usually do not replace a solution reached according to Proposition 52* with a fundamentally different one.

57* The veto is perceived as the most effective means the government members who are not directly interested can use against a solution reached according to Proposition 52*.

58* The government members who are not directly interested make use of the veto in the sense of Proposition 57* relatively infrequently.

59* The reactions of the members of Parliament who are not directly interested are anticipated relatively precisely and are taken into consideration to a large extent throughout the process leading to a solution in the sense of Proposition 52*.

60* The directly interested members of Parliament who have participated in reaching a solution according to Proposition 52* usually support this solution in Parliament.

61* The decision-making process usually has such a big time lag with respect to the existing stress that the members of Parliament who are not directly interested feel constrained not to delay the decision any longer.

62* The members of Parliament who are not directly interested usually do not replace a solution reached according to Proposition 52* with a fundamentally different one.

63* The veto is perceived as the most effective means the members of Parliament who are not directly interested can use against a solution reached according to Proposition 52*.

64* The members of Parliament who are not directly interested make use of the veto in the sense of Proposition 63* relatively infrequently.

65* The political parties tend to enter the decision-making process more actively only when a solution according to Proposition 52* has already been reached.

66* The opinions of the political parties tend to be influenced significantly by persons who have participated in reaching a solution according to Proposition 52*.

67* The pressure groups that perceive themselves to be directly interested tend to participate in negotiating a compromise according to Proposition 52*.

68* The reactions of the individual citizens to a potential referendum are anticipated relatively precisely and are taken into consideration to a large extent throughout the process leading to a solution according to Proposition 52*.

69* The directly interested groups tend to use the referendum and popular initiative more often than any other groups.

70* The referendum and popular initiative are used primarily as a threat to influence the decision-making process according to one's own goals.

71* A referendum or a popular initiative is taken only when a compromise according to Proposition 52* has not been achieved successfully.

72* Directly interested groups also tend to participate in the execution of a decision.

2. FOUNDING A UNIVERSITY IN THE CANTON OF AARGAU

The propositions developed from the case study concerning federal subsidies to the university cantons will now be tested by a case study about the founding of a university in Aargau. This case study also concerns university policy; it is different from the first primarily because it takes place at the cantonal rather than the federal level, and because the decision was subjected to the obligatory rather than the optional referendum. I will test the propositions one after the other to see to what extent they are confirmed by the second case study.

*Proposition 19**:

Parliament tends to start the formal decision-making process.

It was Parliament, not the government or the administration, that started the formal decision-making process. On June 4, 1962, Jakob Hohl submitted the following motion in the Great Council, which is the cantonal Parliament: "The traditional university cantons cannot fulfill the demands made on them as a consequence of the great increase in the number of students. At the same time it may be said that the contribution of our canton to the furtherance of science does not correspond to what is economically possible. The government is requested to take steps towards founding a university in the canton of Aargau. Cooperation on this project with other interested cantons should take place to the extent that this is possible."[33]

Hohl belonged to the Independent party, which at that time had only eight of the two hundred seats in the cantonal Parliament. Not long after the submission of this motion Hohl left the Independent party, but in the following election he won two seats with his own party that he called The Party for Education and Progress. With respect to party alignment, then, Hohl was a definite outsider, yet his motion passed. This incident confirms my earlier observation that members of nongovernment parties are able to articulate demands to the system in a relevant way. When Hohl made his motion, government and administration had not yet concerned themselves with university affairs in any way. The question was also new for the other members of the Great Council because Jakob Hohl had neither discussed his motion with his own party nor with other parties. In contrast, the motion that Weibel had made in the federal Parliament had been signed by members from all major parliamentary groups before he submitted it. Therefore, it seems that the political system of Switzerland is open to parliamentary motions about which a widespread consensus has been obtained before they are submitted, and to motions that are undertaken without prior discussion. It would be interesting at some time to classify and study a greater number of parliamentary motions to see what variables set them apart with respect to this criterion.

*Proposition 20**:

> The formal decision-making process tends to start with a time lag rather than a time lead with respect to the stress situation in question.

It has already been stated that a marked stress had existed in the Swiss university system since the mid-1950s when the number of students began to increase strongly and a multitude of new needs arose in research and instruction. The *one* response of the political system of Switzerland was the decision to provide federal subsidies to facilitate the expansion of the existing universities. A second response to the stress situation could have been to found new universities. Whether that response would have been found expedient from the financial and other points of view could only have been judged had extensive studies of the whole set of problems been made. The political system of Switzerland would have registered a time lead if such studies had been concluded at the time of the onset of the stress. Practically speaking, this would have been possible, since in the late forties data were already available on which a prognosis of the development of the Swiss university system ten to fifteen years ahead of time could have been based. It would also have been possible to work out beforehand the criteria that would have justified the founding of a new university. Since nobody had made these preparations, there was no time lead in the decision-making process; on the contrary, a considerable time lag had accrued. The question of the founding of new universities was first expressed by the government member responsible for education in the canton of Basel-City. In a speech at the celebration honoring the five-hundred-year history of the University of Basel in 1960, he had stated: "We want no mammoth universities, but places in which human education and the care for the creative and spiritual powers of young persons may come to their right. And therefore the call is issued today, when we are together in friendly intercantonal concord: let us found a new university in our country."[34] But he did not specify who was to found the new university, nor did he take further steps to see that his proposal was realized. According to Article 27 in the Federal Constitution, the federation had the authority "to found a university and other institutions of higher learning in addition to the existing technical university." But at the federal level no one took up the proposal. The federal government did not take advantage of the time lead by urging any of the nonuniversity cantons to found a university. The canton of

Aargau was the one nonuniversity canton, which, with respect to population and economic power, was best fitted to start a university.[35] But no one in the Aargau government or among its major parties echoed the call for the founding of a new university. Not until two years later did the motion of the outsider Jakob Hohl come up, and he was not even aware of the call from Basel-City. Only then were efforts also beginning to be made in the canton of Lucerne to found a new university.

If one glances at the way the question of the founding of new universities was approached, it is hard to avoid the impression that there was something random about it. Although it was a question of national importance, there was no agency in all of Switzerland that took action in a systematic way. Neither the federal authorities, the conference that regularly brings together all cantonal government members concerned with education, or any other agency set about investigating the problem of the founding of new universities. It was more by chance than anything else that two cantons were finally ready to approach the problem. In view of the fact that the start of the decision-making process was left so much to chance it was no wonder that a considerable time lag had resulted.

*Proposition 21**:

> When Parliament has started the formal decision-making process, the initiative tends to be transferred from Parliament to the government.

*Proposition 22**:

> At the government level, only the department in charge tends to become active at that point, not the government as a whole.

The Parliament of the canton of Aargau debated the Hohl motion on February 5, 1963. At that time the opinions on the question were still very diffuse, because, in contrast to the Weibel motion in the previous case study, the Hohl motion had not articulated an already existing consensus, but had attacked the problem for the first time. In the Aargau case, Parliament authorized the government to pursue the matter and did not attempt to keep the initiative by undertaking the necessary investigations itself. Furthermore, in conformity with Proposition 22*, it was the Department of Education rather than the government as a whole that was activated at that point. The government member responsible for education declared in the Great Council that he was ready to accept the Hohl motion on the assumption that he was instructed only to make a report, not to undertake measures that implied that the founding of a university in Aargau was a fait accompli. The Great Council agreed to the lesser commitment and the motion was accepted, 99 to 1.

*Proposition 23**:

> The department in charge tends to negotiate further procedures with the directly interested persons.

To determine the procedure to be used in studying the Hohl motion, the Department of Education sought the help of a professor at the University of Basel. The professor, who lived in the canton of Aargau, outlined a plan that included the following inventory of questions: (a) Was there a need for a new university? (b) What kind of structure should a new university have? (c) What procedures were necessary to found the university? (d) What financial questions should be considered? (e) What legal problems should be expected? (f) Would the university emphasize areas of specialization?

The working plan for the study of these questions as proposed by the professor follows:

1. A full-time expert for university affairs should be appointed temporarily.
2. The full-time expert should be responsible to a small working group of experienced people who would fix the guidelines for the investigations and evaluate the results.
3. A representative study commission should be nominated. It should include the directly interested groups and the major political forces in the Aargau canton, federal authorities, and professors from all Swiss universities. It should assist the full-time expert and the working group, help to make particularly knowledgeable individuals available for specific questions, and set up the connection to the existing universities and the political forces.
4. The full-time expert and the working group should have facilities made available to them from the different administrative departments (e.g., the Department of Construction, the Department of Statistics, the Auditing Department, and the cantonal hospital). When dealing with questions that concerned the faculties and departments to be set up, coordination with other universities in certain research areas, and so on, it would be necessary to call in outside experts.

In preparing this working plan, the professor contacted the Federal Department of the Interior, some university officials, and representatives from the different kinds of schools in Aargau. Of particular importance was a meeting about the Aargau university question that was held on June 14 and 15, 1963, at the appeal of the cultural foundation Pro Argovia in the Philipp-Albert-Stapfer-Haus at Schloss Lenzburg. The list of invited persons was drawn up with the help of the professor. A total of ninety-six people were invited; fifty-six of them, mainly representatives of the political authorities, the educational institutions, and various cultural institutions, were from the Aargau canton. The other invited persons were representatives of the Swiss universities, the federal authorities, and the canton of Lucerne, which was also interested in founding a university. In general, then, the meeting included all persons in and out of Aargau who were directly interested in the question of the founding of a new university. This opportunity for direct contacts was not provided for in a given institutional framework, but was created ad hoc. The crucial point was that the directly interested persons could meet without lengthy formal procedures. The meeting was opened by the president of the Swiss National Science Foundation, who gave a survey of the Swiss university system. Primarily, the discussions served the purpose of providing and exchanging information; no decisions were made. Even more relevant than the formal discussions were the many informal small-group discussions.

As far as Proposition 23* is concerned, the directly interested parties were the existing Swiss universities, the federal authorities, the canton of Lucerne, and the representatives of the educational system in Aargau. Through the discussions at Schloss Lenzburg and through additional personal contacts, the professor commissioned by the Department of Education of the Aargau canton learned how most of the directly interested persons wished to proceed. To a large extent, these opinions were incorporated in the working plan which the professor submitted to the Department of Education and which the department accepted in large part.

In the case study at the federal level, the information-gathering phase started without further contact with Parliament once the head of the Department of the Interior and the directly interested persons had agreed about procedures. Because the costs of the scheduled investigations in the Aargau case study were so great—200,000 francs in all—the decision had to be made by Parliament, according to the cantonal laws. A larger amount would have required a popular decision. The institutional obligation to present the matter in Parliament again before the real investigations began delayed the decision-making process one year. Although the Department of Education and the directly interested persons had been in agreement about further procedures in the summer of 1963, Parliament did not make its decision until the summer of 1964. However, the delay made it possible to subject the compromise reached by the Department of Education and the directly interested persons to a feedback process. There were differences of opinion at the governmental level. Two of the five government members were of the opinion that in comparison with other public projects, the creation of a university at Aargau was not urgent; in their view it was indiscreet to undertake expensive studies at this time. They proposed waiting temporarily to see what decisions would be made at the federal level and in the university cantons in the next few years. According to them, the Hohl motion did not have to be written off because it would be possible to return to it later on.

Since the two other government members agreed with the head of the Department of Education, there was a bare 3 to 2 majority for the procedure. The head of the Department of Education came from the Swiss People's party; one of the two government members who supported him was a Free Democrat and the other was a Social Democrat; of the two dissenting members, one was a Free Democrat and the other was a Christian Democrat. Thus the alignment did not follow party lines. It is particularly noteworthy that the two Free Democrats had different opinions, a fact that illustrates the earlier observation that there is low party discipline in Switzerland. In the seventeen-member commission of Parliament preparing the matter, similar differences of opinion could be found. This commission provides a beautiful example of the efforts that were made to reach a compromise from many different points of view. I think it is worthwhile to follow some of the discussion:[36]

The head of the Department of Education submits the following proposal of the government majority: "An amount of 250,000 francs is to be appropriated for the continuation of the investigations concerning the founding of a university in Aargau."

Member A would like the problem to be investigated for all of Switzerland and proposes that the canton of Aargau give the necessary money for the investigation to an agency on the federal level.

Member B, a declared opponent of an Aargau university, seconds the proposal of member A.

The professor commissioned by the Department of Education, who also participates in the session, declares that the proposal of Member A would be virtually impossible to effect.

Member C, who presides over the session, supports Member A

in the sense that he agrees it should be made more explicit that the matter is of concern not only to Aargau, but to all of Switzerland.

At this point Member C moves that the commission adjourn. The motion is accepted unanimously.

At the beginning of the second session Member A proposes the following: "An appropriation of 250,000 francs is to be made to investigate the way in which the canton of Aargau should participate in the task of furthering the Swiss university system."

Member D would welcome a unanimous appearance of the commission in the plenary session of Parliament. He proposes the following compromise: "An appropriation of 250,000 francs is to be made to continue the investigations concerning the question of the founding of a university in Aargau from the perspective of Switzerland as a whole."

Member E proposes the following: "A comprehensive examination should be made to determine if and how the canton of Aargau can participate in the task of furthering the university system, and, in particular, whether a university is to be founded in Aargau.

Member B would like to insert "Swiss" before "university system" in the proposal of Member E.

Member A withdraws his proposal in favor of that of Member E.

The commission takes a vote. The proposal of Member E as amended by Member B receives eight votes, the government proposal receives five votes.

Member F, who voted for the government proposal, declares that he would settle for the proposal of Member E, if the plenary session of Parliament was to decide in favor of it.

As president of the commission, Member C announces that he will present both versions to the plenary session and he will stress that the difference is one of formulation only.

This passage from the deliberations of the commission clearly shows how the attempt was made to find a compromise between two opposed points of view. The aim of the discussion was not to accentuate the existing difference, but to mitigate it. In spite of all efforts, unanimity was not achieved, but the remaining difference was dismissed as a mere question of formulation. In the plenary session of Parliament the formulation of the majority in the commission won out with a vote of 82 to 25.

To what extent has Proposition 23* been confirmed by the Aargau case study? At first the course of events corresponded closely to the proposition, since it was primarily the Department of Education and the directly interested persons who made up a plan for further procedures. However, because of the financial scope of the investigations, it became mandatory for the government and Parliament to participate in those procedures. Because of this extra step, the plan for the investigations was delayed, but it was not basically changed. Thus the influence of the Department of Education and the directly interested persons was considerable enough in the Aargau case so that Proposition 23* was confirmed to a large extent.

*Proposition 24**:

> Many of the directly interested persons who participate in the preparliamentary decision-making process also tend to be members of Parliament.

This proposition is not valid for the Aargau case study. The professor commissioned by the Department of Education, a resident of the canton, was not a member of Parliament. The representatives of the existing universities, the federal officials, and the officials of the canton of Lucerne could not be members of the Aargau Parliament because they were not residents of Aargau. The teachers at the higher schools of the canton were ineligible as members of Parliament because they were cantonal employees. Although role accumulations did not exist between Parliament and the directly interested persons, it was possible to establish mutual channels of communication. The first important step in this direction was taken with the Lenzburg discussions, to which ten members of Parliament and the directly interested persons were invited. The professor who was commissioned by the Department of Education also took part in the sessions of the parliamentary commission and his presence further contributed to the communication between Parliament and the directly interested persons. The professor was an active member of a cantonal political party, and in that role he was also brought in touch with members of Parliament. Throughout this case study we will see many other channels of communication between members of Parliament and the directly interested persons. For the moment it is important to note that the absence of role accumulations had functional equivalents in many different ways. Therefore, Proposition 24* can probably be considered valid here if reference is made not specifically to role accumulations, but rather to active channels of communication between the members of Parliament and the directly interested persons.

*Proposition 25**:

> Negotiations about further procedures between the department in charge and the directly interested persons tend to take place away from the public view.

The university professor commissioned by the Department of Education had his discussions with the existing universities, the federal authorities, and the canton of Lucerne outside the public eye. The public did not know when the discussions were held or who the participants were. Only specific persons were invited to the discussions, which took place at Schloss Lenzburg behind closed doors, although in this case the fact of the meeting itself was made known to the public.

*Proposition 26**:

> Even at the beginning of the decision-making process alternatives that are based on new and unusual combinations of information tend to be ignored.

The Hohl motion had a relatively narrow formulation; it was aimed directly at "the founding of a university in Aargau," and it did not mention other ways in which Aargau could contribute to higher education.

At the beginning of the discussions there was a strong tendency to consider information from the past primarily, particularly information that had to do with the founding of the first Aargau gymnasium in the nineteenth century.[37] It was believed that that event could provide some guidelines for the founding of a university. Therefore, the scope of innovation had been considerably restricted at the start of the decision-making process because only the founding of a university was to be studied, and that primarily on the basis of stored information. It then turned out that no consensus was reached among the directly interested persons, the government members, and the members of Parliament concerning the principle of the founding of a university. The conflict resulting from this situation increased the scope of innovation: instead of limiting the investigations to the different alternatives involved in founding a university in Aargau, Parliament decided that the comprehensive questions of whether and in what manner the canton of Aargau could participate in the task of furthering the entire Swiss university system should be examined.

In the case study at the federal level, the scope of innovation was restricted from the beginning, because nobody disagreed with the basic principle that the solution should consist of federal subsidies. Proposition 26* thus seems to be valid primarily if there is a definite consensus. On the other hand, the Aargau case study indicates that a conflict situation may contribute to an increase in the scope of innovation. In the case of very sharp conflict there is the possibility that each party will stick to its own opinion, which again may reduce the scope of innovation. It might be worthwhile at some time to investigate the variables on which the scope of innovation depends, and in that context it would be particularly interesting to study the functions of social conflicts.

The institutional framework of the decision-making process in the Aargau case may have produced some decrease in the scope of innovation. Of primary relevance was the federal structure of Switzerland. Because the decision-making process was started in a specific subsystem rather than at the level of the system as a whole, some solutions became less likely, if not impossible. It was extremely difficult, for example, to concretize solutions in which more than one canton would found a new university. If the decision was to have been made for all of Switzerland, it would presumably have been easier to increase the scope of innovation.

*Proposition 27**:

The department in charge tends to entrust experts from outside the administration with the gathering of information.

*Proposition 28**:

The nonadministration experts also tend to be directly interested persons.

*Proposition 29**:

The directly interested persons tend to have an authoritative voice in the selection of the nonadministration experts whom the department in charge entrusts with the gathering of information.

*Proposition 30**:

The department in charge also tends to entrust nonadministration experts with the task of innovation.

*Proposition 31**:

The innovation experts from outside the administration also tend to be directly interested persons.

*Proposition 32**:

The directly interested persons tend to have an authoritative voice in the selection of nonadministration experts whom the department in charge entrusts with the innovation function.

*Proposition 33**:

Role accumulations tend to exist between information and innovation experts.

Because there was almost complete role accumulation between information and innovation experts in the Aargau case, the functions of information gathering and innovation tasks were handled by the same persons. The full-time expert for university affairs provided for in the working plan was the first to be appointed. The appointment was prepared by the professor who had drafted the working plan. After making inquiries in the Federal Department of the Interior, he asked the secretary of the Labhardt Committee if he would be interested in the position. The secretary accepted the offer and a meeting with the head of the Department of Education of the Aargau canton was set up. The head of the department immediately sanctioned the appointment and the working contract that had already been prepared by the university professor before the meeting. The government as a whole, which had the formal authority in this matter, sanctioned the choice on September 10, 1964.

The working plan provided for the selection of a working group. The university professor had a decisive say in the selection of the group. He discussed the matter with two teachers from the gymnasium, and together they reached the conclusion that, in addition to themselves, the committee should comprise the following members: another teacher from the gymnasium, a chief medical doctor at the cantonal hospital, a physicist at the Federal Institute for Reactor Research, which is located in Aargau, a chief editor from a newspaper, and the first secretary from the Department of Education. The medical doctor and the physicist were part-time university lecturers. The head of the Department of Education agreed to the proposed selection and submitted it to the government as a whole, which then formally appointed the working group on October 8, 1964.

The working plan also provided that a large study commission was to be constituted. The preparations for the commission were made by the working group that had been appointed in the meantime. The group made up a list of all the organizations and institutions that should be represented in the study commission. From the canton the list included the political parties, the economic interest groups, scientific and cultural societies, the churches, the press, women's organizations, schools, hospitals, and some special institutions such as the cantonal library and the superior court. In a second stage the number of representatives for each organization and institution was determined. Then the personal composition of the commission was discussed. Many persons were unclear as to which organizations and institutions they should represent because of their frequent role accumulations. For instance, which group should a person with leading roles in a party as well as in an economic interest group represent? The role accumulations enabled the selection system to be more flexible than might otherwise have been expected.

The individual organizations and institutions were then asked in writing which representatives they would like to send to the study commission. The official letter did not say which persons the working group had already considered. But the individual members of the group used informal means within their sphere of influence to see to it that those persons who were most agreeable to the group were designated as representatives, and, except in a few instances, their nominees were appointed. In order not to overestimate the influence of the working group, it should be remembered that the group was able to use vast amounts of stored and current information to anticipate the acceptability of the nominations. It was able to accurately anticipate, for example, that schools would like to be represented by their principals. On the basis of this information the working group made no attempts to propose other nominations. In other cases, the question of representation was not as clearly determined a priori, so that the influence of the working group became more obvious.

The federal authorities, the five universities of the German-speaking part of Switzerland, and the bilingual University of Freiburg were the groups that needed representation from outside the canton. To represent the federal authorities, the working group nominated the chief of the section for university affairs in the Federal Department of the Interior and the federal delegate concerned with questions of atomic energy. The heads of the corresponding federal departments were asked to approve these two nominations. The nominations were made explicit in official letters. Both the department heads approved the nominations.

In determining who the university representatives were to be, the working group first decided that each university should be represented by two professors, but care was to be taken to represent all major academic disciplines. It was further decided that the professors to be nominated should be connected somehow with the canton of Aargau, if possible, and at the same time should hold leading positions in agencies (such as the Swiss Council of Science) that were concerned with university policy for all of Switzerland. On the basis of these criteria the working group made up a list of professors who then were asked in writing if they would cooperate. In this case, the working group did not ask the universities as institutions for their approval.

The working group nominated a study commission with a total of fifty-five members; of these, forty were to come from within the canton of Aargau and fifteen from outside it. The head of the Department of Education agreed to the proposed nominations and presented them to the government as a whole, which made the formal appointments without changes on April 22, 1965. Although the government was informed what organizations and institutions the individual members in the study commission were supposed to represent, the published report of the government appointments made a distinction only between members from within and outside the canton of Aargau. An information barrier was thus introduced at this point which prevented the public from clearly understanding which groups were represented in the study commission. Because of the frequent role accumulations it was not possible for an outsider to identify the represented groups from the list of members. The main function of this information barrier was to prevent a public conflict about the composition of the study commission. This is another example of how conflicts are prevented in Switzerland by the holding back of information.

The procedure described so far confirms Propositions 27* and 32*. According to Propositions 27* and 30* the experts came from outside the cantonal administration for the most part: only one of the eight members of the working group, the first secretary of the Department of Education, belonged to the cantonal administration. The three teachers and the chief medical doctor of the cantonal hospital did receive their salaries from the canton, but they were not seen as representatives of the general administration. Nor did they see themselves as part of the administration, a point they made clear at different times, particularly in a joking manner on informal occasions. Only one of the fifty-nine members of the study commission belonged to the general administration of the canton. Furthermore, it is worth noting that the full-time expert for university affairs did not have the status of a cantonal official; he worked on a contractual basis in an office at his own home.

The information and innovation experts can for the most part be called directly interested persons, according to Propositions 28* and 31*. The university representatives, for example, were directly interested in the question of whether a new university should be founded, since their own development depended, to a large extent, on the solution of this question. The federal representatives were also directly interested persons because of the financial support expected of the federation.

It is somewhat harder to determine the degree of interestedness of the information and innovation experts from the canton of Aargau itself. Among the eight members of the small working group the full-time university professor was, as representative of an existing university, most directly interested in the question. The three teachers at the gymnasium were directly interested because the founding of a university would displace the gymnasium as the highest level of education in Aargau. The chief medical doctor at the cantonal hospital and the physicist at the Federal Institute for Reactor Research were directly interested as part-time university lecturers, but also as representatives of their institutions, because the founding of a university might change the status of the cantonal hospital and the institute. Six of the eight members were thus more or less directly interested persons in the sense of Propositions 28* and 31*. This does not necessarily mean that these members limited themselves to represent their direct interests; it only means that they had roles whose pattern might be changed by the founding of a university.

The first secretary of the Department of Education and the chief editor of a newspaper can be seen as not directly interested members of the working group. The editor was also a member of the cantonal Parliament, which enabled him to become a channel of communication between the directly interested persons and Parliament. In the case study at the federal level this communication was brought about by role accumulations between members of Parliament and directly interested persons; in the Aargau case the nomination of a member of Parliament as a member of the working group was a functional equivalent for the missing role accumulations. The important thing is that in both cases a link between Parliament and the directly interested persons had been established.

Although many directly interested persons from outside Aargau were represented in the study commission, many directly interested persons from the canton of Aargau were represented as well. Directly interested organizations and institutions such as schools, hospitals, and cultural and scientific societies had been overrepresented in the composition of the commission. Furthermore, groups such as political parties that were not directly interested were often represented by persons who were directly interested. These two factors contributed to the fact that sixteen of the forty Aargau members of the study commission were active in teaching or research and thus directly interested. Even more than the working group, the study commission was comprised of persons whose main function was to constitute channels of communication to Parliament. Eight of the forty commission members from the canton of Aargau were members of the cantonal Parliament. Two members belonged to the federal Parliament, a fact that was also relevant to the decision-making process, since the founding of a new university had to be considered at the federal level later in connection with federal subsidies.

The analysis of the composition of the working group and of the study commission has shown that the directly interested persons formed a large majority. However, very different levels of interestedness could be found, and both groups also included persons who were not directly interested. The working group and the study commission were thus not set up in a way such that they were pure aggregates of directly interested persons who would later have to confront the interests of Parliament, the administration, and the political parties. Rather, direct communication between the directly interested persons and most other important political groups could already be found in the working group and the study commission.

According to Propositions 29* and 32*, the directly interested persons were mainly mutually coopted. The government, which had the formal authority of appointment, contented itself with sanctioning the nominations made to it. This does not necessarily mean that the government had no influence at all; it must be remembered that the persons who made the nominations had to anticipate, often on the basis of stored information, how expert groups had to be composed in order to gain the stamp of approval of the government. For example, frequent reference was made to cases in which not all regions and religions in the canton were represented in the appropriate proportions, a situation that led to a rejection of nominations by the government. If such information about cases from the past had not been considered with due respect, the proposed nominations would hardly have been able to pass through the government without opposition. Within the limits of the existing system of norms, the interested persons were relatively free to decide how they would coopt each other. A most complex mixture of overlapping delegation and appointment mechanisms developed. At the formal level, it was generally the delegation principle that was predominant, and at the informal level, it was the appointment principle, but there was a tendency to appoint those who had the highest chances of being delegated, and to delegate those who had the highest chances of being appointed. In general, this selection procedure was characterized by mutual bargaining which tended to blur the responsibility for the final choice. In conclusion, it may be stressed once more that Propositions 27* through 33* were confirmed to a high degree with respect to the appointment of the full-time expert, the working group, and the study commission.

*Proposition 34**:

> Information experts tend to receive an abundant and heterogeneous flow of information through many channels of communication.

Determining what contribution the canton of Aargau could make to the Swiss university system presupposed information concerning the gaps in academic disciplines that were to be closed by the founding of a new university. The recognition of such gaps implied information about the future needs of the Swiss university system and about plans to expand the existing universities. Because a cantonal subsystem acted for the whole system, the Aargau information experts were confronted with the task of collecting information that was not primarily related to the subsystem of the canton of Aargau, but to the political system of Switzerland as a whole.

When the Aargau information experts assumed their duties in the fall of 1964, the Labhardt Report had just been published. The Labhardt Committee had been the first agency to attempt a survey about the future needs of the Swiss university system. All the information that had been prepared by the Labhardt Committee, which was much more comprehensive than the later committee report, was now made available to the Aargau by virtue of the fact that the secretary of the Labhardt Committee was appointed as the Aargau full-time expert for university affairs. Thus, by exchanging a carrier of information, a channel of communication between the federal and the cantonal levels had been established relatively easily. The efficiency of this channel was further increased by the fact that the Aargau expert for university affairs kept up a part-time appointment as secretary to the Labhardt Committee. After concluding its report, the Labhardt Committee still had certain additional studies to do for the federal authorities. In particular, its prognosis of the trend in the development of the number of students had to be continued and tested on the basis of new information. The role accumulation between the secretary of the Labhardt Committee and the Aargau expert also made this new information available to the canton of Aargau. In addition, the canton was equipped with many channels of communication by which it received information from the federal authorities. For example, of the thirteen members of the Aargau study commission, four belonged to the Swiss Council of Science. The latter were not official representatives from the Council of Science, but they participated in the study commission in a personal capacity. Consequently, a broad range of information from the Council of Science reached the Aargau study commission because the four members of the Council of Science often expressed rather different opinions. Information flowed relatively freely and abundantly between the Council of Science and the Aargau study commission because of their informality of communication.

Informal connections similar to the ones between the council and the study commission also existed within two other advisory organs of the federal government—the Swiss National Science Foundation, a foundation run almost exclusively by federal funds, and the Federal Expert Commission for Questions of Expansion and Coordination of Medical Education, a commission that was appointed by the Federal Department of the Interior. The foundation was represented by its president and two other members, the medical expert commission by its president. Not official delegates, either, these persons participated in a personal capacity in the Aargau study commission, and since they were not restricted in their freedom of expression by their institutions, their interaction with the other members of the study commission provided a rich flow of information. Later on, communication with the federation was further broadened with the election, in the spring of 1965, of a new head of the Aargau Department of Education, who was also a member of the federal Parliament. As a whole, the relations between the canton of Aargau and the federation were characterized by an extensive communication system through which very varied bits of information about the opinions and intentions of the federal authorities flowed to the canton of Aargau.

The existing universities also provided heterogeneous information to the canton of Aargau. In order to get information about the expansion plans, the Aargau expert for university affairs established an initial channel of communication by visiting the heads of the departments of education of the university cantons and the university presidents. Because the latter had usually not taken the trouble to agree on a common position before the Aargau expert's visit, they presented considerable differences of opinion to him. In order to receive somewhat more homogeneous information from the university cantons, the Aargau decided to make the communication more formal by putting the questions in writing at the government level. This approach did not yield the desired results for the following reasons. First, the government parties in Switzerland have a relatively great independence from the government; thus an opinion of the government in no way commits the parties represented in the government. Second, all important decisions about the expansion of a cantonal university are subject to referendum, and the people are even less committed than the parties to a government decision; thus the responses of the governments of the university cantons are relatively nonreliable and other types of information have to be taken into account. For example, the Aargau experts had to consider how the political parties, the economic interest groups, the mass media, the individual professors, etc., in the university cantons viewed the question of the expanding of the existing universities. In the sessions of the small working group such bits of information were exchanged in great number and compared with the opinions of the cantonal government. The result was usually a very varied mosaic of opinions.

In conclusion, it may be said that Proposition 34* has been confirmed clearly. The federation and the university cantons did not collect and sum up their information so that it reached the canton of Aargau in a homogeneous form. Instead, the information flow from the subsystems of the federation and the university cantons was characterized by a very strong heterogeneity.

Proposition 35*:

The information experts tend to homogenize the heterogeneous information that they receive.

Proposition 36*:

The information experts tend to regulate conflict by the principle of amicable agreement and not by majority principle.

Proposition 37*:

The decision-making process among the information experts tends to be strongly informal.

Proposition 38*:

The information experts tend to include all potential information experts in their consensus.

In validation of Proposition 35*, the information experts homogenized the heterogeneous information they received and were able to predict that the shortage of capacity following the expansion of the universities would be the precise figure of 4,600 places in 1975. Propositions 36*, 37*, and 38* were also validated. The main participants were the eight members of the working group and the full-time expert for university affairs who met almost once a week for a session usually lasting a whole day. The received information was checked for its reliability and the extreme figures were eliminated. If at first there were different interpretations of the received information, they were always evened out without the group ever having to take a formal vote. A special function in such evening-out processes was performed by the common lunch. Seats at the meal were frequently distributed so that members with divergent interpretations sat next to each other and thus had the opportunity to reach an agreement in an informal manner. The informal interactions, then, were thus not used to form groups along the existing differences of opinion: instead, they helped to bridge differences and to reach unanimity. As far as I could tell, no member of the group ever suggested that a majority opinion be reached. A unanimous opinion was always aimed at, and interactions among members with similar views were less frequent than interactions among members with differences of opinion. A group member who endangered the unanimity of the group was courted rather than isolated.

Propositions 36* to 38* were confirmed in the sense that the information experts regulated their conflicts primarily in an informal manner and according to the principle of amicable agreement. There was also the tendency to include all potential information experts in the consensus. The information experts from the canton of Lucerne, which was also concerned with the question of the founding of a new university, met informally and frequently with the full-time expert from Aargau to homogenize the information that originated in the federation and the university cantons. The success of these efforts was shown by the fact that both cantons agreed on the same figure with respect to the shortage of the capacity at the existing universities.

The tendency to homogenize the information and to include all the potential experts in the consensus showed up in many fields. An interesting example was the procedure for calculating the costs of different university models. The same architect who had assisted the Labhardt Committee was called in. When the architect, the full-time expert for university affairs, and the eight members of the working group had agreed on the same figures, an inventory was taken of possible dissenting voices. Potential critics within the cantons were the cantonal building engineer and the chief official for hospital affairs; these two persons were contacted and they were successfully included in the consensus.

*Proposition 39**:

The information experts tend to forward only homogenized information.

*Proposition 40**:

An exception to Proposition 39* is made for the department head in charge and his officials who usually also have access to the nonhomogenized information.

*Proposition 41**:

Information emanating from the information experts tends not to be subject to a systematic examination.

The information homogenized by the working group was summarized in a report published in June, 1967.[38] The drafts of this report, already homogenized to a considerable degree, were presented to the study commission, which was considerably less active than the working group, having met only four times in full session. The nonhomogenized information was, for the most part, not submitted to the study commission. Only the working group had access to the records of the talks between the full-time expert and the heads of the departments of education of the university presidents. Proposition 39*, then, was already valid to some extent as far as the working group and the study commission were concerned, since a filter existed between the two bodies that in general let only homogenized information through. However, the study commission was not completely closed to heterogeneous information. There were many informal channels of communication by way of which heterogeneous information from the working group reached the study commission. Moreover, there were also some cases in which the working group distributed heterogeneous information at the formal sessions of the study commission. In accordance with Proposition 40*, the government member in charge and his officials had access to the nonhomogenized information, particularly after 1965 when the newly elected head of the Department of Education himself took office as president of the working group. He took part in almost all the sessions of the group and thus gained familiarity with all of the information. Both of the top officials in the Department of Education gained the same familiarity because they also participated regularly in the sessions of the working group.

In the spring of 1967, when the report of the working group was ready for the press, the four government members not directly involved were invited to look at the unprinted version. But they did not receive any information beyond the scope of the report. The government did have hearings with the working group in two half-day sessions, but these hearings were nothing more than oral presentations of the homogenized information from the report. The government would only have been able to get hold of heterogeneous information if it had had at its disposal information experts who were independent of the working group. But such experts were not easily found since the working group had included most potential information experts in its consensus. Thus, in spite of its hearings, the government could not in the strict sense of the word check the information it had received.

Parliament received the report only in printed form. It deliberated it first in a nineteen-member commission. For information the commission relied primarily on the head of the Department of Education and on the full-time expert for university affairs. Since both of them had participated significantly in the preparation of the report, questioning them hardly constituted a real test of the information contained in the report. The parliamentary commission also visited the universities of Basel and Konstanz in order to obtain more information. There they met primarily with persons who had already been included in the consensus of the working group, so that the visits were not valid tests of the information contained in the report.

The parliamentary groups of the political parties were informed by oral presentations from the full-time expert for university affairs. Some of the groups also invited members of the working group to give a presentation. Neither the parliamentary commission nor the parliamentary groups were able to systematically check the information contained in the report. Because all major parties were represented in the government, there was no large opposition party that could have used its own experts to check the government information. In conclusion, Propositions 39* to 41* have been clearly confirmed. The working group had an extensive information monopoly.

Proposition 42*:

> The quantitative information emanating from the information experts tends to be communicated more precisely than the qualitative information.

The information experts established that the deficiencies in the university system were greatest in the medical sciences and in education. In the medical sciences the deficiencies depended more on quantitative factors; in education the deficiencies were more qualitative. Although education was treated more extensively in the report than the medical sciences, it turned out that information about the medical sciences was communicated more precisely and more comprehensively to the government, to Parliament, to the press, and so on. In other cases, too, quantitative information was communicated better than qualitative information.

*Proposition 43**:

The point of reference for judging the credibility of the information collected by the information experts tends to be the composition of the expert groups.

Proposition 43* was confirmed in the Aargau case study. To stress the quality of the information contained in the report, those prestigious persons who had taken part in the work of the Aargau study commission—the presidents of the Council of Science, the National Science Foundation, and the Federal Expert Commission for the Expansion and Coordination of Medical Education—were frequently referred to. Such references were evidently aimed at increasing the credibility of the information.

*Proposition 44**:

The innovation process tends to start long before the information gathering has been completed.

The development of the decision-making process was not such that the collection of information and the innovation process had to take place in two separate sequences. In confirmation of Proposition 44*, the information collection and innovation processes were undertaken, to a large extent, at the same time. In 1964, when the working group began the collection of information, it also started the innovation process. There was a reciprocal exchange between the information collection and the innovation process, since the innovation process was based on the information that had been collected up to that point and the collection of the information was guided by the evolution of the innovation process.

*Proposition 45**:

The innovation experts tend to work out their proposals by the trial-and-error method.

The preparation of the proposal about the Aargau contribution to the Swiss university system was not arrived at deductively by inferring a concrete solution from general principles. The procedure was rather one of trial and error.

At the second session of the working group the full-time expert for university affairs had proposed that the model of a postgraduate institute be studied first. He had received the stimulus for this proposal in his role as secretary of the Labhardt Committee, which had stressed repeatedly the necessity of increasing postgraduate education. It was thus through role accumulation that a federal agency started the innovation process in the canton of Aargau.

The model of a postgraduate institute was concretized in several sessions of the working group. At the proposal of the editor in chief it was agreed to develop the model for the field of city and regional planning. During the spring and summer of 1965 the model developed by the working group was the "trial" submitted for examination to authorities such as the head of the Federal Department of the Interior, the heads of the departments of education of the university cantons, the university presidents, the members of the study commission, and various organizations and individuals in the field of city and regional planning. The responses received showed the extent of "error" according to which the model did not correspond to the expectations that had been made concerning Aargau's best contribution to the Swiss university system. The working group attempted afterward to change the model according to the received reactions.

From a cybernetic point of view the whole process worked as a feedback mechanism. The working group communicated its proposal to those persons whom it perceived to have a politically relevant opinion; those persons in turn communicated their reactions back to the working group which then corrected its proposal in accordance with these reactions. According to my observations, the feedback process was goal-changing as well as goal-seeking. The members of the working group tried not only to orient their behavior to the received reactions, but they also tried to change the reactions themselves.

On the basis of the first feedback process the model was revised in that it now referred to planning problems in general rather than to city and regional planning in particular. This new version was subjected to a second feedback process in August, 1965, this time at the government level. The Federal Council, all cantonal governments, and the executives of the major cities were asked for their opinion. On the basis of the new reactions the model was revised again.

Even before the first model had been completed, the working group went about developing additional models, namely, for a school of education, an academy for the medical sciences, a school for advanced studies in economics and public administration, and a complete university. Models for the financial support of the existing universities and for the setting up of dormitories in the existing universities were also developed. These models were also subjected to feedback processes by directly interested persons; for example, education authorities, schools, and teachers' associations were questioned about the school of education.

*Proposition 46**:

The innovation experts tend to proceed in a predominantly informal way in working out their proposals.

The working group once again proceeded very informally with the innovation process and many relevant transactions took place outside the formal sessions, particularly during the common lunch breaks.

The feedback processes between the working group and the persons directly interested in the individual models had also taken place in a very informal manner, but often behind a screen of formal procedures. For example, the model of a school for advanced studies in economics and public administration was submitted for consideration to the federal authorities in the institutionally prescribed way; the latter answered the canton of Aargau via the same channel. The formal procedures were merely measures that sanctioned the informal interactions. The official in the Federal Personnel Bureau in charge of this matter bypassed the formal hierarchy and contacted the Aargau expert for university affairs directly. Then several informal discussions took place in the federal building during which the Aargau expert was introduced to a university professor called in as adviser by the Federal Personnel Bureau. The adviser invited the Aargau expert to his private home to discuss the matter further. The permeation of formal and informal interactions, with the stress on the latter, was characteristic of the innovation process as a whole. The interactions of the working group with the Swiss Society for City and Regional Planning, the Swiss Teachers' Association, the medical schools, and many other organizations and institutions developed in a similar way.

*Proposition 47**:

Different groups of innovation experts do not tend to work out alternatives independently of one another.

*Proposition 48**:

Proposition 47* also tends to obtain if the institutional environment of the innovation process changes because, due to frequent role accumulations, roughly the same persons participate in the decision-making.

The Aargau government had appointed three agents to perform the innovation process: the full-time expert for university affairs, the working group, and the study commission. But three alternative solutions did not develop from this tripartite division. The relations between the full-time expert and the working group were so close that the former actually acted as secretary for the latter; he wrote the invitations, kept the records, and usually prepared the written reports for the session. During the deliberations of the working group the full-time expert had a role pattern similar to that of the other members of the group. The dates and agendas of the sessions of the study commission were determined by the working group. The members of the working group regularly participated in the sessions of the study commission, and the president of the working group presided at the sessions of the study commission.

The full-time expert, the working group, and the study commission were closely interdependent, a fact that made it impossible for one of them to act independently of the two others. Consequently, the innovation processes of the three agents were closely connected and formed more or less a whole as outlined in Proposition 47*.

The institutional division in this case remained the same during all of the innovation process so that Proposition 48* is not applicable.

*Proposition 49**:

The major part of the innovation process tends not to become manifest to the public.

All sessions of the working group and the study commission took place behind closed doors. The feedback processes to which the individual models were subjected were not publicly visible, since the written opinions of the various organizations and institutions were not published.

Although the Labhardt Committee had not informed the press until the report of the committee was published, the Aargau working group had staged three press conferences prior to the publication of the report. However, only summary reports about the development of the innovation process were given. The informal aspects of the process were hardly even mentioned so that, in spite of the press conferences, the public had relatively little information.

Proposition 50*:

Representatives of the Department of Finance tend to be called in toward the end of the innovation process.

Proposition 51*:

The innovation process tends to develop in a way such that the scope of innovation decreases gradually.

Proposition 52*:

The department in charge, the directly interested persons, and the Department of Finance finally tend to agree on a common solution.

The functions of innovation and decision-making converged sharply. It was not a matter of several distinct alternative solutions being available at the end of the decision-making process among which a decision would have to be made. The convergence of the functions was due primarily to the phenomenon described in Proposition 47* that states that different groups do not participate independently of one another in the innovation process.

As the functions of innovation and decision-finding overlapped more and more, the scope of innovation became narrower and narrower. First, both extreme solutions—the building of a completely new university and a mere financial contribution to the existing universities—were excluded. However, they were not formally ruled out; they were explicitly mentioned in the report as possible alternatives, but it was agreed that they could not be considered seriously, and consequently, they were soon outside the real scope of innovation. Second, the scope of innovation was further narrowed by the fact that the school for advanced studies in economics and public administration and the school of planning were excluded. The two remaining models—an academy for the medical sciences and a school of education—were finally assimilated into a single model with two departments.

When the scope of innovation had been restricted to this one model, a representative of the Department of Finance was called in, a step that is in conformity with Proposition 50*. The working group then discussed the financial aspects of realizing this model with the representative.

Proposition 53*:

If it is not possible to find a common solution for all points according to Proposition 52*, the controversial points tend to be left out and their solutions put off to a later time.

There were many controversial points about the model containing a department of medical sciences and a department of education. For example, it had to be decided whether the program of the department of medical sciences should be started at the fifth or the seventh semester; also, a decision had to be made to what extent the cantonal hospital in Baden should be involved in addition to the cantonal hospital in Aargau. There were also different opinions concerning the philosophy of the whole model, the intensity of cooperation with existing universities, and many other things.

In confirmation of Proposition 53*, these controversial points were left out and their solutions put off to a later point in time. A period of five years was proposed during which these questions were to be followed up. Putting off solutions was also a frequently practiced pattern of easing conflicts in other respects.

*Proposition 54**:

> The reactions of the government members who do not participate directly are anticipated relatively precisely and are taken into consideration to a large extent throughout the process leading to a compromise in the sense of Proposition 52*.

Because of the resignation of two elected officials, two new members of government were elected in the spring of 1965. The working group discussed this event in relation to the university question, exchanging many stored and current bits of information about the position of the two newly elected members with respect to university policy. The group also attempted to anticipate how the previous head of the Department of Education, who had become the head of the Department of Finance, would behave in the future.

The working group anticipated the reactions of the members of government more or less continuously. This anticipation process was almost always informal and took place primarily at the meals they had together. As most of the members of the working group combined their roles with many other roles in the political life of the canton, a rich flow of information was activated. One member of the group, for instance, belonged to the Commission for City and Regional Planning and, in that capacity, he met regularly with the head of the Department of Construction.

Later negotiations with the government showed that the reaction of the individual government members had been anticipated relatively precisely. For example, the working group had predicted correctly that the previous head of the Department of Education would take a more negative position about the university question after switching to the Department of Finance. Proposition 54* was also confirmed in the sense that the working group aimed at orienting its behavior to the reactions of the government. On the other hand, it also attempted to influence the reactions of the government members through informal channels. Thus the feedback process could be considered goal-changing as well as goal-seeking.

Proposition 55*:

> The decision-making process usually has such a big time lag with respect to the existing stress that the government members who are not directly interested feel constrained not to delay the decision any longer.

Proposition 56*:

> The members of government who are not directly interested usually do not replace a solution reached according to Proposition 52* with a fundamentally different one.

Proposition 57*:

> The veto is perceived as the most effective means the government members who are not directly interested can use against a solution reached according to Proposition 52*.

Proposition 58*:

> The government members who are not directly interested make use of the veto in the sense of Proposition 57* relatively infrequently.

In the spring of 1967, when the university question formally reached the government, the members of the working group perceived that the veto was the most effective measure the government could use to show its disapproval of the proposal. On the other hand, the government did not consider it its task to work out fundamentally different solutions, nor was it equipped to do so, having no special staff at its disposal. It was hardly possible to call in experts from outside the administration, since most of them had already been included in the consensus of the working group. It should also be understood that the decision-making process already showed such a big time lag that the government felt reluctant to lose more time by preparing a counter-proposal of its own.

After deliberations lasting more than five months, during which time the working group was given two hearings, the government decided not to make use of its veto power and to forward the proposal to Parliament practically unchanged. This pattern of behavior should not be interpreted to mean that the government had exerted no influence at all; it should be remembered that the working group had anticipated the reactions of the government and that it had also oriented its behavior strongly to these anticipated reactions.

*Proposition 59**:

> The reactions of the members of Parliament who are not directly interested are anticipated relatively precisely and are taken into consideration to a large extent throughout the process leading to a solution in the sense of Proposition 52*.

There were many channels of communication between the working group and Parliament that made it possible for the working group to anticipate the reactions of Parliament relatively precisely. The shortest channel of communication was formed by the editor in chief who was a member of the working group and at the same time a member of Parliament. Furthermore, eight members of Parliament were members of the study commission. Finally, it is important to note that most members of the working group had other political roles in the canton and thus had many opportunities to get directly in touch with many members of Parliament. The working group took pains to orient its proposals to the anticipated reactions of Parliament; at the same time it also attempted to change the reactions of Parliament according to its own goals. It attempted to do this informally by letting its members have personal conversations with the important members of Parliament.

*Proposition 60**:

> The directly interested members of Parliament who have participated in reaching a solution according to Proposition 52* usually support this solution in Parliament.

*Proposition 61**:

> The decision-making process usually has such a big time lag with respect to the existing stress that the members of Parliament who are not directly interested feel constrained not to delay the decision any longer.

*Proposition 62**:

> The members of Parliament who are not directly interested usually do not replace a solution reached according to Proposition 52* with a fundamentally different one.

*Proposition 63**:

The veto is perceived as the most effective means the members of Parliament who are not directly interested can use against a solution reached according to Proposition 52*.

*Proposition 64**:

The members of Parliament who are not directly interested make use of the veto in the sense of Proposition 63* relatively infrequently.

In the spring of 1968 the parliamentary commission approved the proposal of the working group unanimously and practically without changes. This showed that the working group had anticipated the reactions of Parliament relatively precisely. The parliamentary commission needed fifteen sessions to reach this result. The head of the Department of Education and the full-time expert for university affairs participated in these sessions by representing the proposal of the working group. In conformity with Proposition 60*, the members of Parliament who, in one way or another, had participated in negotiating the proposal, supported it in the parliamentary commission. The abovementioned editor in chief was a member of the working group and now also belonged to the parliamentary commission. The parliamentary commission also included three members who had been in the study commission; two other members of the parliamentary commission, the mayor of the city of Aarau and a member of the cantonal Council of Education, had also been relatively strongly involved in the decision-making process up to this time. These members of the parliamentary commission identified themselves to a relatively large extent with the proposals of the working group. Consequently, the role accumulations between the preparliamentary stage and the parliamentary stage reduced to a minimum any polarization between government and Parliament in the deliberations of the parliamentary commission.

However, a certain polarization did exist among the members because of each member's earlier participation in the decision-making process. On one side were the head of the Department of Education, the full-time expert for university affairs, and the six members of Parliament who had been active in negotiating the proposal; on the other side were the thirteen members of Parliament, who had hardly participated in the decision-making process so far. The aim of the first group was to convince the second group to accept its proposal. It is important to note that, because representatives of all parties had been included in the preparliamentary stage, both groups were heterogeneous with respect to party affiliation. The deliberations of the parliamentary commission were characterized by the tendency to regulate conflicts by amicable agreement rather than by majority decisions. It was often stressed on formal and on informal occasions that it was important for the commission to appear in the full session of Parliament with a unanimous position. If a majority and a minority opinion confronted each other, the commission president tended to declare the question not yet ready for discussion and to postpone the decision to a later session. The postponement tactic made it possible to seek an informal compromise. This procedure was successful because there were many informal interactions across party lines. For example, members of the commission usually did not group according to party lines during lunch breaks.

When the parliamentary commission had reached unanimity, it decided to inform the parliamentary groups and to make a definitive decision on the basis of their reactions. During the deliberations in the parliamentary groups something unexpected happened: the canton of St. Gallen publicly stated that it intended to found a medical school. This caused the agreement among the experts to break down. The experts that had been called in by the canton of Aargau had previously come to the conclusion that there was a need for *one* additional medical school in Switzerland and that the establishment of one in the canton of Aargau would cover this need. It now appeared that the Aargau experts had not considered the canton of St. Gallen seriously enough; they had been of the opinion that the financially relatively weak canton, which already had a university of economics and social sciences, could not be a serious candidate for a medical school.

When the parliamentary commission met again, it was necessary to discuss the new situation rather than the opinions of the parliamentary groups. The commission could no longer refer to the unanimity of the university experts, since there was no longer one opinion on the founding of a new medical school in Aargau. Would the commission make a decision independently of the experts or would it send the matter back to them? During the deliberations of the commission it was made clear that Parliament was not expected to seek a solution independently; the parliamentary commission perceived itself primarily as a veto group that could return "unripened" proposals. It decided to give the matter back to the Department of Education so that the department could review the situation. The behavior of the commission confirmed Proposition 62* and 63*.

On the basis of the Aargau case study the hypothesis may be formulated that Parliament makes use of its veto power primarily when consensus among the experts breaks down. It will be seen in a later context that this hypothesis has been confirmed in other case studies.

The working group prepared an extra report for the parliamentary commission retaining in principle the model of a university with both a department of medical sciences and a department of education, but it emphasized the needs of the department of education. With regard to the medical sciences, it was decided for the time being that only an internship hospital should be erected, while the question of further expansion at a later date was left open. This solution acknowledged the most recent development in St. Gallen and again the parliamentary commission was in unanimous agreement.

On October 1, 1968, full debate took place in Parliament. The unanimity achieved in the commission showed itself in the debate in that all parliamentary group spokesmen declared their agreement. Only two outsiders were in opposition in the final vote.

Before the proposal was submitted to the people of Aargau in a referendum, the Aargau authorities introduced still another intermediary stage by asking the federal authorities if the university project could count on the payment of federal subsidies. Important federal officials had been called in as experts in their personal capacities in an earlier phase and had participated significantly in developing the Aargau project; they were now asked for their support through formal channels. These contacts with the federal authorities caused another delay in the decision-making process of more than a year. The government of the canton of Aargau informed the Parliament on October 2, 1969, that the federal authorities agreed to support the project.[39] The Parliament then confirmed its approval of the university project on February 17, 1970. All parliamentary group spokesmen again were positive. This time, too, only two outsiders voted against the project.

Proposition 65*:

The political parties tend to enter the decision-making process more actively only when a solution according to Proposition 52* has already been reached.

Proposition 66*:

The opinions of the political parties tend to be influenced significantly by persons who have participated in reaching a solution according to Proposition 52*.

*Proposition 67**:

> The pressure groups that perceive themselves to be directly interested tend to participate in negotiating a compromise according to Proposition 52*.

Propositions 65, 66, and 67 were clearly confirmed. When nominations for the study commission were being considered, the political parties were thought to be as significant as the pressure groups; nevertheless, the pressure groups enjoyed a stronger influence. This happened because the representatives of the pressure groups were backed far more strongly by their organizations than the party representatives. Whereas the parties had hardly concerned themselves with the university question during the preparliamentary stage, pressure groups (such as the chamber of commerce) had developed a broad body of opinion about the matter at hand. The difference between the parties and the pressure groups can be explained partly by the fact that the pressure groups as a rule are much better staffed than are the political parties.

In the deliberations in the study commission the representatives of the pressure groups were often able to present well-founded opinions as a result of their preparation. Furthermore, they were clearly perceived in their roles as pressure group representatives in contrast to the party representatives who, because they usually expressed only their personal opinions, were frequently not seen as representatives of a party. The fact that most party representatives also held many other political roles contributed to the diffuse picture they presented to others.

The priority position of the pressure groups was particularly obvious when the university models were submitted to different organizations. Although the political parties were not asked for their opinion of the issues, the working group did request the views of many pressure groups. For example, the model of a school for advanced studies in economics and public administration was submitted for review to the following special-interest organizations: the Association of Aargau Officials and Employees, the Association of Aargau Notaries, the Association of Swiss Local Communities, the Association of Cantonal and Local Community Employees, the Swiss Merchants' Association, the Swiss Association of Public Employees, the Swiss Union of Commerce and Industry, the Aargau Chamber of Commerce, the Zurich Chamber of Commerce, the Chamber of Commerce of Central Switzerland, the Chamber of Commerce of St. Gallen, the Solothurn Chamber of Commerce, and the Berne Chamber of Commerce.

As the political parties gradually became more involved after the preparliamentary stage, their positions were significantly influenced by persons who had already participated in the preparliamentary stage, and, in confirmation of Proposition 66, the representatives from the pressure groups were particularly active within the parties.

*Proposition 68**:

The reactions of the individual citizens to a potential referendum are anticipated relatively precisely and are also taken into consideration to a large extent throughout the process leading to a solution according to Proposition 52*.

*Proposition 69**:

The directly interested groups tend to use the referendum and the popular initiative more often than any other groups.

*Proposition 70**:

The referendum and popular initiative are used primarily as a threat to influence the decision-making process according to one's own goals.

*Proposition 71**:

A referendum or a popular initiative is taken only when a compromise according to Proposition 52* has not been achieved successfully.

In contrast to the decision of the case study at the federal level, the question of whether a university was to be founded in Aargau was subject to an obligatory rather than an optional referendum. Consequently, Propositions 69* through 71* are not applicable because it was determined a priori that the people would have the last word. Thus there was no chance to use the referendum as a threat to influence the decision-making process. Although it was still possible to introduce a popular initiative, no one took that action.

During the whole decision-making process, the reactions of the people were anticipated by the decision-makers. Most formal and informal discussions ended with the question of whether the people would give its approval. Since there was no organized opposition to the university project, the estimates of public opinion were diffuse and hard to make. The results of referenda about other questions were used as one basis for information. Attempts were made to draw conclusions from referenda about hospital proposals, for example, since the university was to contain a department of medical sciences. The anticipation process was also based to a high degree on contacts with the "man in the street." Finally, an attempt was made to use scientific opinion polls, which was a relatively new way of anticipating the reactions of the citizenry in Switzerland. The University Association of Aargau, a private organization that was promoting the idea of a university in Aargau, sponsored an opinion survey on the university question that was carried out by a scientific institute in the summer of 1968.

Generally speaking, a distinct trend could be observed during the whole decision-making process to take into account the wishes of the people as they had been anticipated by various methods. The people of Aargau accepted the proposal on May 10, 1970, with 31,460 votes for the proposal and 28,945 votes against it.

Proposition 72*:

The directly interested groups also tend to participate in the administration of a decision.

This proposition cannot be evaluated because the execution of the decision had not started at the conclusion of the present study.

3. OTHER DECISION-MAKING PROCESSES

At the time I finished the German version of this study only three other systematic studies about political decision-making processes in Switzerland were available: Christopher Hughes's study of the federal law in 1949 concerning the working contracts of commercial agents;[40] Beat Alexander Jenny's study of the federal decree in 1955 concerning federal subsidies to the Fuel Corporation of Ems;[41] and Gerhard Kocher's study about the partial revision in 1964 of the Health and Accident Insurance Law.[42]

In the following section I shall examine the extent to which the propositions developed so far apply to these three case studies.[43]

*Proposition 19**:

Parliament tends to start the formal decision-making process.

In the case of the law concerning the working contracts of commercial agents, the formal decision-making process was started in 1938 when the Union of Swiss Commercial Agents petitioned the Federal Bureau for Industry, Trade, and Labor. The union demanded that the working conditions of the agents be regulated by law, which had not been the case up to that time.[44]

In the case of the Fuel Corporation in Ems, the problem came to a head in 1955 with the expiration of a contract between the federation and the corporation, which had been made in 1941 in connection with the wartime economy. During 1953 four motions had been made in Parliament with regard to this problem. At approximately the same time, several directly interested groups had contacted the federal department in charge of this matter.[45] The Swiss Union of Commerce and Industry, the Association of Swiss Synthetic Silk Factories, and the Swiss Society for Chemical Industry were directly interested because they saw federal support to the Fuel Corporation as an unfair distortion of the market. Because the corporation was a major buyer of wood, the forestry organization and the wood industry were also directly interested. The trade unions saw themselves as directly interested because of the problem of maintaining the number of jobs in Ems. Finally, the automobile associations were directly interested because the fuel produced in Ems had to be mixed with imported gasoline.

The revision of the Health and Accident Insurance Law was also started simultaneously by parliamentary motions and by petitions of directly interested organizations to the department in charge. In this case the organizations of the medical doctors and the health insurance societies were primarily involved.[46]

To what extent does Proposition 19* apply to Hughes's, Jenny's, and Kocher's case studies? It does not apply to the working contracts study because Parliament did not participate at all in the first sequences of the decision-making process. It was a petition of an interest group to the department in charge that started the formal decision-making process. Hughes comments that the organization "did not (as it might have done) contact a friendly deputy but went straight to the Federal Bureau for Industry, Trade and Labor."[47] By the parenthetical remark Hughes evidently wants to say that the organization might just as well have chosen the parliamentary way. But why was another alternative used in this case? If we are not satisfied with considering this a random occurrence, we must look for a hypothesis. It might be that the parliamentary solution was avoided because the question was thought to be of too little importance. It appears from the case studies about the Fuel Corporation and the Health and Accident Insurance Law that there may be something to this hypothesis. In both of these latter studies, the directly interested organizations contacted the department in charge. But why did they choose to engage Parliament as well? It may be because both questions were perceived to be politically very important. In a general form, then, the hypothesis could read as follows: The more important the political problem in question is perceived to be, the more frequently Parliament is engaged at the beginning of the formal decision-making.

To what extent does Parliament perform a gatekeeper function at the outset of the formal decision-making process? Is it Parliament that effectively determines whether decision-making can really start? If any member of Parliament demands that a formal decision-making process be started, rarely will a full session of Parliament oppose the demand. The early history of requests for federal support to the cantonal universities does, however, contain exceptions. In 1946, when two members of Parliament from Geneva submitted a motion requesting the preparation of a bill for federal support to cantonal universities, Parliament rejected the motions and thus stopped the decision-making process before it really was started. As Parliament usually is generous in accepting motions from its members, it is possible that a great many demands could overload the system. However, such motions are usually shelved unless the directly interested groups really show a desire to pursue the matter. For example, this mechanism was used in the study concerning the federal subsidies for the cantonal universities. After the acceptance of the parliamentary motion, when the head of the Federal Department of the Interior met with the heads of the Departments of Education of the university cantons, the university presidents, and other directly interested persons, he said at the beginning of the meeting: "Today the questions are (1) to clarify whether the need for support of the universities exists, and (2) if it does, to investigate how to proceed toward obtaining that support."

Since everyone agreed that the need for support existed, the decision-making process could begin. The manner in which the question was posed, however, makes it clear that the participants did not merely consider themselves executors of a parliamentary decision; they wanted to determine for themselves whether it was worthwhile to continue the decision-making process. If they had reached a negative conclusion, the matter would probably have come to an end. In this context it would be interesting to study in detail the circumstances that prevent parliamentary motions from being followed up. I assume for the time being that opposition on the part of the directly interested persons is a decisive variable.

Does this really mean that the directly interested persons rather than Parliament determine whether a decision-making process is to be started? The answer can only be given with qualifications: The directly interested persons have a considerable veto power that they can use against Parliament, but only with relatively unimportant questions can they start the decision-making process without engaging Parliament. In important matters, however, Parliament, for its part, can use its veto power against the directly interested persons in the sense that it can prevent the decision-making process from beginning if it wants to. That Parliament uses this veto power relatively infrequently does not necessarily mean that it has only limited influence. The directly interested persons seem to anticipate the reactions of Parliament relatively precisely and they usually do not try to start the decision-making process until they are certain that Parliament will not use its veto power. If this hypothesis were to be confirmed, it would mean that the approval of both Parliament and the directly interested persons are needed to actually start a decision-making process.

What is the function of the government in starting the decision-making process? In none of the five case studies did the government as a whole play a significant role in the first phases of the decision-making process. In contrast to the government as a whole, the head of the department in charge participated intensively in the decision-making process from the beginning. In no case, however, was he the only driving force behind the decision-making process. Like Parliament and the directly interested persons, the head of the department in charge can use his veto power to stop or at least extensively delay a decision-making process. All this leads us to the hypothesis that the decision-making process cannot really get started unless Parliament, the directly interested persons, and the head of the department in charge do not oppose it.

A distinctive quality of the Swiss political system is that the decision-making process can also be started by a popular initiative. As this method was not used in any of the five case studies, I have to use unsystematic observations to describe it. Individual citizens will rarely stand up and spontaneously organize a popular initiative. The rule is that the popular initiative is used by well-organized groups such as political parties and economic interest groups. The popular initiative has two main functions. It can be used as a threat to influence an ongoing decision-making process. In this respect it is more or less a functional equivalent of the referendum. It was used, for example, in the case of the revision of the Health and Accident Insurance Law when the health insurance societies threatened the other groups alternatively with the referendum and the initiative.[48] A second function of the popular initiative is to make a demand publicly more visible than it would be by a motion in Parliament or a petition to the department in charge. In this respect the initiative has a great importance in election campaigns.

It is now necessary to revise Proposition 19* as follows:

The decision-making process does not really tend to start until Parliament, the directly interested persons, and the department in charge agree.

It rarely happens that individual citizens spontaneously organize a popular initiative.

The popular initiative is used almost exclusively by strongly organized groups such as political parties and economic interest groups.

The popular initiative serves to make political demands more visible and to exert pressure in an ongoing decision-making process. The initiative frequently exerts pressure by threat rather than by action.

Proposition 20*:

> The formal decision-making process tends to start with a time lag rather than a time lead with respect to the stress situation in question.

Proposition 20* is clearly confirmed by Hughes, Jenny, and Kocher. In all three cases the decision-making process was started when the stress on the system was already strongly apparent. It would have been easiest to anticipate the stress in the case of the Fuel Corporation, because it had already been decided in 1941 that the contract between the corporation and the federation would expire at the end of 1955. In spite of this, preparations for a regulation after 1955 did not start until 1953. At that time the stress was already very grave because at the end of 1953 the corporation had already completed the delivery of the contractually fixed amount of fuel to the federation. Therefore, it became necessary to resort to a temporary solution for 1954 and 1955.[49] Instead of preparing a solution several years ahead for the time after 1955, the problem was allowed to escalate, and there was no reaction until the stress was very acute. A similar time lag existed in the cases of the working contracts law and the revision of the Health and Accident Insurance Law.

The reasons why the political system of Switzerland waited so long to react to an actual stress situation in all five cases may be found in the circumstances described in revised Proposition 19*. For one thing, it seems to be important that Parliament, the directly interested persons, and the department in charge all have a right to veto the launching of the decision-making process. This "stalemate" position prevents each group from daring to move forward prematurely and running the risk of being put down by the veto of another group. It is also relevant in this context that the government as a whole infrequently takes a leadership role in this phase.

Which variables influence the extent of the time lag before the decision-making process begins? A first hypothesis could be that the more controversial the political question, the greater the time lag. An example of this is the revision of the Health and Accident Insurance Law. Between 1952 and 1954 a revision had already been attempted, but considerable differences of opinion had appeared among the members of the expert commission. Consequently, the revision was stopped; it was evidently preferable to have a time lag than to make latent conflicts manifest by trying to reach a decision.[50] A second hypothesis could be that the more ambiguous the allocation of competence among the departments, the greater the time lag. For instance, in 1938 when the Organization of Swiss Commercial Agents brought its request to the Federal Bureau for Industry, Trade, and Labor, a bureau that is under the jurisdiction of the Federal Department of Economic Affairs, it knocked on the wrong door, because the matter really belonged to the Federal Department of Justice and Police. But it took three years before the Federal Bureau for Industry, Trade, and Commerce reached the conclusion that the matter really fell within the jurisdiction of the Federal Department of Police and Justice.[51] A third hypothesis could be that the more ambiguous the claim of competence of the governmental level (federal, cantonal, or local) to which the question belongs, the greater the time lag. For example, Switzerland began the construction of highways with a great time lag compared to other countries because it was not possible to decide how the matter should be divided among the three levels for a long time.

In conclusion, the following hypothesis may be postulated with respect to Proposition 20*: The more controversial the question, the more ambiguous the allocation of competence among the departments, and the more ambiguous the claim of competence among the governmental levels, the greater the time lag between the onset of the stress situation and the beginning of the formal decision-making process.

*Proposition 21**:

When Parliament has started the formal decision-making process, the initiative tends to be transferred from Parliament to the government.

*Proposition 22**:

At the government level only the department in charge tends to become active at that point, not the government as a whole.

*Proposition 23**:

The department in charge tends to negotiate further procedures with the directly interested parties.

In the case of the working contracts law, Parliament did not participate in beginning the decision-making process. In confirmation of Proposition 21* it also remained inactive during the first sequences of decision-making. At the government level it was the department in charge that became active at that point.

In the case of the Fuel Corporation and the revision of the Health and Accident Insurance Law, Parliament was active in starting the decision-making process, but took no further initiatives immediately afterward. The government as a whole remained inactive at first, and left the matter to the department in charge.

The individual departments are legally free to proceed with the decision-making process in any way they wish up to the point when they present a proposal to the government as a whole. In practice, it has been the norm for the departments to work closely with the directly interested persons in this sequence, but it is not determined exactly who is to be considered directly interested, and how they are to be consulted. In my own case studies from the field of university policy the procedure was that the departments in charge called in a relatively small group of directly interested persons to discuss the development of the decision-making process. This procedure, expressed in Proposition 23*, also seems to have been confirmed by Hughes, Jenny, and Kocher, although none of these authors, presumably because of lack of data, describe it in much detail. Hughes, for instance, is content to note that, at the beginning of the decision-making process, a conference had taken place between the administration "and the representatives of certain interests. The conference requested the Department of Justice to submit a draft."[52] It is worth noting that this quotation suggests that the directly interested persons helped decide what the future procedure was to be. The studies of Jenny and Kocher also show that the department in charge had conferred, to some extent at least, about the further development of the decision-making process with those who were directly interested.

*Proposition 24**:

> Many of the directly interested persons who participate in the preparliamentary decision-making process also tend to be members of Parliament.

In Hughes's, Jenny's, and Kocher's studies, persons who were both directly interested and members of Parliament participated in the preparliamentary phase of decision-making.[53] It is interesting to note that the individual interest groups were represented by members of

Parliament in very different ways. In the case of the Fuel Corporation, the confrontation took place between the chemical industry and the forestry industry. The Swiss Society for Chemical Industry was not represented by any member of Parliament in the discussions with the department in charge, but the forestry lobby moved forward with two members of Parliament.[54] In the case of the Health and Accident Insurance Law, the lobby of the health insurance societies included many more members of Parliament than that of the medical doctors.[55]

Do the interest groups, which let themselves be strongly represented by members of Parliament in the preparliamentary phase of decision-making, have a disproportionately great influence? Are they able to anticipate the reactions of Parliament more precisely? At the moment we do not have the data to postulate hypotheses on these questions.

In connection with Proposition 24* it is important to emphasize that there is only slight polarization between Parliament and the directly interested persons because of the frequent role accumulations; a strong reciprocity is more characteristic of the relationship. It would therefore not be correct to assert that Parliament was cut off during the first sequences of the decision-making process; that assertion would be valid for Parliament as an institution, but not for many of its members.

*Proposition 25**:

> Negotiations about further procedures between the department in charge and the directly interested persons take place away from the public view.

This proposition was confirmed by Hughes, Jenny, and Kocher. In a later context I will postulate the hypothesis that the confidentiality of this sequence of decision-making is a condition of the great capacity to compromise shown by the Swiss political system.

*Proposition 26**:

> Even at the beginning of the decision-making process alternatives that are based on new and unusual combinations of information tend to be ignored.

A meaningful evaluation cannot be provided for Hughes's study with regard to Proposition 26* because the study provides too little data.

In the revision of the Health and Accident Insurance Law, the scope of innovation was kept as narrow as possible at the beginning of the decision-making process by ignoring the controversial question of a change in doctors' rights. This decision was made at a session including the department in charge and representatives for both health insurance societies and the Doctors' Association. Afterward, a short time before the parliamentary deliberation, the doctors withdrew from this position and demanded that the controversial question be included in the revision of the law.[56] The change of position constituted a considerable widening of the scope of innovation, which made the finding of a common solution even more difficult. This study invites the hypothesis, which I will develop in more detail later, that the limitation of the scope of innovation is an important condition of the great capacity to compromise in the Swiss political system.

In the case of the Fuel Corporation, the forestry industry, the timber industry, agriculture, and the labor unions all attempted to limit the scope of innovation in the beginning by considering only those solutions that were based on the previous wartime economy situation. But this intention was thwarted by the chemical industry, which introduced a set of alternative solutions. No generally accepted compromise was achieved by these measures and a referendum campaign had to be fought.[57]

Proposition 26* has thus been confirmed insofar as both case studies attempted to keep the scope of innovation as narrow as possible, both times unsuccessfully, however, because of the breaking away of individual interest groups. Why did Jenny and Kocher choose such cases? I assume that both authors were primarily interested in decision-making processes in which conflicts become visible to the outside observer. Conflicts do not often reach the public, of course, when, thanks to a narrow scope of innovation, a compromise can be reached early. A study by Erich Gruner states that out of 871 bills investigated at the federal level only 69 were brought to a referendum.[58] It would be regrettable if research that is done because of a more favorable data situation concentrated on decision-making processes in which a referendum took place or in which a referendum could be prevented only at the last moment (as in the case of the Health and Accident Insurance Law), because that emphasis would not give a representative picture of the decision-making processes in Switzerland. It would be a great advantage to use some sampling methods in the selection of the decision-making processes to be investigated.

*Proposition 27**:

> The department in charge tends to entrust experts from outside the administration with the gathering of information.

*Proposition 28**:

The nonadministration experts also tend to be directly interested persons.

*Proposition 29**:

The directly interested persons tend to have an authoritative voice in the selection of the nonadministration experts whom the department in charge entrusts with the gathering of information.

*Proposition 30**:

The department in charge also tends to entrust nonadministration experts with the task of innovation.

*Proposition 31**:

The innovation experts from outside the administration also tend to be directly interested persons.

*Proposition 32**:

The directly interested persons tend to have an authoritative voice in the selection of nonadministration experts whom the department in charge entrusts with the innovation function.

*Proposition 33**:

Role accumulations tend to exist between information and innovation experts.

Proposition 33* is confirmed by Hughes, Jenny, and Kocher. However, role accumulations have led the three authors to distinguish insufficiently between information gathering and the innovation process. As a rule, they describe both processes in terms of one role pattern, and it is therefore not possible to differentiate between information and innovation experts in examining Propositions 27* through 32*.

In the case of the working contracts law, nonadministration experts seemed to have participated less in the gathering of information and in the innovation process than was the case in our two university policy case studies. At least, the first three drafts of the bill were made by the administration itself; not until afterward were experts from outside the administration called in. The appointed expert commission consisted of fourteen members at first, and twenty-two members later on. An official from the administration was president, whereas in the university studies, an expert from outside the administration was president in one case, and the head of the department in charge in the other. In accordance with Propositions 28* and 31*, the nonadministration experts in Hughes's study were nearly always directly interested persons, often representatives of the commercial agents and their employers. A university professor, who functioned as a legal expert, was the least directly interested person. Hughes's study gives no information about the manner in which the selection of the nonadministration experts was determined (Propositions 29* and 32*).[59]

In the case of the Fuel Corporation, many nonadministration experts assisted in the gathering of information and in the innovation process. However, in contrast to the two university policy case studies and Hughes's study, no formal expert commission was appointed; a more informal procedure was chosen, with ad hoc conferences and correspondence between the department in charge and nonadministration experts. In accordance with the Propositions 28* and 31*, the experts—in this case, representatives for the chemical industry, the forestry industry, the employees, and the automobile associations—were largely directly interested. The canton of Graubuenden, the home canton of the Fuel Corporation, also participated in the decision-making. It is worth noting that the government members of the canton of Graubuenden developed role patterns similar to those of the other directly interested parties.

The department in charge also took pains to include experts who were not directly interested. The head of the department in charge expressed the desire to call in "independent experts" to examine some of the technical chemical problems of the corporation.[60] But, as Jenny describes in detail, the chemical industry succeeded in getting at least one of their trusted men elected.

In the case of the revision of the Health and Accident Insurance Law, many directly interested persons from outside the administration, such as representatives for the doctors and the health insurance societies, also participated in the information gathering and in the innovation process. These experts were consulted in a manner similar to those in the case of the Fuel Corporation, i.e., not in the setting of a formal expert commission, but by several ad hoc conferences and through correspondence. Kocher suggests that the day-by-day informal contacts between federal and interest group officials also had great importance. The almost daily contacts between the department in charge and the health insurance societies were facilitated by relatively frequent exchanges of jobs among officials. In many cases these contacts were nearly indispensable to the federal administration because certain statistics were compiled only by the health insurance societies.[61]

In conclusion, Hughes's, Jenny's, and Kocher's case studies

have confirmed that directly interested experts from outside the administration are very often called in for the information gathering and the innovation processes. The studies also confirmed that the directly interested persons often strongly influence the selection of these experts. The experts were consulted in a great variety of ways, ranging from the appointment of formal expert commissions to day-by-day informal contacts. It would be interesting to study how the forms of expert consultation influence the decision-making process. In the case of the Fuel Corporation, the department in charge had separate conferences with the individual interest groups. Was that a reason why no universally accepted compromise came about? Would a compromise have been possible if all the directly interested persons had been brought together in one expert commission? We still have too little information to postulate meaningful hypotheses about these questions.

Proposition 34*:

The information experts tend to receive an abundant and heterogeneous flow of information through many channels of communication.

Proposition 35*:

The information experts tend to homogenize the heterogeneous information that they receive.

Proposition 36*:

The information experts tend to regulate conflict by the principle of amicable agreement and not by the majority principle.

Proposition 37*:

The decision-making process among the information experts tends to be strongly informal.

Proposition 38*:

The information experts tend to include all potential information experts in their consensus.

Proposition 39*:

The information experts tend to forward only the homogenized information.

Proposition 40*:

An exception to Proposition 39* is made for the department head in charge and his officials who usually also have access to the nonhomogenized information.

*Proposition 41**:

Information emanating from the information experts tends not to be subject to a systematic examination.

*Proposition 42**:

The quantitative information emanating from the information experts tends to be communicated more precisely than the qualitative information.

*Proposition 43**:

The point of reference for judging the credibility of the information collected by the information experts tends to be the composition of the expert groups.

These propositions refer to the process of information gathering, which is just barely described in the case studies by Hughes, Jenny, and Kocher. The three authors do not show who received what information from whom at what time and through which channels, and whether the information content was changed. Thus an important part of the decision-making process is not considered. For example, these gaps become clear in the case study about the Fuel Corporation. In order to arrive at a decision in this case, information about the economic conditions and the chemical-technical conditions of the corporation were of great importance. But we hardly learn anything about how this information was gathered and communicated. Questions such as the following are left without answers: To what extent have the commissioned experts homogenized the information that they received? How did this homogenization process come about? Were other potential information experts included in the consensus? Did the head of the department in charge also have access to the nonhomogenized information? Did the parliamentary commission and the full session of Parliament have access to this information? If we know that Jenny did not even have access to the written report of the experts,[62] it becomes evident that he could learn very little about the information process.

This example shows that an analysis of a decision-making process can be very incomplete if one has to rely on a post facto analysis of written documents. Both Hughes and Kocher offer little observational data about the information-gathering process. When Kocher mentions that the basis for the drafting of the bill was a report of the Federal Department of the Interior containing "commentaries and statistics,"[63] it would have been nice to know to what extent information from the health societies had been included in these commentaries and statistics.

Had the information contained in the department report first been compared with and then changed after the consultation with representatives of the health societies? As a whole, the few fragmentary references in the studies by Hughes, Jenny, and Kocher are not adequate to evaluate whether Propositions 34* through 43* have been confirmed.

*Proposition 44**:

The innovation process tends to start long before the information gathering has been completed.

Since Hughes, Jenny, and Kocher barely describe the manner in which the information was gathered, the nature of the relationship between information collection and innovation was not made clear in their studies. One never really knows whether certain bits of information served as the basis for innovation, or if, on the other hand, they were used to support a solution that had already been reached.

*Proposition 45**:

The innovation experts tend to work out their proposals by the trial-and-error method.

In none of the case studies did the innovation process proceed by attempting to gradually deduce the solution from general principles. In accordance with Proposition 45*, concrete individual proposals were the subjects of an intensive feedback process during a prolonged period. Since I have already described this trial-and-error method in my two university policy case studies, it would be redundant to cite additional illustrative examples from Hughes, Jenny, and Kocher.

*Proposition 46**:

The innovation experts tend to proceed in a predominantly informal way in working out their proposals.

Because Hughes, Jenny, and Kocher relied on a post facto analysis of written documents almost exclusively, major parts of the informal decision-making process were not accessible to them. However, on the basis of many gaps in the descriptions of the cases, it could be assumed that the innovation process frequently developed informally, but that the informal means were not evident in the written documents. Can an analysis of written sources truly comprehend the character of the innovation process to a satisfactory extent at all or is it not primarily the result of the process that is registered in written sources? In the studies by Hughes, Jenny, and Kocher, there is never a reference to conversations by phone, common lunch breaks, or other informal means of communication. Might it not be that the innovation process primarily took place on such informal occasions, and that the result was ratified afterward in a more formal manner?

*Proposition 47**:

> Different groups of innovation experts do not tend to work out alternatives independently of one another.

In the case of the working contracts law, the innovation process took place within a single expert commission that included representatives for the commercial agents as well as for their employers. The study confirmed Proposition 47*, therefore, because the different groups of innovation experts did not prepare alternative proposals independently of one another.

In the case of the revision of the Health and Accident Insurance Law, the department in charge, the health insurance societies, and the doctors each tended to develop its own alternatives. This might have resulted in forcing the government and Parliament to choose among different alternatives. This development did not seem desirable to the department in charge, and it attempted to unify the separate innovation processes by calling common conferences and by informal measures. It is remarkable that the health insurance societies and the doctors also made efforts to work together in the innovation process. The presidents and the secretaries of the two organizations met at a conference without the participation of the federal authorities.[64] It becomes increasingly clear that, even with the strong ideological antagonisms that existed, the predominant goal was that the innovation process should result in a jointly prepared compromise. In this specific case, however, it finally turned out that the antagonisms between the health insurance societies and the doctors were too strong for the innovation processes to merge completely.

The Fuel Corporation's situation was similar to that which developed with the Health and Accident Insurance Law. There were strong efforts to unify the innovation process of the different groups, but these efforts were not completely successful.

These investigations are not sufficiently broad to allow for a comprehensive hypothesis about the variables that determine whether the innovation process takes place within one or more groups. The case study of the Health and Accident Insurance Law, however, suggests that the extent to which the rank-and-file members of the different interest groups participate in the decision-making might be important. It turned out that the Doctors' Association was less willing to proceed jointly with the health insurance societies the more active its rank-and-file members became. It may be that the elite members of the organization are more familiar with the norms that are dominant in political decision-making processes than the nonelite members and they therefore take greater trouble to conform to them.

*Proposition 48**:

> Proposition 47* also tends to obtain if the institutional environment of the innovation process changes because, due to frequent role accumulations, roughly the same persons participate in the decision-making.

This proposition is not applicable to Hughes's, Jenny's, and Kocher's case studies because the institutional environment hardly changed during the course of the decision-making.

*Proposition 49**:

> The major part of the innovation process tends not to become manifest to the public.

This proposition was clearly confirmed by Hughes's, Jenny's, and Kocher's studies. In reference to a very important phase of the innovation process, Kocher writes: "All discussion took place closed to the public, no reports were released to the press, and the organization periodicals did not mention them."[65] There are similar references to the confidential character of the innovation process in the works of Hughes and Jenny. With regard to the consequences of this confidentiality, Kocher makes the following statement, which needs to be examined more closely: "The confidential character furthered . . . the objectivity of the political discussion. The 'initiated' from all camps knew that they could not fool each other. Terminological shadow-boxing and tricks are of no avail among professionals."[66]

*Proposition 50**:

> Representatives of the Department of Finance tend to be called in toward the end of the innovation process.

In the case of the working contracts law, the Department of Finance was not called in during any phase of the decision-making process; obviously, that bill had no financial ramifications. On the other hand, the Department of Justice and Police, which was in charge of the drafting of the bill, was in communication with the Department of Economic Affairs. In the case of the Fuel Corporation, the Department of Finance was itself in charge; it maintained contacts with the Department of Economic Affairs, the Department of Defense, and the Department of Justice and Police. In the revision of the Health and Accident Insurance Law, the Department of the Interior, which drafted the proposal, contacted the Department of Finance.

Consequently, it seems that Proposition 50* has to be modified in three respects. First, it is possible that the Department of Finance may not be consulted; second, other departments may be consulted in addition to the Department of Finance; and third, these interdepartmental contacts may take place both in earlier phases of and at the end of the innovation process.

An expert commission presided over by Otto Hongler had described the cooperation among the departments in its report as follows:

> Associate consultation *(Mitberichts-verfahren)* is the procedure by which all departments involved are consulted in writing prior to the decision of the Federal Council. It is used not only if a matter falls within the jurisdiction of several departments (connected or interdepartmental matters), but also when a question pertaining to a specific department may be of interest to other departments (e.g., with questions about legal principles that relate to the Department of Justice and Police or financial matters that relate to the Department of Finance). In this procedure each interested department gives its comments or its consent in writing to the department primarily in charge. Efforts are made to eliminate differences of opinion by a sort of exchange of notes. Then the matter is submitted to the Federal Council as a unified proposal, if possible agreed to by all departments and agencies involved.[67]

The Hongler Report restricts its description to the formal procedure. It does not mention the possibility of informal interactions—which I encountered in both university policy case studies—in which one department invites officials from another department to a conference, or an informal conversation takes place among officials of the same level "over a cup of coffee."[68] If the informal interactions among the departments are considered in addition to the formal procedures, the Hongler Commission's statement that differences of opinion are eliminated "by a sort of exchange of notes" is not quite appropriate because the example is far too reminiscent of strongly formalized international relations. But in the political system of Switzerland interactions among the different departments of the administration are not characterized by a strong formality. According to my observations, the formal exchange of notes referred to by the Hongler Commission frequently registers a prior decision arrived at by informal means.

In its modified form Proposition 50* now has the following

content: The department in charge tends to contact other interested departments before the proposal reaches the government; these interdepartmental contacts are usually carried out in a strongly informal way.

*Proposition 51**:

The innovation process tends to develop in a way such that the scope of innovation decreases gradually.

*Proposition 52**:

The department in charge, the directly interested persons, and other interested departments finally tend to agree on a common solution.[69]

In the cases studied by Hughes, Jenny, and Kocher, efforts were made to narrow the scope of innovation to the point at which a compromise could result almost automatically. Since it was possible to achieve an agreement in the preparliamentary procedure, the strategy of letting the innovation and decision-making processes converge seemed to be successful in all three cases. But each time one of the directly interested organizations disengaged during the parliamentary stage by moving away from the compromise. In all three cases, the lower organizational levels repudiated the leaders of their organizations. Kocher gives this description of the way in which the Doctors' Association refused to follow their leaders: "The opposition against the outcome of the negotiation was strong and intense. . . . the 'doctor parliament' did not vote for the compromise and thus disavowed its own delegation, i.e., the top leadership of the Doctors' Association, at the negotiation."[70]

Do directly interested parties frequently refuse to accept an already settled compromise? Because we have no representative sample of this kind of decision-making process available, this question cannot be answered conclusively. On the basis of unsystematic observations, however, I assume that Hughes, Jenny, and Kocher considered rather exceptional cases perhaps because of favorable data. In the decision-making processes that confirm Proposition 52*, the data situation is much less favorable than when conflicts among those directly interested are articulated in Parliament.

It would be particularly interesting to examine the variables that determine whether the decision-making processes follow the pattern of Propositions 51* and 52*. For the moment, I would like to postulate the following:

The probability that the scope of innovation gradually decreases and that a lasting agreement results between the department in charge, the directly interested persons, and other interested departments, is greater, (1) the smaller the scope of innovation at the onset of the decision-making process (cf. Proposition 26*), (2) the less publicly manifest the innovation process becomes (cf. Proposition 49*), (3) the more the innovation process takes place within a single group (cf. Proposition 47*), and (4) the less the nonelite members of the system participate in the innovation process (cf. Proposition 52*).

Proposition 53*:

If it is not possible to find a common solution for all points according to Proposition 52*, the controversial points tend to be left out and their solutions put off to a later time.

In the decision-making processes studied by Hughes, Jenny, and Kocher, the effort to leave out controversial points and to put off their solutions to a later time could be found everywhere, but such attempts were not always successful.

Proposition 54*:

The reactions of the government members who do not participate directly are anticipated relatively precisely and are taken into consideration to a large extent throughout the process leading to a compromise in the sense of Proposition 52*.

Proposition 55*:

The decision-making process usually has such a big time lag with respect to the existing stress that the government members who are not directly interested feel constrained not to delay the decision any longer.

Proposition 56*:

The members of government who are not directly interested usually do not replace a solution reached according to Proposition 52* with a fundamentally different one.

Proposition 57*:

The veto is perceived as the most effective means the government members who are not directly interested can use against a solution reached according to Proposition 52*.

Proposition 58*:

The government members who are not directly interested make use of the veto in the sense of Proposition 57* relatively infrequently.

Propositions 56* and 58* were confirmed by Hughes, Jenny, and

Kocher. In none of the three cases did the government members who were not directly interested attempt to replace the solution proposed by the department in charge with a fundamentally different one. Nor did the government as a whole use the veto and refer the proposal back to the department in charge. Does this mean that the government as a whole had no influence in these decision-making processes? This question cannot be answered conclusively because the three authors did not investigate the extent to which the reactions of the government were anticipated and considered at the drafting of the proposal.

The manner in which the government members who were not directly interested perceived their own roles and how they were perceived by other participants were not examined by Hughes, Jenny, and Kocher so that we have no information with respect to Proposition 57*. Nor do we learn much about the extent of the time pressure that the government experienced in the sense of Proposition 55*.

Proposition 59*:

> The reactions of the members of Parliament who are not directly interested are anticipated relatively precisely and are taken into consideration to a large extent throughout the process leading to a solution in the sense of Proposition 52*.

Hughes, Jenny, and Kocher do not pay much attention to anticipation processes as they are used with regard to Parliament. The authors studied Parliament's influence mainly within the narrow perspective of its actual reactions. They do not give credence to the possibility that Parliament's influence was affected by the participants in the preparliamentary phase when Parliament's reactions were anticipated and considered in the preparliamentary proposals.

Proposition 60*:

> The directly interested members of Parliament who have participated in reaching a solution according to Proposition 52* usually support this solution in Parliament.

Proposition 61*:

> The decision-making process usually has such a big time lag with respect to the existing stress that the members of Parliament who are not directly interested feel constrained not to delay the decision any longer.

Proposition 62*:

> The members of Parliament who are not directly interested usually do not replace a solution reached according to Proposition 52* with a fundamentally different one.

*Proposition 63**:

The veto is perceived as the most effective means the members of Parliament who are not directly interested can use against a solution reached according to Proposition 52*.

*Proposition 64**:

The members of Parliament who are not directly interested make use of the veto in the sense of Proposition 63* relatively infrequently.

Proposition 60* was not confirmed by the revision of the Health and Accident Insurance Law, because the doctors disassociated themselves from the compromise reached in the preparliamentary phase a short time before the parliamentary debate. Consequently, the representatives of the Doctors' Association and the health insurance societies were antagonistic and did not form a united front in Parliament. As a result, the members of Parliament who were not directly interested became mediators. Would these members use the mediator role to work out a solution of their own contrary to Proposition 62*? Although the decision-making process had already suffered from a considerable time lag, Parliament was reluctant to search for a decision on its own. One of the members who was not directly interested referred to the fact that "the question is not yet ripe for solution, the problem too difficult to be solved satisfactorily in this unusual way. The opportunities for Parliament to be active in a creative way in the legislative process are somehow restricted. . . . Before Parliament forces a solution, the Federal Council should once more negotiate with the doctors and the health insurance societies."[71] This opinion won general approval and clearly shows that Parliament does not primarily perceive itself as a creative legislative power, but rather as a veto power against "not-yet-ripe" proposals. After the veto of Parliament a new compromise was found between the department in charge and the directly interested groups. But again the doctors repudiated the compromise under pressure from rank-and-file members. Only in this extreme situation did Parliament finally choose to work out a solution of its own.

In the case of the working contracts law, Parliament again referred the proposal back to the department in charge when a directly interested group refused to accept the compromise that had been reached in the preparliamentary stage. In contrast to the Health and Accident Insurance Law, however, a new and enduring compromise formula was reached the second time. Parliament then did nothing but sanction the new formula. Because Jenny has basically restricted his description to the preparliamentary procedure, the case of the Fuel Corporation could not be tested against Propositions 60* through 64*.

It can be concluded, then, that the directly interested persons in Parliament do as a rule form a united front to defend the compromise reached in the preparliamentary stage. In such cases Parliament does not usually make major changes. If, in exceptional cases, the directly interested persons do not accept a compromise that has been achieved in the preparliamentary stage, Parliament in general does not use the opportunity to work out its own solution; instead, it tends to veto the proposal and to send it back to the department in charge in the hope that it can reach a new compromise with the directly interested groups. Only when the directly interested groups find it definitively impossible to reach an agreement does Parliament attempt to decide the central question itself. But in such cases the decision-making process is frequently discontinued so that the problem can "ripen." In order to correctly estimate the influence of Parliament, it is important to remember that during the decision-making process in the preparliamentary stage, the reactions of Parliament are usually anticipated relatively precisely and are seriously considered.

Proposition 65*:

> The political parties tend to enter the decision-making process more actively only when a solution according to Proposition 52* has already been reached.

Proposition 66*:

> The opinions of the political parties tend to be influenced significantly by persons who have participated in reaching a solution according to Proposition 52*.

In the decision-making processes studied by Hughes, Jenny, and Kocher, the political parties participated either little or not at all in the preparliamentary stage. The position of the political parties was significantly determined by persons who had already participated as directly interested individuals in the preparliamentary procedure. Does this mean that the political parties merely functioned as satellites of the interest groups? If there has been *verzuiling* between the interest groups and the political parties, that situation might indeed have been probable—in fact, the parties would hardly have been able to withdraw from the influence of the interest groups. But in reality the interest groups and the parties crosscut each other in large measure. During the deliberations concerning the revision of the Health and Accident Insurance Law, for example, the main proponents of both the Doctors' Association and the health insurance societies belonged to the same political party, the Christian Democratic party. Thus the influence of the two interest groups was more or less counterbalanced within the party, a situation that gave a relatively large amount of freedom to the party members who were not directly interested. This was manifested by the fact that the Christian Democratic party did not vote unanimously in the parliamentary debate.[72] In summary, I would like to formulate the following hypothesis concerning the relationship between interest groups and parties: The influence of interest groups on parties is greatest when their relationship is characterized by *verzuiling* and the interest groups have reached a compromise with one another.

Proposition 67*:

> The pressure groups that perceive themselves to be directly interested tend to participate in negotiating a compromise according to Proposition 52*.

Having referred repeatedly to the important functions of interest groups in the preparliamentary stage, I can summarize their importance by stating that the interests of the directly interested persons were represented in the case studies primarily by interest groups and not by political parties. In the case of the Fuel Corporation, for example, the interests of the workers of the corporation were represented in the preparliamentary stage by the trade unions and not by the Social Democratic party.[73]

Proposition 68*:

> The reactions of the individual citizens to a potential referendum are anticipated relatively precisely and are taken into consideration to a large extent throughout the process leading to a solution according to Proposition 52*.

Many references in Hughes, Jenny, and Kocher indicated that Proposition 68* was confirmed to a large extent in the decision-making processes that they studied. The anticipated reactions of the people were considered implicitly and often explicitly. The participants in the decision-making process were used to orienting their behavior to the wishes of the people, at least to some extent. In order to illustrate how openly referendum considerations are made, I cite the following opinion given by Tschudi, a member of the federal government, during the deliberations of the Health and Accident Insurance Law in Parliament: "The great difficulty is that we will fail with a proposal which stipulates a legal division into classes. . . . It is to be granted by all means that, from a purely social policy point of view, good reasons could be presented for this proposal. . . . But with the structure of our population, there is not the least chance to get through with this proposal."[74]

Proposition 69*:

The directly interested groups tend to use referendum and popular initiative more often than any other groups.

Proposition 70*:

The institutions of referendum and popular initiative are primarily used as a threat to influence the decision-making process according to one's own goals.

In the cases studied by Hughes, Jenny, and Kocher, only the directly interested groups used the referendum and the initiative. This is an important point to note because it is occasionally suggested that in Swiss democracy the people themselves use the referendum and the initiative. However, the case studies show that these two institutions are primarily battle instruments in the hands of the directly interested groups. As stated in Proposition 70*, these battle instruments were primarily used as threats to influence the decision-making process in conformity with one's own goals. Although institutionally quite different, the referendum and the initiative were more or less functionally equivalent as threats.[75] The forms in which the threat of referendum or initiative were expressed varied strongly; they ranged from covert allusions at informal occasions to formal publicly proclaimed decisions by interest groups and party agencies. In summary, I should like to postulate the following hypotheses:

The probability that a decision-making process can be influenced according to one's own goals by threats of referendum or initiative is greater, (1) the more supporters the group using the threat has in its following, (2) the more effectively the group using the threat can produce the impression that it can actually mobilize its supporters in a referendum, (3) the larger the financial resources of the group using the threat, (4) the more the group using the threat is able to produce the impression that it will actually use the financial resources in a referendum, and (5) the less explicitly and the less publicly the threat is articulated (very explicit and publicized threats are easily perceived as blackmail, which may produce resistance on the part of the other groups).

It is obvious that it takes great skill to use the threat of referendum or initiative effectively. The threat must be clearly expressed so that it is taken seriously without giving the impression that it is blackmail.

Proposition 71*:

> A referendum or a popular initiative is taken only when a compromise according to Proposition 52* has not been achieved successfully.

In the case of the working contracts law, a compromise was finally achieved in the second attempt. Neither a referendum nor an initiative was called for, in accordance with Proposition 71*. The proposition was also maintained in the case of the Fuel Corporation, during the course of which there was no compromise and the referendum was used.

The situation was more complicated with regard to the revision of the Health and Accident Insurance Law. After the achieved compromise had fallen apart twice and the doctors had prevailed during most of the parliamentary procedure, the health insurance societies might have been expected to call for a referendum, but they did not. According to Kocher, they declined to call for a referendum because the rules of the referendum do not allow only the points of conflict to be submitted to a popular vote. However, if the proposal as a whole had been subjected to a referendum, the health insurance societies would have risked the advantages that they had gained in the revision. This point of view was expressed by a member of Parliament as follows: "After all, the bill brings to everyone an abundance of advantages that cannot be disregarded and should suppress existing desires for a referendum."[76]

In deciding whether a referendum is to be taken, additional factors besides the risking of achieved advantages may be important. Such factors as the costs of a referendum and the influence of a referendum campaign on future relations with other groups might be considered. This area of research has hardly been approached.

Proposition 72*:

> The directly interested groups also tend to participate in the execution of a decision.

A clear indication that Proposition 72* was confirmed by the Health and Accident Insurance Law can be found in the following remark from a representative for the health insurance societies: "The Federal agencies concerned with the execution [of the decision] have approached the task with much psychological skill combined with understanding and consideration—no trace of tyrannical decrees or edicts. The honest will toward cooperation was even expressed in detailed discussions of questions of form."[77] In the case of the Fuel Corporation there was no executive phase because the federal support for the Fuel Corporation fell away after the negative result of the referendum. The case study concerning the working contracts law did not include any reference to the executive phase.

CHAPTER VI
The Input of Support

In this chapter I will first compare the output performance of the political system of Switzerland with those of other political systems. Next I will investigate how the output performance of the Swiss system is perceived by its citizens. Finally, I will inquire to what extent the input of support flowing into the system depends on the perception of the output performance, and how the input of support is articulated and aggregated.

1. THE OUTPUT PERFORMANCE OF THE POLITICAL SYSTEM OF SWITZERLAND COMPARED WITH THAT OF OTHER POLITICAL SYSTEMS

Herman Weilenmann and Karl W. Deutsch have compared the output performance of Switzerland with that of its four neighbors—Austria, France, the Federal Republic of Germany, and Italy—and with Great Britain, Sweden, the United States, and the Soviet Union.[1] As a point of reference they used the *World Handbook of Political and Social Indicators*.[2]

Weilenmann and Deutsch distinguish the following eight dimensions of output performance: (a) economic development, (b) health care systems, (c) communications systems, (d) educational systems, (e) equality, (f) political stability, (g) decentralization, and (h) density of population and immigration. Forty indicators are used for all eight dimensions, the number of indicators per dimension varying between three and nine. When all eight dimensions are used, Switzerland ranks ahead of the United States, the Federal Republic of Germany, Great Britain, Sweden, Austria, France, Italy, and the Soviet Union. Weilenmann and Deutsch comment on this result as follows: "What our data do show is that the Swiss have succeeded in a political and social system that works in terms of these values, which they share with many other peoples. They have demonstrated that high levels of decentralization and equality can be made to work long and well in a crowded country with no special resources, and they can produce higher levels of overall performance in regard to many values than can be observed in centralized unitary states. Switzerland thus shows a possible alternative pathway to modernity. For federalists and democrats anywhere in the world this should be good news."[3] One might argue that the output performance should be categorized along other dimensions than the ones used by Weilenmann and Deutsch. It would certainly also be possible to find fault with the indicators chosen to measure the individual dimensions. Such criticisms, however, would not fundamentally change the overall results: the output performance of the political system of Switzerland is relatively high in comparison with other countries.

In a grouping of the results by the individual dimensions and indicators, Weilenmann and Deutsch conclude that in areas in which development progresses most rapidly internationally, the output performance of Switzerland is lowest. Take, for example, its communications system: "Switzerland ranks high in the use of older and in part more active forms of communication, such as domestic and international letter-writing and the use of newspapers, but it ranks relatively low among our nine advanced countries in the use of such modern—but also passive—media of communication as motion pictures, radio and television. . . . It seems characteristic of a certain Swiss conservatism to be reluctant to accept novelties."[4] In the field of educational affairs, in which the development of other nations probably has been most dynamic, Switzerland's relative lag behind other nations becomes quite apparent. Weilenmann and Deutsch draw this conclusion: "In the years ahead, Swiss industry and economic life may find it hard to recruit enough highly trained native personnel. . . . At present, young Swiss scientists often go abroad in search of better opportunities while some Swiss firms have research carried out abroad."[5]

Francesco Kneschaurek has suggested rather forcefully that the Swiss educational system, especially at the university level, lags increasingly behind those of other countries. "The education index in our country has not gone up at the same rate as the average prosperity since 1950: whereas at the beginning of the fifties Switzerland was close to the basic correlation between the education index and the prosperity existing in most countries, it has since then moved away from this basic correlation."[6] The backwardness of Switzerland in higher education is expressed in table 16.

Hence Switzerland assumes a leading position with respect to its output performance in comparison with other countries, but it lags behind in some dynamic areas, particularly in education and communications.

2. THE OUTPUT PERFORMANCE OF THE POLITICAL SYSTEM OF SWITZERLAND IN THE PERCEPTION OF ITS CITIZENS

The influx of support into the system does not depend directly on the objectively determinable output performance; the perception of

TABLE 16. STUDENTS IN EUROPEAN COUNTRIES, BETWEEN 20 AND 24 YEARS OF AGE, IN 1965 (IN PERCENTAGES)

Nation	Percent
France	23.9
Finland	22.6
Belgium	22.6
Holland	20.9
Sweden	19.1
Denmark	13.6
Italy	13.2
West Germany	12.3
England	12.2
Norway	11.5
Austria	9.2
Switzerland	5.7
Turkey	4.9

Source: *Wissenschaftspolitik Mitteilungsblatt des Schweizerischen Wissenschaftrates* 2 (1968):11. This journal is published by the Swiss Council of Science.
Note: This table does not include foreign students.

the output performance by the citizens of the system has to be considered as an intervening variable. How are the citizens informed about the output process? The citizens are most directly informed if they themselves belong to the formal decision-makers, i.e., if they themselves are the political authorities. In a study I made of the city of Thun, I had to determine, on the basis of information from the city hall, how many voters were active as political authorities at the local, cantonal, or federal level by the end of 1963. I had to consider a great variety of agencies, including local school boards, local construction commissions, and so on. I found that a total of 330 citizens, or 4 percent of the population of Thun, had political authority at the local, cantonal, or federal level at that time. It was not possible to determine precisely what percentage of the population had held political authority in the past. On the basis of the average age and the average period in office of the current political leaders, it was possible to estimate that roughly 10 percent of the Thun citizenry had political authority at the end of 1963 or had held political authority in the past.

In a representative survey of the suburban community of Belp near Berne, 21 percent of the respondents said that they had held public office.[7] The considerably higher percentage of politically active citizens in Belp might be explained by the fact that Belp had something like six times fewer inhabitants than Thun, although the number of public offices was not correspondingly smaller. As a result of the comparison of these two communities I would like to postulate that the citizens of a community have a better chance of holding public office the smaller the number of inhabitants in the community. This hypothesis was confirmed in a study by Urs Jaeggi in the rural community of Blumenstein between Berne and Thun, which at the time of the survey had about four times fewer inhabitants than Belp.[8] In Blumenstein 32 percent of the citizens had held public office, a percentage considerably larger than that of Thun and of Belp. In both Guggisberg and Lenk, two rural communities in the canton of Berne, where the population was half that of Belp, the hypothesis was less clearly confirmed.[9] In these two communities, 19 and 20 percent of the populations, respectively, had held public office—percentages that were considerably higher than Thun's. But the percentages were not higher than Belp's, although, according to the hypothesis, they should have been because of their smaller populations. The reason for this deviation from the hypothesis was that the number of role accumulations was much higher in Guggisberg and Lenk than in Belp. The degree of role accumulation thus seems to be another variable which, in addition to the size of the community, determines what percentage of the citizens holds public office.

Membership in a political party is a second means by which the citizenry can become informed about the output process. Not only do political parties articulate the demands of the citizens to the system, but they also communicate information about the output process of the system to the citizens. It has already been shown that, on the average, 15 to 20 percent of the Swiss citizens belong to a party. The economic interest groups also perform the same functions. It is important to remember that roughly four times as many citizens belong to economic interest groups as to political parties.

Another means of communication by which information about the output performance of the system can reach the ordinary citizens are personal conversations with the decision-makers. These conversations often take place within the institutional framework of a party or an interest group. According to a study I made in the canton of Berne concerning the interactions between the cantonal legislators and the ordinary citizens,[10] the interactions were quite different in rural and urban environments. In the rural district of Seftigen, only 13 percent of the respondents had never talked with any of the six cantonal legislators from their district. In the city of Berne, on the other hand, 33 percent had never talked to a cantonal legislator. This finding is particularly remarkable because the city of Berne sends thirty-four members to the cantonal legislature, almost six times as many as the district of Seftigen.

The citizenry may also be informed about the output performance of the political system through small-group discussion. In Belp, the population was asked whether it discussed politics frequently or infrequently, and where the discussions took place.[11] Table 17 shows the results of this inquiry:

TABLE 17. FREQUENCY AND PLACE OF POLITICAL DISCUSSION IN THE COMMUNITY OF BELP IN 1960 (IN PERCENTAGES)

Place	Discussed Politics Frequently	Discussed Politics Infrequently	Discussed Politics Occasionally
In the family	24	42	34
At the job	19	60	21
With neighbors	8	75	17
At the local inn	7	83	10
In voluntary organizations	7	83	10

A study of the 20- to 35-year-old citizens in urban areas also showed that political discussions most frequently take place in the family and at the job.[12]

Finally, the mass media communicate information about the output performance of the political system to the individual citizens. When asked how often they had read a newspaper for more than twenty minutes per day within the past week, the 20- to 35-year-old citizens in urban areas answered as follows: (1) five days or more (30 percent); (2) three or four days (15 percent); (3) one or two days (17 percent); (4) never (37 percent); 2 percent gave no information.[13]

In the same study I placed the respondents in a hypothetical situation by presenting them with four newspaper articles with political content. For each article I asked if they definitely would read it, definitely would not read it, possibly read it. The results were as follows:[14]

a. Would read an article about social security problems:

definitely	54%
definitely not	23%
possibly	22%
no information	1%
total	100%

b. Would read an article about NATO:

definitely	48%
definitely not	21%
possibly	30%
no information	1%
total	100%

c. Would read an article about the federal Parliament:

definitely	42%
definitely not	27%
possibly	30%
no information	1%
total	100%

d. Would read an article about elections in Italy:

definitely	25%
definitely not	48%
possible	26%
no information	1%
total	100%

Depending upon the topic, then, 20 to 50 percent of the citizenry in urban areas declared that they would definitely not read the article in question. A roughly similar percentage stated that they would definitely read the article. I asked the 20- to 35-year-old citizens in urban areas whether they tune in to the discussions on radio and television before federal referenda are taken.[15] Their responses follow:

a. Would listen to the round-table discussions on radio before federal referenda:

usually	17%
occasionally	25%
seldom	20%
never, but do have a radio	33%
never, do not have a radio	4%
no information	1%
total	100%

b. Would watch the round-table discussions on television before federal referenda:

usually	16%
occasionally	17%
seldom	9%

never, but do have a television set	7%
never, do not have a television set	48%
no information	3%
total	100%

In addition, I asked whether they had followed the radio discussions about the popular initiative for the banning of nuclear armaments: 18 percent had heard the whole program, 16 percent had heard only a part, and the rest had not even turned the radio on.[16]

In order to compare the means by which the citizens are informed, I did a special study of eleven communities. I investigated the sources through which the citizens were informed about the nine most prominent questions in federal politics.[17] Table 18 shows that reading newspapers and discussions at the job with friends and family form the most important channels of communication through which information about the issues of federal politics are communicated. It should be noted that at the time of the survey (winter 1961–62) many voters did not yet have television sets. In their recent national survey in 1972 Sidjanski and Kerr found that 52 percent of the citizens watch a political show on television at least once a week. The increasing importance of television was marked by the fact that 31 percent of the respondents considered television the most important influence in the formation of their political opinions, although 33 percent still believed newspapers to be the most important influence.[18]

TABLE 18. VOTERS EXPOSED TO AT LEAST FIVE OF NINE POLITICAL ISSUES WITHIN THE LAST MONTH AND LAST HALF-YEAR (IN PERCENTAGES)

Mode of Exposure	Within Last Month	Within Last Half-Year
Listening to radio broadcasts	11	41
Attending public meetings	3	13
Watching television programs	3	9
Discussions at the job	29	76
Discussions with family, neighbors, friends, etc.	28	69
Discussions with friends in one's organizations	10	24
Reading newspaper articles	43	83

How are the different channels of communication related to one another? All the studies I have done so far show that the voter who gets much information from one channel of communication also tends to get much information from other channels of communication.[19] The following groups receive information from a great variety of sources: upper- and middle-status groups; persons who are not geographically or socially mobile; socially well-integrated persons; men; older people (with the exception of the very old); and rural people.[20]

Up to this point I have discussed the structure of the system of communication between the output processes and the citizens. An important question at the present time is the following: What information flows through which channels of communication with what degree of filtering? The problem of filtering is particularly interesting. The extent to which the mass media filter the information about the output process and the ideologies with respect to which they perform the filtering have yet to be investigated. On the basis of some of my studies, however, I can attempt to determine the level of information that is available to the citizenry.

There is a great deal of evidence to prove that the individual citizen is not well-informed about the institutional setting of the output process on the federal level. We can use the federal tax system as an example. Of the two most elementary concepts of the federal tax system cited in one of our studies, 47 percent of the respondents did not know about one, and 39 percent did not know about the other.[21]

More important than the citizen's lack of information about the institutional setting of the output process is his unfamiliarity with the actual development of the decision-making process. An example from another one of my surveys will prove the point. When asked whether a major change in the party composition of the Federal Council would have an effect on their own occupational and private life, 14 percent of the respondents said that it would, 71 percent said that it would not, 12 percent said that it "depends," and 3 percent gave no answer.[22] Seventy-one percent of the voters were evidently so unfamiliar with the decision-making mechanisms that they were not able to realize how a major change in the party composition of the Federal Council would influence the output process and how the changed output performance would affect their lives. These results may be partly due to the fact that there are relatively small differences in the goals of the major parties. Since a major part of the decision-making process takes place away from the public eye, it is also possible that the influence of the Federal Council is closed to many citizens. It is important in this context to remember that Switzerland has no political leaders with a high nationwide visibility. The political play of power remains relatively anonymous to the outside world and, unlike the British system, it is not personalized by the confrontation between the prime minister and leader of the opposition. In Switzerland there are no symbolic figures with whom people can identify.

The picture is somewhat different for the local level. The citizen's knowledge of the local institutions is certainly not much greater than it is of the federal institutions. In Belp, for instance, only 34 percent of the respondents knew who elects the local construction commission. On the other hand, the political leaders are much more visible than they are at the federal level. Ninety-eight percent of the respondents in Belp knew what the occupation of the mayor was and 90 percent knew where he lived.[23]

How do the citizens evaluate the information they receive about the output process? It might be useful to distinguish between the process itself and its results. By the process, I mean the ways in which these decisions come about; by the results, I mean the substance of the political decisions.

It has already been stated that a far-reaching consensus exists with respect to the content of the political decisions. There is much less unanimity of public opinion about the process by which the decisions are reached. Table 19 is based on a survey I made, the results of which testify to the critical positions taken by the public.[24]

TABLE 19. ATTITUDES TOWARD POLITICAL DECISION-MAKING IN SWITZERLAND (IN PERCENTAGES)

Items	Yes	No	No Information	Total
There are often incapable people among our authorities because connections are more important than ability.	68	28	4	100
You have to have gray hair to be taken seriously in politics.	53	44	3	100
The most important political decisions take place behind closed doors.	47	49	4	100
In spite of our democratic institutions the bureaucracy can do almost everything it wants to.	34	65	1	100
The individual does not count in politics.	32	66	2	100

The criticisms expressed in table 19 are of a diffuse nature: they are directed not at particular persons, but at the political elite in general. Just as there are no symbolic figures in Switzerland with whom the people can identify, neither are there any against whom criticism can be directed. Nor is criticism based on clearly defined matters such as corruption or inefficiency. The real substance of the criticism is that the work of the political elite is virtually unknown to the public, and therefore the public cannot really understand how political decisions are made. Many citizens have the impression that everything takes place in smoke-filled rooms where the bureaucracy is supposed to have a great influence. The members of the political elite are reproached for holding their offices too long and for fraternizing too much. This attitude is exemplified in a statement often used by the public: "They do what they want to, anyway."

It is no wonder that such a diffuse criticism of the decision-making process has arisen. After all, it actually does take place almost entirely away from the public eye, and those who participate in it are connected by a network of role accumulations so complex that it is hardly comprehensible to the outside observer. It is also true that the political elite is replaced relatively infrequently. The criticism is not completely justified, however, because it must be remembered that the political leaders attempt to anticipate and consider the reactions of the rank-and-file members of the system during the decision-making processes. Therefore, it cannot be assumed that the elite "do what they want to, anyway" or that "the individual does not count in politics." In the present context, it is not our task to judge whether the criticism is objectively true, but to record it as a politically relevant phenomenon.

3. THE ARTICULATION AND AGGREGATION OF SUPPORT

Elections are not a very useful means of dissent in Switzerland because all major parties participate in the government. Thus the voters do not have the opportunity to replace the government team with the opposition team. That election results are perceived to have little importance can be seen in the results of a survey in which the following question was asked: "The National Council will be elected shortly. Do you think that something will change in your occupational and private life because of the outcome of these elections?" Eight percent of the respondents said yes, 76 percent said no, and 16 percent did not express any opinion.[25] Intensive studies have shown that the voters who wish to express dissent through the elections do so most often by not voting.[26]

A second means of articulating dissent is by voting for the small parties that do not participate in government. The Independent party, the Anti-Alien party, the Republican party, and the Communist party especially are the parties that represent the protest vote. In contrast, voting for one of the major parties is a way to articulate consensus.

The referenda offer far greater opportunities for the expression of dissent. Hans Huber makes the point graphically: a no in the referendum acts as a "valve" through which "the surplus steam can be let out and the pressure can be reduced."[27] Huber's metaphor seems appropriate because it expresses the fact that with a no in a referendum most citizens do not only take a position with regard to a concrete question, but, in the act of articulating dissent, they help themselves psychologically by "letting off steam." A no in a referendum is dysfunctional if it seems to the public that the proposal would change the status quo too little, because negative results in a referendum often mean that no change will be made at all. Referenda are less useful for progressive citizens who want to change the status quo than for those who support it. Therefore, although the conservative members of the system generally content themselves with articulating their dissent in the referenda, the progressive members more frequently resort to other means such as protest marches and demonstrations.

The articulation of consent is expressed by a vote for the government parties and the acceptance of government proposals in the referenda. In addition, attendance at the patriotic events of the marksmen, the gymnasts, the yodelers and the singers, and the annual Federation Day celebrations on August 1 can be seen as support for the system. Flying the Swiss flag all over the country and the usual willingness to serve in the army are other expressions of consent. Consensus depends on the output performance of the system and, to a very large extent, on a well-developed ideology. The ideology is based on the perception that Switzerland is a special case in world history, and, because of its uniqueness, comparisons with the output performance of other systems are almost irrelevant. The point is often made in public debates that foreign examples are irrelevant because Switzerland, with its own peculiarities, has to arrive at its own solutions.

Although its citizens believe that Switzerland is a special case, they think that it can serve as a model for other countries. Daniel Frei suggests that "the idea of a republican-democratic model, the idea of peaceful reconciliation among different cultures, and the idea of a humanitarian-charitable activity" are three aspects of the Swiss model.[28] Since the Swiss believe that they are at once a special case and also a model for the world in many respects, a strong ideology has developed among the citizenry in Switzerland. In the Belp survey 97 percent of the respondents declared they were happy to be Swiss.[29]

CHAPTER VII

Descriptive Propositions about the Political System of Switzerland

In this chapter I will summarize the political system of Switzerland in 145 general propositions. These propositions are not meant to be unique to Switzerland—many may also apply to other countries. Another qualification is in order: the propositions are not meant to be valid for all periods of Swiss history. If I do not specify otherwise, the propositions describe the political system of Switzerland in the 1960s and in the early 1970s.

1. THE INPUT OF DEMANDS

1 On all levels of the system—the federal, the cantonal, and the local—the political parties tend to participate in the government according to their numerical strength.

2 An exception to Proposition 1 is that the government seats that cannot be claimed without numerical ambiguity by one single party usually are decided by the majority principle.

3 Another exception to Proposition 1 is that parties that do not recognize the fundamental principles of the Swiss political system are excluded from participating in government even if their claim can be established without numerical ambiguity.

4 The use of amicable agreement in the formation of the government is not dependent upon whether a party or a coalition of parties has an absolute majority.

5 The use of amicable agreement in the formation of the government is not dependent upon the number of parties with a proportional claim to participate in government.

6 Amicable agreement is not used so extensively in the formation of government that the government parties must reach a formal agreement on the policies to be pursued by the government.

7 This lack of a formal government program enables the government parties to perceive the government as a legitimate recipient of demands that are in opposition to government policy.

8 The opposition of a government party to government policy does not lead to the fall of the government because certain institutional provisions prevent that occurrence.

9 It is possible within the given institutional framework to cause individual government members to lose their seats, but that is done only in exceptional instances. More frequently, individual members of government are forced to resign "voluntarily" by informal sanctions.

10 Political parties that do not participate in the federal government because of lack of numerical strength may nevertheless have political relevance if they have government representation at the cantonal or the local level.

11 Political parties that participate at no level in the government may nevertheless have political relevance if they can use their right to popular initiative and referendum successfully.

12 As a consequence of Propositions 10 and 11 the number of parties that are politically relevant is relatively high. However, the exact number cannot be given because a potential use of the right to initiative and referendum may also be politically relevant.

13 Most nongovernment parties do not act in opposition to government policy as a matter of principle.

14 As a consequence of Propositions 7 and 13 interests are not aggregated by the Swiss party system in a way that allows for a clear distinction between government and opposition parties.

15 Most parties crosscut important subcultures such as languages, regions and cantons, and to a somewhat smaller extent, religious groups, occupational groups, and voluntary organizations.

16 Party discipline is relatively low in Switzerland.

17 As a consequence of Propositions 1 through 16 the input processed by the Swiss party system is relatively diffuse.

18 The pattern of regulating political conflicts by amicable agreement was learned early in the history of the federation.

19 At the federal level the elite groups of all parties together total about 500 to 600 persons.

20 Party leaders often hold several other politically relevant roles. Frequently a party leader is also (a) a member of Parliament, (b) a member of the leadership group of another politically relevant intermediary group, and (c) a member of the leadership group at a lower party level.

21 The elite groups of the parties overlap with the top of the formal party hierarchy in the sense that most members of the party hierarchy belong to the elite group. The elite groups, on the other hand, also include persons with no function at the top of the formal party hierarchy.

22 The most reliable information from the party rank and file reaches the elite groups of the parties primarily through the following channels: (a) role accumulation at the local and the federal party levels, (b) other intermediary groups, and (c) referenda results. In contrast, the ordinary party members have little opportunity in elections to articulate their demands unambiguously, since the political system of Switzerland makes a vague distinction between government and opposition parties.

23 The following categorical groups communicate with the party elite at a below-average rate: (a) foreign workers, (b) women, (c) the lower social strata, (d) young and very old persons, (e) geographically and socially mobile persons, (f) socially less well-integrated persons.

24 A strong social norm motivates the elite groups to orient their decision-making toward the effective or anticipated reactions of the ordinary party members.

25 If the elite groups violate Proposition 24, the ordinary party members rarely resort to formal sanctions such as voting the elite out of office. More frequently, the roles that the members of the party elite have accumulated are withdrawn from them. This sanction usually causes these persons to resign "voluntarily" from the elite group of the party because the party role cannot easily be "played" without the accumulation of the other politically relevant roles.

26 The decision-making process within the elite groups of the parties is generally such that the role of innovation falls to relatively small groups, which as a rule include not more than twenty to thirty members.

27 These groups consist primarily of persons who are perceived to be experts in the issues related to the innovation.

28 The expert groups include persons with leading positions in the formal party hierarchy and persons in subordinate positions in the formal organization of the party.

29 The amount of influence among the individual members of the expert groups tends not to vary greatly from one to the other.

30 The expert groups tend to regulate conflicts not by the majority principle but by the principle of amicable agreement.

31 If the expert groups cannot regulate a conflict by the principle of amicable agreement they tend to defer the decision.

32 The individual expert groups are in a relatively close feedback relationship with the rest of the members of the party elite group.

33 The nonexperts in the party elite group are perceived as generalists with respect to the issue of a specific expert group.

34 A member of a generalist group on one topic may belong to an expert group on another topic.

35 The generalist group may include generalists in a narrower sense, that is, persons who are not experts in any particular topic, but who, to some extent, are specialists in synthesizing the individual topics.

36 The expert groups tend to anticipate the reactions of the generalist group relatively precisely and to make their decisions according to these anticipated reactions.

37 The expert groups tend to anticipate the reactions of the generalist group on the basis of stored as well as current information. The stored information, which originates mainly in the personal experience of the group members, is a relatively reliable basis for the anticipation process because the membership of the expert as well as the generalist groups changes relatively infrequently, and the political process in Switzerland is relatively continuous. The current information is usually transmitted to the expert groups through many role accumulations.

38 There is a tendency to reduce conflicts between the expert and the generalist groups by moving important decisions from the statutorily provided institutions to prior meetings in an ad hoc environment not visible to the public.

39 If the expert groups violate Proposition 36, they are rarely subjected to a formal sanction such as a vote censure. More frequently, the experts in question are no longer taken seriously by the other groups and, as a rule, the experts resign "voluntarily" because their role no longer appears tenable.

40 Politically relevant elite groups exist not only at the federal level, but also at the lower levels, including the local party level. The communication between the various party levels consists primarily of role accumulations.

41 Taken together, the members of the elite groups at all party levels are approximately 5 percent of the electorate.

42 The economic interest groups are as pluralistic as the political parties.

43 The economic interest groups can articulate demands to the political system not only via the political parties, but also through direct channels of communication.

44 The economic interest groups have considerably larger membership bodies than the political parties.

45 The economic interest groups have considerably larger financial resources than the political parties.

46 The economic interest groups have considerably more full-time officials than the political parties.

47 As a consequence of Propositions 43 through 46 the economic interest groups do not play the role of mere satellites of the political parties, but have considerable influence of their own.

48 In general, there is no *verzuiling* between the political parties and the economic interest groups.

49 An important exception to Proposition 48 exists in the trade unions which have a distinct *verzuiling* with the parties.

50 Information between political parties and economic interest groups is usually transmitted by role accumulations.

51 Conflicts between economic interest groups are usually regulated by the principle of amicable agreement.

52 The economic interest groups assume an ambivalent position with respect to government policies in that none of them support or oppose government policies as a matter of principle.

53 The decision-making process between the political parties and between the economic interest groups is often congruent.

54 In addition to the political parties and the economic interest groups, a large number of voluntary associations articulate demands to the political system.

55 Voluntary associations articulate demands to the political system by way of the political parties and the economic interest groups, and also through direct channels of communication.

56 In general, there is no *verzuiling* between the voluntary associations on the one hand and the political parties and the economic interest groups on the other.

57 Information between the voluntary associations and the political parties and economic interest groups is usually transmitted by role accumulations.

58 Most voluntary associations have an ambivalent position with respect to government policies similar to that of economic interest groups in that they neither support nor oppose government policies as a matter of principle.

59 The decision-making process in the voluntary associations is often congruent with that of the political parties and the economic interest groups.

60 Switzerland has a very high number of newspapers relative to the size of the population.

61 In spite of increasing interpaper cooperation, centralization of the newspaper system is still relatively low.

62 The *verzuiling* between political parties and newspapers is declining.
63 Even newspapers aligned with a specific political party may occasionally oppose the official party line.
64 The communication between the political parties and the newspapers consists primarily of role accumulations between the elite groups of the parties and the editorial staffs of the newspapers.
65 There are no government newspapers which would support government policies as a matter of principle.
66 The newspapers of the Communist party and, to a lesser extent, those of the Independent party, as well as some politically nonaligned papers are more or less in fundamental opposition to government policies.
67 The only radio and television license is held by a partly public and partly private nonprofit institution.
68 Radio and television rarely articulate their own demands to the system. Their main function is to serve as amplifiers for the articulation of the demands of the political parties, the economic interest groups, the voluntary associations, and the newspapers.
69 There are three linguistically mixed cantons in the border area between the French- and the German-speaking parts of Switzerland in which language and cantonal boundaries do not coincide.
70 The Jura separatists demand that the crosscutting boundaries in the canton of Berne be changed and an independent French-speaking canton of Jura be formed.
71 So far it has not been possible to regulate the conflict described in Proposition 70 by amicable agreement.
72 The Jura separatists have started to force their demands with some acts of terror.
73 There are many role accumulations between the intermediary groups and the formal decision-makers.
74 The formal decision-makers delegate many functions in the decision-making process to intermediary groups.
75 As a consequence of Propositions 73 and 74 most channels of communication from the intermediary groups to the formal decision-makers are brief and not visible to the public.
76 If the intermediary groups articulate demands publicly, they make the demands primarily to show their supporters that they are active rather than to influence the formal decision-makers.
77 The federal, the cantonal, and the local levels communicate

reciprocal demands to one another, and in so doing they often use the same channels of communication as the intermediary groups.

78 As a consequence of Propositions 73 through 77 the transition from the input to the output processes is very diffuse.

2. THE OUTPUT OF AUTHORITATIVE DECISIONS

79 The decision-making process does not really tend to start until Parliament, the directly interested persons, and the department in charge agree.

80 The government as a whole does not tend to participate in the onset of the decision-making process.

81 It rarely happens that individual citizens spontaneously organize a popular initiative.

82 The popular initiative is used almost exclusively by strongly organized groups such as political parties and economic interest groups.

83 The popular initiative serves to make political demands more visible and to exert pressure in an ongoing decision-making process. The initiative frequently exerts pressure by threat rather than by action.

84 The formal decision-making process tends to start with a time lag rather than a time lead with respect to the stress situation in question.

85 After the onset of the decision-making process the department in charge tends to take the initiative whereas Parliament and the government remain passive.

86 The department in charge tends to negotiate further procedures with the directly interested persons.

87 Many of the directly interested persons who participate in the preparliamentary decision-making process also tend to be members of Parliament.

88 Negotiations about further procedures between the department in charge and the directly interested persons tend to take place away from the public view.

89 Even at the beginning of the decision-making process alternatives that are based on new and unusual combinations of information tend to be ignored.

90 The department in charge tends to entrust experts from outside the administration with the gathering of information.

91 The nonadministration experts also tend to be directly interested persons.

92 The directly interested persons tend to have an authoritative voice in the selection of the nonadministration experts whom the department in charge entrusts with the gathering of information.

93 The department in charge also tends to entrust nonadministration experts with the task of innovation.

94 The innovation experts from outside the administration also tend to be directly interested persons.

95 The directly interested persons have an authoritative voice in the selection of nonadministration experts whom the department in charge entrusts with the innovation function.

96 Role accumulations tend to exist between information and innovation experts.

97 Information experts tend to receive an abundant and heterogeneous flow of information through many channels of communication.

98 The information experts tend to homogenize the heterogeneous information that they receive.

99 The information experts tend to regulate conflict by the principle of amicable agreement and not by the majority principle.

100 The decision-making process among the information experts tends to be strongly informal.

101 The information experts tend to include all potential information experts in their consensus.

102 The information experts tend to forward only the homogenized information.

103 An exception to Proposition 102 is made for the department head in charge and his officials who usually also have access to the nonhomogenized information.

104 Information emanating from the information experts tends not to be subject to a systematic examination.

105 The quantitative information emanating from the information experts tends to be communicated more precisely than the qualitative information.

106 The point of reference for judging the credibility of the information collected by the information experts tends to be the composition of the expert groups.

107 The innovation process tends to start long before the information gathering has been completed.

108 The innovation experts tend to work out their proposals by the trial-and-error method.

109 The innovation experts tend to proceed in a predominantly informal way in working out their proposals.

110 Different groups of innovation experts do not tend to work out alternatives independently of one another.

111 The department in charge tends to contact other interested departments before a proposal reaches the government; these interdepartmental contacts are usually carried out in a strongly informal way.

112 The major part of the innovation process tends not to become manifest to the public.

113 The innovation process tends to develop in a way such that the scope of innovation decreases gradually.

114 The department in charge, the directly interested persons, and other interested departments finally tend to agree on a common solution.

115 If it is not possible to find a common solution for all points according to Proposition 114, the controversial points tend to be left out and their solutions put off to a later time.

116 The reactions of the government members who do not participate directly are anticipated relatively precisely and are taken into consideration to a large extent throughout the process leading to a compromise in the sense of Proposition 114.

117 The decision-making process usually has such a big time lag with respect to the existing stress that the government members who are not directly interested feel constrained not to delay the decision any longer.

118 The members of government who are not directly interested usually do not replace a solution reached according to Proposition 114 with a fundamentally different one.

119 The veto is perceived as the most effective means the government members who are not directly interested can use against a solution reached according to Proposition 114.

120 The government members who are not directly interested make use of the veto in the sense of Proposition 119 relatively infrequently.

121 The reactions of the members of Parliament who are not directly interested are anticipated relatively precisely and are taken into consideration to a large extent throughout the process leading to a solution in the sense of Proposition 114.

122 The directly interested members of Parliament who have participated in reaching a solution according to Proposition 114 usually support this solution in Parliament.

123 The decision-making process usually has such a big time lag with

respect to the existing stress that the members of Parliament who are not directly interested feel constrained not to delay the decision any longer.

124 The members of Parliament who are not directly interested usually do not replace a solution reached according to Proposition 114 with a fundamentally different one.

125 The veto is perceived as the most effective means the members of Parliament who are not directly interested can use against a solution reached according to Proposition 114.

126 The members of Parliament who are not directly interested make use of the veto in the sense of Proposition 125 relatively infrequently.

127 The political parties tend to enter the decision-making process more actively only when a solution according to Proposition 114 has already been reached.

128 The opinions of the political parties tend to be influenced significantly by persons who have participated in reaching a solution according to Proposition 114.

129 The reaction of the individual citizens to a potential referendum are anticipated relatively precisely and are taken into consideration to a large extent throughout the process leading to a solution according to Proposition 114.

130 The directly interested groups tend to use the referendum and popular initiative more often than any other groups.

131 The referendum and popular initiative are used primarily as threats to influence the decision-making process according to one's own goals.

132 A referendum or a popular initiative are only taken when a compromise according to Proposition 114 has not been achieved successfully.

133 Directly interested groups also tend to participate in the administration of a decision.

3. THE INPUT OF SUPPORT

134 The output performance of the political system of Switzerland is relatively high.

135 The output performance of the political system of Switzerland is lowest in those areas characterized by rapid development.

136 The average citizen does not tend to be well informed about the

nature of the political decision-making process and the consequences of political decisions.

137 There are few political figureheads with whom the average citizen can associate the successes or failures of the system.

138 As a consequence of Propositions 136 and 137 most citizens criticize the system in a diffuse way by blaming "those at the top" rather than a person or group of persons.

139 Elections constitute a relatively dysfunctional channel of communication for the articulation of dissent because all major political parties participate in government. Dissent during elections is most likely to be articulated by abstaining from voting or by voting for small nongovernment parties.

140 Referenda are a more functional channel of communication for the articulation of dissent than elections.

141 The referendum is not an effective way to articulate dissent for those who are interested in a change of the status quo because a no in a referendum may contribute to the maintenance of the status quo.

142 As a consequence of Proposition 141 the citizens most interested in changing the status quo articulate their dissent relatively often by other means such as protest marches.

143 A yes in a referendum, voting for the major parties, and participation in the elections are means of articulating consensus.

144 The consensus flowing into the political system of Switzerland is based not only on the output performance of the system, but also on the strongly held ideology of its citizens.

145 This ideology is based primarily on the fact that the Swiss tend to consider their country a special case in many respects.

PART THREE:

A THEORY OF HOSTILITY IN SUBCULTURALLY STRONGLY SEGMENTED POLITICAL SYSTEMS

CHAPTER VIII
Testing the Individual Hypotheses

Having investigated the political system of Switzerland and having summarized the most important findings in 145 propositions, I will now attempt to determine whether the initial hypotheses outlined in chapter I apply to Switzerland. I shall be concerned primarily with the federal level of government, but I shall also refer to the cantonal level occasionally. In a strict sense, a test of this kind would be possible only if reliable and valid cross-national and cross-cantonal yardsticks were available to measure the variables in the hypotheses, but unfortunately, no such yardsticks are available. For example, what exactly is meant by a *high* number of autonomous intermediary groups (Hypothesis 2*)? In principle it would be possible to develop yardsticks for this hypothesis and others, but that task is clearly outside the scope of this study. Consequently, I can test the initial hypotheses only in a rather loose sense. On the basis of my knowledge of the literature, I will try to determine, in an impressionistic way, how Switzerland compares with other Western countries with regard to the variables of the different hypotheses. I will restrict these comparisons explicitly to Western countries because my impressionistic comparisons would be even less reliable if they included Communist countries and countries of the Third World. Although it may be possible to make a reasonable judgment about whether the number of autonomous intermediary groups is relatively high or low in Switzerland in comparison with other Western countries, it would be much more difficult to make a reasonable judgment about that matter in Communist countries or countries of the Third World because very uneven things would have to be compared. In spite of these limitations, I do not mean to disavow the goal of a general theory that would apply to all subculturally strongly segmented political systems.

Comparisons on the cantonal level will also be rather impressionistic, although hard data are sometimes available on this level. I might add that the testing of hypotheses against case studies is often done in the relatively loose manner proposed here. Lijphart's study of the Netherlands[1] and Eckstein's study of Norway[2] were both made in this manner.

First of all, we have to determine whether Switzerland is subculturally strongly segmented and thus belongs to the theoretical universe of this study. As far as I can tell from the literature, all observers of the Swiss political system agree that Switzerland belongs in this theoretical universe.[3] This study, too, gives ample evidence that Switzerland has strongly segmented subcultures. The decision-making processes have shown how often subcultural units act on an independent basis, and that being a member of a particular subculture is often politically valuable. The description of the various decision-making processes should also have demonstrated that intersubcultural hostility—the dependent variable of this study—is at a rather low level in Switzerland. This observation is confirmed by other scholars.[4] We have also seen that there is an exception to this generally low intersubcultural hostility in the canton of Berne where the Jura problem has given rise to a relatively high level of intersubcultural hostility.

I will now discuss the initial hypotheses as they apply to the political system of Switzerland.

*Hypothesis 1**:

> In a political system with strong subcultural segmentation, the more often political decisions are made by amicable agreement, the more probable is a low level of intersubcultural hostility.

Since all major political parties participate in the government in proportion to their numerical strength (Proposition 1), the government is formed primarily by amicable agreement at all levels of the political system of Switzerland. The majority principle, as a rule, is used only when a party cannot unambiguously demonstrate its proportional claim to a government seat, and when parties that do not recognize the fundamental principles of the democratic system of Switzerland are excluded from participation in government (Proposition 2 and 3). On the other hand, the use of amicable agreement in the formation of the government does not depend upon whether one party or a coalition of parties has the absolute majority, nor is it important how many parties can make a proportional claim to a share in government responsibility (Propositions 4 and 5). Amicable agreement is predominant not only in the process of the formation of the government but also in the decision-making process as a whole. It is the method of conflict resolution at the onset of the formal decision-making process when the head of the department in charge and the directly interested groups usually come to an agreement about the procedure to be chosen (Proposition 86). There is also a strong tendency among the experts to regulate conflicts by amicable agreement during the information-gathering phase

(Proposition 99). The innovation process usually proceeds in a way such that the scope of innovation is decreased gradually until a common solution finally appears (Propositions 113 and 114). If it is not possible to reach agreement about all points, there is a tendency to avoid the controversial points and to postpone their solution to a later time rather than to seek a solution by a majority vote (Proposition 115).

The decision-making process within the political parties, the economic interest groups, and the voluntary associations is also characterized by a predominance of the principle of amicable agreement (Propositions 30, 31, 38, 51, 53, 59). In conclusion, conflict resolution in which the majority principle has priority does not seem to be a necessary condition for low intersubcultural hostility. The Swiss experience challenges the following assertion by Lipset: "If the outcome of the political game is not the periodic awarding of effective authority to one group, unstable and irresponsible government rather than democracy will result."[5] As examples of "unstable and irresponsible government," Lipset cites Italy before fascism and the Third and Fourth Republics of France, "which were characterized by weak coalition governments, often formed among parties having major interest and value conflicts with each other."[6] The Swiss example shows that a political system without a clear and homogeneous government majority is not necessarily unstable and that it is capable of having low intersubcultural hostility.

Hypothesis 2*:

> In a political system with strong subcultural segmentation, the higher the number of autonomous intermediary groups, the more probable is a low level of intersubcultural hostility.

Hypothesis 2* is in no way refuted by the Swiss experience. First, the number of political parties in Switzerland is relatively high. It should be noted that the four parties forming the government at the federal level are actually independent, because each of these parties takes the liberty of opposing government policy at its discretion (Proposition 7). In addition to the four parties participating in the federal government, there are a considerable number of other parties with government responsibility at the cantonal or local levels (Proposition 10). Even parties that do not participate in government at any level because of their lack of sufficient support may have political relevance because of the referendum and the popular initiative. This relevance may only be potential (Proposition 11). Finally, it is important that the lower party levels are relatively autonomous in their dealings with the federal parties (Proposition 40).

The economic interest groups show a similar pluralism (Proposition 42). It should be remembered that the economic interest groups do not play the role of mere satellites of the parties, but have a considerable influence of their own (Proposition 47). The factors contributing to the influence of the economic interest groups are the following: (a) crosscutting rather than a *verzuiling* exists between the political parties and the economic interest groups (Proposition 48), (b) the economic interest groups can also articulate their demands to the system through direct channels of communication (Proposition 43), and (c) the economic interest groups usually have far more members, more financial resources, and more full-time officials than the political parties (Propositions 44, 45, and 46).

In addition to the political parties and the economic interest groups, a large number of voluntary associations also articulate demands to the political system in a relevant way (Proposition 54). Because most voluntary associations crosscut with the economic interest groups and the political parties, they have a relatively high degree of autonomy (Proposition 56). This autonomy is also increased by the fact that they can articulate demands to the system not only through parties and economic interest groups, but also through direct channels of communication (Proposition 55).

Switzerland has a high number of newspapers in relation to its population (Proposition 60). In spite of an increasing cooperation among newspapers, the centralization of the newspaper system is still relatively low in Switzerland in comparison with other countries (Proposition 61). In general, the newspapers are relatively autonomous and are not dominated by the political parties. Even newspapers affiliated with a political party occasionally choose to oppose the official party line (Proposition 63).

Only one corporation has a radio and television license (Proposition 67), but this corporation articulates its own demands to the political system only to a slight degree. The main function of radio and television is to serve as amplifiers for the articulation of the demands of the political parties, the economic interest groups, the voluntary associations, and the newspapers (Proposition 68).

By and large the number of political parties, economic interest groups, voluntary associations, and newspapers seems to be very high in Switzerland. Furthermore, most of these groups seem to have a relatively strong autonomy. Consequently, there is no evidence that Hypothesis 2* is refuted by the Swiss case. The political system of Switzerland seems to be characterized, in William Kornhauser's words, by "a plurality of independent and limited-function groups."[7]

Hypothesis 3*:

In a political system with strong subcultural segmentation, the more the major cleavages crosscut one another, the more probable is a low level of intersubcultural hostility.

Although there is usually a crosscutting rather than a *verzuiling* between political parties, economic interest groups, voluntary associations, and newspapers, an important exception exists with the trade unions, which show a strong *verzuiling* with different political parties (Proposition 49). Most political parties crosscut language groups, regions, and the cantons strongly, and religious and occupational groups somewhat less strongly (Proposition 15).

Switzerland is also characterized by a strong overlap between government and opposition parties in the sense that there are no distinctive lines between the two groups (Proposition 14). Most intermediary groups overlap strongly with the formal decision-makers of the system (Propositions 73 and 74), and there are strong tendencies to overlap between the federal, cantonal, and local levels of government (Proposition 77). Consequently, the evidence shows that Hypothesis 3* applies to Switzerland, where, in the words of Lipset, "groups and individuals have a number of crosscutting, politically relevant affiliations."[8]

Hypothesis 4*:

In a political system with strong subcultural segmentation, the less one of the subcultures has a hegemonial position, the more probable is a low level of intersubcultural hostility.

The strong crosscutting tendencies in Switzerland make for a multitude of subcultures. For example, since language and religious groups crosscut each other, a distinction has to be made in the French-speaking part of Switzerland between a Protestant and a Catholic subculture. Each of these subcultures is again divided into cantonal subcultures (Proposition 15).

It is important to emphasize that the phenomenon of crosscutting in Switzerland creates genuine subcultures rather than mere statistical groups. For example, it would seem that Protestants in the canton of Freiburg and German-speaking people in the canton of Wallis are genuine subcultures. Detailed study would be needed to determine the exact number of subcultures in Switzerland. In the present context, however, the main point is that crosscutting and subcultural segmentation do not necessarily exclude each other, as is frequently assumed. The Swiss example shows that it is not only possible to have a unidimensional segmentation, which by definition excludes major crosscuttings, but also a multidimentional segmentation. In summary, I agree with Arend Lijphart, who has described the relations among the Swiss subcultures in terms of "a multiple balance of power."

Hypothesis 4* might also explain the relatively high level of intersubcultural hostility in the Bernese Jura (Proposition 72). The people of the Jura are a minority subculture in practically every respect: they are French-speaking, predominantly Catholic, and a numerical minority within the canton of Berne. Consequently, the German-speaking part of the canton of Berne, which is predominantly Protestant, is perceived as a hegemonial subculture by the people of the Jura. According to Hypothesis 14* a situation of this kind would lead to the likelihood of high intersubcultural hostility, which is actually the case in the relationship between the Jura and the remainder of the canton of Berne.

Hypothesis 5*:

In a political system with strong subcultural segmentation, the less frequent the interactions among the nonelite of the various subcultures, the more probable is a low level of intersubcultural hostility.

Hypothesis 6*:

In a political system with strong subcultural segmentation, the more frequent the interactions among the elite of the various subcultures, the more probable is a low level of intersubcultural hostility.

Although it seems to me that Hypothesis 5* is to some degree refuted by the Swiss experience, Lijphart suggests the contrary in the following: "One important factor in the explanation of political stability in religiously and linguistically heterogeneous Switzerland is that many of the cantons, where much of the country's decentralized politics takes place, are quite homogeneous. For instance, the eight cantons and half-cantons of the Sonderbund plus Ticino and Appenzell-Inner-Rhoden are not only overwhelmingly Catholic, but also linguistically homogeneous with only two exceptions (Valais and Fribourg).)"[10]

According to Lijphart, the homogeneity of the cantons leads to "distinct lines of cleavage and . . . high internal cohesion."[11] It should be remembered that the Sonderbund existed in the first half of the nineteenth century and united the cantons representing the politically conservative wing of Catholicism. The cantons of the Sonderbund were internally homogeneous, and presented "distinct lines of cleavage" to the outside.

But it was exactly this cleavage structure that eventuated in hostility and violence, and led to the last civil war in Switzerland. Today the cantons are less set apart from one another. This development was hastened by increasing geographic mobility. In 1860, 88 percent of the population still lived in the canton of their birth, but in 1960 only 62.5 percent did so.[12] The increasing geographic mobility has made for a much greater mixture of religions and languages in the cantons. An outstanding example of this heterogeneity is the canton of Geneva, which used to be almost entirely French-speaking and Protestant; according to the 1970 census only 65 percent of the population was still French-speaking and only 38 percent was Protestant.[13]

In contrast to Lijphart's assumption, I conclude that there are no "distinct lines of cleavage" between the Swiss cantons. In general, the boundaries between the cantons and between other subcultures are relatively diffuse. Consequently, interactions between the various subcultures are also relatively frequent at the mass level. For instance, the cantonal, linguistic, religious, and party lines are intertwined in an extremely complicated way at the border between the cantons of Berne and Freiburg.

If we wish to examine interactions from outside the political realm, we might note that sports events do not often take place within subcultural boundaries. In gymnastics, for instance, the Swiss Workers' Gymnastics Association and the Swiss Catholic Gymnastics Association are relatively unimportant in comparison with the politically and religiously unaffiliated Federal Gymnastics Association, whose tournaments unite gymnasts from all Swiss subcultures. In a similar way, the federal shooting competitions and other sports events also bring about interactions on the nonelite level among the various subcultures. The army also serves to bring about contacts among the nonelite members of the different subcultures. Every physically fit Swiss man has to serve in the armed forces and also has to pass regular military courses until he is fifty. It should also be mentioned here that, after leaving school, many German-speaking Swiss spend a year with a French-speaking family, and this interaction, too, increases contacts among the subcultures.

In conclusion, it may be said that the following statement by Lijphart does not seem to apply to Switzerland: "Clear boundaries between subcultures have the advantage of limiting mutual contacts and, consequently, of limiting the chances of ever-present potential antagonisms from erupting into actual hostility."[14] What exactly does Lijphart understand by limited mutual contacts? How numerous should the interactions among nonelite members of the various subcultures be to qualify as "limited" in Lijphart's sense? As he does not give a precise answer to this question, it is difficult to test the hypothesis in a strict sense. This criticism also applies to Lorwin, who speaks of "few contacts" in the same context.[15]

Hypothesis 6*, however, seems to apply to Switzerland. Lijphart describes the conditions of "low" hostility as follows: "The leaders must be able to break through the barriers to mutual understanding caused by subcultural differences, and to establish effective contacts and communication across these cleavages."[16] The previously mentioned factors that lead to frequent interactions among the nonelite of the individual subcultures are also at work at the elite level. An important additional factor at the elite level, however, is the frequent accumulation of different elite roles. For instance, role accumulation can be found between (1) the various intermediary groups—the political parties, the economic interest groups, the voluntary associations, and the newspapers (Propositions 20, 50, 57, and 64); (2) the expert and generalist groups within the individual political parties and between the various party levels (Propositions 20, 37, and 40); and (3) the elite groups of the different intermediary groups and the formal decision-makers of the system (Propositions 20 and 73).

As a consequence of the frequent role accumulations and the crosscutting between the different subcultures, the subcultures of the political system of Switzerland are connected by relatively short channels of communication on the elite level. For example, there is a strong overlap between the Free Democratic party, on the one hand, and the Swiss Union of Artisans and the Swiss Farmers' Union, on the other. At the same time, there are many role accumulations between the two interest groups and the party. Therefore, this constellation makes it possible for the leading figures in the two interest groups to come together within the Free Democratic party. The Swiss Union of Artisans overlaps not only with the Free Democratic party, but also with the Christian Democratic party, and, as a consequence of that relationship, one can find leading representatives of the Free Democratic and the Christian Democratic parties within the Swiss Union of Artisans. Relatively short channels of communication also exist between the elite of the cantons, the religious groups, and the linguistic groups. The role accumulations act like relay stations to keep up the flow of communication among the elite of the various subcultures.

Hypothesis 7*:

> In a political system with strong subcultural segmentation, the lower the political participation at the mass level, the more probable is a low level of intersubcultural hostility.

Hypothesis 8*:

> In a political system with strong subcultural segmentation, the higher the political participation at the mass level, the more probable is a low level of intersubcultural hostility.

C. J. Friedrich restates Hypothesis 8* as follows: "Democracy must to a very considerable extent appeal to the efforts, and even the sacrifices, of the individual because it cannot persist without these efforts and sacrifices. Since the individual in a democracy is continuously drawn into state affairs, an interest in this community must of course be cultivated."[17] The most readily available indicator of political participation is the turnout in national parliamentary elections. In the five elections for the National Council between 1951 and 1971 the turnout fluctuated between 57 and 71 percent of the citizens. This is a relatively low figure in comparison with other countries. In referenda the average participation is considerably lower: only 46 percent of the population participated in the nineteen federal referenda from 1959 to 1967.[18] According to my calculations, the elite groups of all political parties at the federal level comprise a total of about 500 to 600 persons, which does not indicate a high level of participation (Proposition 19). If the lower party echelons are included in the total figure, the number of citizens who belong to the elite group of a party increases to about 5 percent of the adult population (Proposition 41).

On the basis of various indicators it has also been shown that the average citizen is generally not well informed about the political decision-making process, nor about the consequences of political decisions (Proposition 136). By and large my observations show that political participation is relatively low in Switzerland. It thus seems that a high political participation is not a necessary condition for a low degree of intersubcultural hostility. A look at the history of Switzerland shows that under certain conditions a high level of political participation may even go with a high level of violence: the highest turnout in a national election took place in 1919, the year after Switzerland experienced its last major violent confrontation with the general strike.[19] The Swiss experience does not show that a high level of political participation *causes* intersubcultural hostility, but it throws some doubt on the hypothesis that a high degree of political participation will lead to a low level of hostility among subcultures at all times.

Hypothesis 9*:

> In a political system with strong subcultural segmentation, the more congruent the role expectations between politics and other social fields, the more probable is a low level of intersubcultural hostility.

This hypothesis is further elaborated by Almond and Powell as follows: "In a stable political system the socialization process is usually homogeneous and consistent. The family authority pattern, the teacher-pupil relationship in schools, the interaction of employer and employee, and direct contacts with the political system tend to establish and maintain a given type of political orientation. . . . in a homogeneous process the elements influencing the individual do not seriously conflict either with each other or with his adult political activities and expectations."[20] Hypothesis 9* seems to apply to Switzerland because the pattern of conflict regulation used in the political area frequently is used in other social areas as well. I have shown that conflicts are predominantly regulated by amicable agreement not only in political parties, but also in economic interest groups, voluntary associations, and in other intermediary groups (Propositions 53 and 59). It is also important that the patterns of conflict regulation are usually relatively congruent between the local, the cantonal, and the federal levels (Proposition 40). There are no systematic data available about the regulation of conflicts in the private economic sector. But it may be of importance that there are frequent role accumulations between the private economic sector and the political arena. It may also be relevant in this context that there are many changes of positions from the private economic sector to the public administration, and vice versa. Both factors—the role accumulations and the change of positions between the political arena and the private economic sector—make it appear possible that conflicts in the private economic sector are not regulated much differently from the way they are regulated in the political sector. There are no systematic data about the regulation of conflict in schools and in families. Impressionistically, I have noted nothing in these areas that would seriously contradict Hypothesis 9*.

*Hypothesis 10**:

> In a political system with strong subcultural segmentation, the greater the opportunities for the articulation of dissent, the more probable is a low level of intersubcultural hostility.

Since all major political parties participate in government, elections do not generally constitute a very functional channel for the articulation of dissent. Abstaining from voting or voting for small nongovernment parties are the only means by which the citizens may articulate a certain amount of dissent in elections (Propositions 22 and 139). The many intermediary groups serve as relatively functional channels for the articulation of dissent (Proposition 22), but the referendum is the most functional means for the expression of dissent in Switzerland (Proposition 140). However, it should be noted that the referendum is not suitable to those who desire a change of the status quo because, as a consequence of a referendum, no action may be taken at all (Proposition 141). According to Almond and Powell, "Groups which have access to established nonviolent channels . . . are less likely to have to resort to violent behavior to transmit their demands."[21] Switzerland seems to be a case in point, and as such, confirms Hypothesis 10*.

*Hypothesis 11**:

> In a political system with strong subcultural segmentation, the lower the input of demands, the more probable is a low level of intersubcultural hostility.

Probably the most remarkable fact about Switzerland is that, because of its policy of neutrality, it is rather unburdened with demands in the foreign policy area. A stronger commitment in international politics would make the often great differences of opinion among the various subcultures with regard to foreign policy a heavy burden for the central government. The strongly federal structure of Switzerland is another factor that relieves the central government of problems. A clear indication of the federal structure may be found in the fact that only 33 percent of the gross public expenditures are spent by the federal government. An indicator from the *World Handbook of Political and Social Indicators* may also be mentioned here. It measures the ratio of centralization in government and is constructed by dividing Variable 1 by Variable 2:

Variable 1: the proportion of the aggregate expenditures of the central government, including social security and public enterprises, in relation to the gross national product

Variable 2: the general government revenue collected at all levels of government—local, regional, and national—in relation to the gross national product[22]

The centralization ratio indicator has a value of .60 for Switzerland, which indicates a very low centralization in comparison with the Federal Republic of Germany (.74), Austria (.84), Italy (.92), France (1.0), Great Britain (.94), and the United States (.77).

It is also important to note that, because of the strong cross-cutting tendency in the Swiss political system, interests are usually aggregated in a way such that many compromises are made within the intermediary groups before the matter reaches the governmental level (Propositions 1 through 78). Switzerland's political system is totally unlike the one in which "the only channels of communication between the two camps would be at the highest level—say when the leaders of the two camps meet in the governing chambers—and all conflict would have to be resolved at this highest level."[23] For example, we have seen that the various language groups often confront one another within the political parties, thereby making it unnecessary for the federal government to deal with the matter (Proposition 15).

If we agree that the small size of Switzerland probably contributes to a lighter load on the political system than other countries may experience, it may be concluded that the Swiss case offers no basis for refuting Hypothesis 11* in any way. In summary, Lijphart's remarks would apply directly to Switzerland: "Any system is more likely to be stable if it does not have to carry burdens that are too heavy. This is of particular significance in consociational systems. Here the management of subcultural cleavages is already a major burden requiring much of the leaders' energies and skills."[24]

*Hypothesis 12**:

In a political system with strong subcultural segmentation, the higher the educational and economic development, the more probable is a low level of intersubcultural hostility.

Most indicators show a high output performance of the political system of Switzerland (Proposition 134). Lipset's statement that "the more well-to-do a nation, the greater the chances that it will sustain democracy" is thus confirmed by the Swiss case.[25] The output performance of the political system of Switzerland is lowest in those areas characterized by a rapid development (Proposition 135).

Hypothesis 13:*

> In a political system with strong subcultural segmentation, the higher the pressures from the international system, the more probable is a low level of intersubcultural hostility.

As a religiously and linguistically mixed small state in a strategic location in the center of Europe, Switzerland was under strong international political pressure for centuries. Although this pressure has decreased with changing patterns in international politics in recent years, many citizens still see Switzerland as occupying a defensive position. If we agree that this defensive position engenders a feeling of solidarity in the citizenry, we would agree that Hypothesis 13* applies to Switzerland.

Hypothesis 14:*

> In a political system with strong subcultural segmentation, the stronger the norm of nonviolence, the more probable is a low level of intersubcultural hostility.

A social norm is strengthened if compliance with it is rewarded and noncompliance punished. When violent conflicts arose in the history of Switzerland, there was always the danger that the great powers of Europe would interfere. One reason for this was the strategic location of Switzerland. Another reason was that internal Swiss conflicts, especially about religion and language, often corresponded to the conflicts in the international system. Interference by the great powers always implied the danger that Switzerland would break down as a political system. In order to avoid this "punishment" the social norm was developed that internal conflicts should be regulated peacefully in the interest of the survival of Switzerland. The pattern of peaceful conflict resolution avoided not only "punishment" by the great powers, but also led to "rewards," since Switzerland was spared as an "island of peace" in the two world wars and also experienced a strong economic development during that time in history. It should be noted in particular that the relative absence of domestic turmoil probably contributed significantly to the fact that Switzerland was able to develop into an international financial center.

The norm of nonviolence developed not only because compliance was rewarded and noncompliance punished, but also because the idea of peaceful conflict resolution always had a high priority in Swiss history. When the federation was founded in 1291, the founding fathers agreed that "if strife should occur among the members of the Federation, then the wisest of the members of the Federation should make up the quarrel between the parties as they see fit."[26] Finally, it should be mentioned that certain institutions and figures in Switzerland—the Red Cross, Henri Dunant, Heinrich Pestalozzi, and Brother Klaus—symbolize the norm of nonviolence throughout the nation.

*Hypothesis 15**:

> In a political system with strong subcultural segmentation, the greater the number of traditional institutions that continue to exist, the more probable is a low level of intersubcultural hostility.

This hypothesis seems to apply to the Swiss case because the political development of Switzerland is characterized by an extraordinary continuity. Traditional institutions and concepts such as the referendum, federalism, neutrality, and a collegial form of government have deep roots in Switzerland.[27]

*Hypothesis 16**:

> In a political system with strong subcultural segmentation, the earlier the right to participate in the making of political decisions is extended to the whole population, the more probable is a low level of intersubcultural hostility.

Universal suffrage for men was introduced in Switzerland in 1848, a very early date when compared with other countries. However, women were given the right to vote only recently and in some rural cantons female suffrage has not yet been granted. Thus Hypothesis 16* does not seem to be applicable to Switzerland insofar as the extension of political rights to women is concerned.

CHAPTER IX

Linkages between the Hypotheses

So far I have dealt with the hypotheses as though there were no relationships between them. In this final chapter I will attempt to ascertain if such relationships exist. I agree with Lehmbruch and Lijphart that the predominant pattern of decision-making among the subcultures of a society is the key explanatory variable in the analysis of the conditions for a low level of intersubcultural hostility. I will now try to answer the following two questions:

1. Under what conditions does a subculturally strongly segmented political system tend toward the decision-making model of amicable agreement?
2. In a subculturally strongly segmented political system, is a decision-making pattern of amicable agreement a sufficient condition for a low level of intersubcultural hostility?

With regard to the first question, I wish to argue that the decision-makers are not altogether free to choose strategies of amicable agreement. There are certain conditions that make it very difficult, perhaps even impossible, to practice amicable agreement. I would like to suggest that these conditions have to do with the cleavage structure and the political role structure of the system. With regard to the second question, my argument is that amicable agreement can prevent high levels of intersubcultural hostility only under relatively rare conditions. More often amicable agreement may even be the cause of hostility because it endangers the innovation capacity of the system and lessens the opportunities for the articulation of dissent. Since majoritarian strategies also have severe shortcomings, the solution for a low level of hostility in a subculturally strongly segmented political system seems to be a mingling of both models.

1. CONDITIONS FOR AMICABLE AGREEMENT

First, I wish to look at the conditions for amicable agreement that have to do with the cleavage structure of the system.

Hypothesis 1:

In a political system with strong subcultural segmentation, the more there is a multitude of cleavages that crosscut one another, the more probable is amicable agreement the pattern of decision-making.

If there is more than one cleavage and if the cleavages crosscut one another, gains on one dimension may compensate for losses on another. The following diagram shows a linguistic cleavage with Language Groups L1 and L2 crosscutting a religious cleavage with Religious Groups R1 and R2. Suppose the members of such a system must decide on a new chief of government, and they elect a member of Language Group L1. Not all members of Language Group L2 have to consider this decision as a defeat. The chief of government will also be a member of a religious group and it is perfectly possible that he will belong to Religious Group R1, so that the members of Language Group L2 who belong to Religious Group R1 at least have the satisfaction of knowing that the new chief of government belongs to their religious group. The only people who will still be totally dissatisfied with the election are those who combine the characteristics of Language Group L2 and Religious Group R2. If there were a third cleavage along racial lines, for example, and if the third cleavage were to crosscut the other two cleavages, part of the dissatisfied group R2 L2 might belong to the same race as the new chief of government, further reducing the number of people who are completely dissatisfied with the decision.

	Language Group L1	Language Group L2
Religious Group R1	R1 L1	R1 L2
Religious Group R2	R2 L1	R2 L2

Because it is possible to compensate for gains and losses within the same decision, I predict that amicable agreement would be a relatively frequent pattern of decision-making when various cleavages crosscut one another. As a caveat I have to add that the hypothesis would not apply if one cleavage is perceived to be much more salient than the other(s). If, in the example above, race was perceived to be much more salient than language and religion, it would not make a real difference to the defeated race group whether or not the new chief of government belonged to their own language and/or religious groups.

If one cleavage is perceived to be much more salient than all others, the situation is about the same as it would be if there were only one cleavage. In the case of a single cleavage, it is often not possible to compensate for gains and losses within the same decision. If language is the only cleavage (or the only one that is perceived to be salient), the election of a new chief of government is a zero-sum game in which the victory of one language group is necessarily a defeat of the other language group(s). Even in such a case, however, it is possible to use the compensation factor. Thus a language group that loses the election for chief of government may possibly win the position of head of the state. Or it may be possible that a losing language group is compensated by a success in a later election. Such compensations, however, are relatively difficult to arrange. Consequently, I predict that amicable agreement would be a relatively infrequent pattern of decision-making in political systems with only one cleavage.

An interesting case that I have not yet discussed is the political system with two or more cleavages superimposed on one another. Superimposed cleavages in our example could mean that practically all members of Language Group L1 belong to the Religious Group R1, and those of Language Group L2 to Religious Group R2. Some scholars reserve the concept of *social fragmentation* for this particular phenomenon.[1] It is usually argued that such a cleavage structure makes it very difficult to attain decisions by amicable agreement. I accept that argument if the comparison is concerned with a crosscutting cleavage structure. I do not agree, however, if it is argued that decisions by amicable agreement are less likely with two or more superimposed cleavages than with a single cleavage. In fact, I would predict a difference in the opposite direction. If two or more cleavages are superimposed on one another, there are more opportunities to compensate for gains and losses within the same decision than there would be in a single-cleavage situation. The attempt to locate a new university may serve as an illustration. If there is only one cleavage—language, for example—the location of the new university is easily perceived in zero-sum terms. But if religion as a second cleavage is superimposed on the language cleavage, it is easier to compensate the losing subculture and thus to transform the zero-sum game into a positive-sum game. A compensating tactic in this case would be to include in the teaching program of the new university the religion of the subculture that has lost with regard to the location of the university.

I do not wish to overwork this argument. Basically, I do not predict great differences between political systems with two or more superimposed cleavages and those with a single cleavage. If there were to be any differences, I would predict that decisions by amicable agreement would be less frequent in systems with a single cleavage than in those with two or more superimposed cleavages. However, my main point is that the frequency of decisions by amicable agreement in both these situations would be much lower than in systems with a multitude of crosscutting cleavages.

Hypothesis 2:

> In a political system with strong subcultural segmentation, the higher the number of subcultures, the more probable is amicable agreement the pattern of decision-making.

The number of subcultures in a society is relatively independent of the number of cleavages in that society because a dimension or criterion of cleavage may be broken down in any number of subcultures. Thus there may be two or more groups in a religious cleavage. The argument for Hypothesis 2, then, is as follows: If there are only two subcultures, a gain for one is easily perceived as a loss for the other. With many subcultures, it is not very clear who loses if one of the subcultures improves its position. This may lead to a logrolling situation in which each subculture cares primarily about its own gains and nobody considers the possible costs of a decision. Let me illustrate this point with the example of segmentation along occupational lines. In a dual structure consisting of employers and employees, each group will tend to consider an improvement in the situation of the other as a decline in its own. On the other hand, if the occupational structure consists of many groups—farmers, artisans, workers, businessmen, etc.—often no one can tell who is paying the price if one of the groups improves its position. This situation would seem to favor decisions made by amicable agreement because no group would feel that it would have to suffer for any decision.

In game-theoretical terms one may say that with a small number of subcultures the political decision-making process is easily perceived as a zero-sum game. With an increasing number of subcultures, the political decision-making process tends to become a positive sum-game. In attempting to link Hypothesis 2 with the foregoing, I would predict a higher probability of amicable agreement in positive-sum games than in zero-sum games.

Hypothesis 3:

> In a political system with strong subcultural segmentation, the less one of the subcultures has a hegemonial position, the more probable is amicable agreement the pattern of decision-making.

Subcultural hegemony may be based on such factors as size, economic wealth, educational level, or military strength. Because it would appear self-evident that a hegemonial subculture would use its position to enforce its point of view, it would seem unnecessary to postulate Hypothesis 3. In some of the Swiss cantons, however, a political party may have an absolute majority but still work with the other parties through amicable agreement. It is even a rule in such cases that the majority party concedes a proportional representation in the government to the other parties. Thus Hypothesis 3 is not as unimportant as it may appear at first. Obviously, certain unusual conditions will lead to decisions by amicable agreement even if one of the subcultures has a hegemonial position (see Hypotheses 4 through 7). Generally speaking, however, a hegemonial subculture will tend to make decisions by majority rule.

Whether a political system with strong subcultural segmentation tends to make decisions more by amicable agreement or by majority rule probably depends not only on the cleavage structure of the system but also on its political role structure. Hypotheses 4 through 7, then, will consider the following variables: (1) political participation, (2) the circulation of incumbents in political leadership positions, (3) the accumulation of political leadership roles, and (4) the congruence between role expectations in politics and in other social fields. These variables probably influence decision-making patterns in any political system. In the present context, however, I am interested only in their relevance to political systems with strong subcultural segmentation.

Hypothesis 4:

> In a political system with strong subcultural segmentation, the more the decision-making process is restricted to persons occupying the highest political leadership positions, the more probable is amicable agreement the pattern of decision-making.

Before I can discuss Hypothesis 4 I will have to consider the differences between the following levels of decision-makers: (1) the general public, (2) the lower elite (the activists), and (3) the higher elite (the top leaders). The difference between the activists and the general public is that the activists hold some political positions and the public holds none. Thus the activists are engaged in a formal way in the political decision-making processes. However, even though they participate in the decision-making processes, the activists do not have a significant amount of power. This lack of power distinguishes them from the top leaders.[2] In the everyday decision-making processes a choice always has to be made between these two alternatives: should the decision-making process be restricted to the top leaders or should it include the activists as well? Within a political party, for example, it is necessary to decide whether a decision should be made by the Executive Committee or by the party convention. Whether or not the public should be included in the decision-making process is a question that does not usually come up at all. Thus it is the difference between the top leaders and the activists that is important for Hypothesis 4. I suggest that the top leaders have a more positive attitude than the activists toward amicable agreement. My arguments are derived from *socialization theory*, *group theory*, and *utility theory*. First, I would like to explain why I think the top leaders would support the norm of amicable agreement relatively strongly.

From the perspective of socialization theory, one might expect that the top leaders have learned on their way up the political ladder that many political problems are too complex to be resolved by a simple vote. They have seen in their political career that successful politics often consists of bargaining in terms of a mutual exchange of gains and losses. It may also be true that those who have learned to bargain outside the political arena have a better chance of entering the top political stratum. Those who reject the norm of bargaining are probably frequently screened out at lower levels in the career line.

Another reason why top leaders frequently prefer amicable agreement to majority rule derives from group theory. We may assume that top leaders interact more often among one another than activists do because the top leaders are less numerous and are more often engaged in politics. Frequent interactions may lead to personal friendships and even to a certain group solidarity among the top leaders. Too much insistence on majority rule may endanger group solidarity. As a rule, top leaders will prefer to resolve their conflicts by amicable agreement because it does not divide a winning group from a losing one and does not threaten group solidarity.

With regard to the argument that derives from utility theory, I assume that the top leaders have more power than the activists. I also assume that a predominant motivation of the top leaders is the desire to maximize their own political power.[3] I do not deny that the top leaders may also be interested in material rewards or in achieving group or community goals, but I believe that political power is their key motivation. If the top leaders have a relatively large amount of power and they want to maximize their power, a strategy of majority rule may be rather risky. It is true that such a strategy would allow the top leaders to be on the winning side of majoritarian decisions and thus to further increase their power. A majority decision, however, also carries the risk of one's being on the losing side. If the top leaders are rational people, and utility theory assumes that they are,[4] then they should be concerned more with possible losses than with possible gains because they have more to lose than to gain. Since they already have power, an additional amount of power is relatively insignificant, whereas the loss of power could seriously threaten their position. In view of this asymmetrical situation with regard to possible gains and losses, a strategy of amicable agreement seems the most rational choice. Such a strategy minimizes the possibility of heavy losses, since nobody is put into a losing minority position. It is true that a strategy of amicable agreement offers no spectacular gains. The gains cannot be reserved to a minimum-winning coalition but have to be distributed among all participants. However, this disadvantage should not concern most top leaders because as rational men they should be less interested in gaining more power than in preventing the loss of power.[5]

A second argument derives from utility theory. This argument assumes that in any political system the top leaders are less numerous than the activists. In modern democracies, applying the majority rule means accepting the "one man, one vote" principle. As a consequence of this principle, the influence of the top leaders is relatively weak on issues that are defined vertically if the issue has to come to a vote. Their influence is greater if a decision is made by amicable agreement because they are able to use their power resources more effectively than they can in a voting decision. Thus in vertically defined issues the top leaders would be expected to prefer decisions made by amicable agreement to those made by majority rule.

Of course, this argument would not apply to issues that are defined horizontally on the level of the top leaders. In such cases some top leaders may well anticipate that their weight would be greater in majoritarian decisions than in decisions made by amicable agreement. But even in such situations a top leader may sometimes prefer a strategy of amicable agreement because choosing a strategy of majority rule would break an important norm among his peer group. This norm-breaking could lead to sanctions by other top leaders that could be more significant than any benefits he might receive as a member of a winning majority. It would be silly to argue that top leaders never choose a strategy of majority rule. But, in the light of the arguments presented above, it seems probable that, in general, the top leaders would prefer to resolve political conflicts by amicable agreement than by majority rule.

I would now like to discuss the decision-making norms of the activists. From the perspective of socialization theory, it is important to note that, compared with the top leaders, activists participate relatively infrequently in political decision-making. Thus the socialization effect of taking part in the actual decision-making process is not as great for the activists as it is for the top leaders. The activists' norms of decision-making are probably shaped more by what they have learned in school and in the mass media than in the political arena. We may assume that in most Western countries the schools and the mass media usually identify democracy with majority rule.

Turning to the perspective of utility theory, we can probably not assume that activists generally have a strong desire to maximize political power. Many activists may primarily want to be near the power-holders and probably do not seek much power for themselves.[6] When activists have to take part in a political decision, their behavior is unlikely to be influenced by considerations of power. The least costly way for them to behave is to rely on the norms of decision-making to which they were socialized. In most cases this will be the norm that they have learned in school and from the mass media, namely, majority rule.

There are always some activists who try to climb the political ladder and who are thus interested in maximizing political power. They have two strategies available to them. They may choose a strategy of amicable agreement by imitating the behavior of the top leaders, or they may choose to use the majority principle and try to be a member of a minimum-winning coalition as often as possible. It would seem that power-seeking activists would have greater success with a strategy of amicable agreement because that strategy would not meet the resistance of the top leaders. Activists who tried to gain power by using the majority principle would frequently be screened out in the lower ranks.

With regard to group theory, it is important to note that interactions among activists are less frequent than they are among top leaders. Consequently, one may not expect activists to develop a group feeling across party lines similar to that of top leaders. The activists tend to identify only with their own party or even with a subgroup of the party. This means that in most political conflicts majority decisions would not disrupt the solidarity of their groups of reference.

In concluding these comments concerning Hypothesis 4, it seems that top leaders are more homogeneous than activists in their attitudes toward amicable agreement and majority rule. The attitudes of top leaders are characterized by a rather uniform support of amicable agreement. In general, activists seem to favor majority rule, but there seems to be considerable variation in their attitudes. Perhaps an explanation for this wide variation could be that the socialization experiences and the motivations for taking part in politics are much more heterogeneous among activists than among top leaders.[7]

Hypothesis 5:

> In a political system with strong subcultural segmentation, the less the incumbents in political leadership positions are circulated, the more probable is amicable agreement the pattern of decision-making.

Often a strategy of amicable agreement is applicable only if there is the possibility that losses in an earlier decision can be compensated by gains in a later decision. This presupposes explicit or implicit agreements over relatively long periods of time. Such arrangements are endangered if the holders of political leadership positions change often. Infrequent changes in political leadership positions create the best climate for a mutual exchange of long-term losses and gains.

Hypothesis 6:

> In a political system with strong subcultural segmentation, the higher the number of political role accumulations, the more probable is amicable agreement the pattern of decision-making.

This hypothesis is also based on the assumption that a strategy of amicable agreement can often be used only if losses in an earlier decision can be compensated by gains in a later decision. This exchange is made easier if the decision-makers interact in different roles. An example may clarify this point: If the leaders of a political party are also leaders in an economic interest group, losses that they might suffer in a party decision can be compensated by gains in a decision within the economic interest group, and vice versa. A caveat has to be made, however, with respect to political systems having a superimposed cleavage structure. In these cases Hypothesis 6 would apply only to decisions within the individual subcultures but not for those between the subcultures. If religion and social class are superimposed cleavages, for example, role accumulations between the church and a trade union should increase the probability of amicable agreement within the specific subculture but not across the subcultures. If, however, religion and social class are crosscutting cleavages, a high number of role accumulations should lead to more amicable agreement not only within the individual subcultures but also across the subcultures.

Hypothesis 7:

In a political system with strong subcultural segmentation, the more often role expectations in politics and in other social fields are congruent, the more probable is amicable agreement the pattern of decision-making.

If role expectations in politics roughly equal those in other social areas, a relatively high role security in politics would result because the participants would already have engaged in similar activities outside the political arena. A high role security is probably an important condition for the successful use of a strategy of amicable agreement. As we have already seen, this strategy often works only if the participants can compensate for losses in an earlier decision by gains in a later decision. This presupposes—and this was the basis for Hypotheses 5 and 6—that the participants in a particular decision meet again later on. But it also presupposes a trust that losses in a decision are in fact compensated by later gains. The probability of such a trust should be higher if the participants have a certain role security because it makes their behavior more predictable. A high predictability in the behavior of the participants is probably one of the most important conditions for the development of mutual trust.

An objection to Hypothesis 7 may be that a strongly held majoritarian norm both in politics and in other social fields does not contribute to amicable agreement. Although that may be true in terms of a short-range perspective, I would expect that a high congruence would lead to such a high predictability of behavior and mutual trust that patterns of amicable agreement might develop in the long run. My general argument is that a high congruence in role expectation contributes to amicable agreement whatever the substance of the role expectations might be. I am aware that this argument—like many others in this book—is highly speculative and can only be confirmed by thorough empirical tests.

I will now combine Hypotheses 1 through 7 by setting up conditions for models that tend toward amicable agreement or majority rule.

AMICABLE AGREEMENT MODEL

Cleavage Structure: There are many cleavages and all of them crosscut one another. Each cleavage is broken down into several subcultures, giving rise to a high total number of subcultures with none of them having a hegemonial position.

Political Role Structure: The political decision-making process is generally restricted to the top leaders. The political leadership positions change infrequently. The number of political role accumulations is high. Role expectations in politics and other social fields are rather congruent.

MAJORITY RULE MODEL

Cleavage Structure: There is only one cleavage and it is broken down into only two subcultures with one of them having a strongly hegemonial position.

Political Role Structure: The political decision-making process is frequently extended to lower elite levels. The political leadership positions change frequently. The number of political role accumulations is low. Role expectations in politics and other social fields are rather incongruent.

---

2. AMICABLE AGREEMENT AND HOSTILITY AMONG SUBCULTURES

Now that we have discussed the conditions of amicable agreement in a subculturally strongly segmented political system, we have to look at the relationship between amicable agreement and intersubcultural hostility. At first glance it seems self-evident that decision-making patterns of amicable agreement lead to a low level of hostility. This is certainly true in short-range terms. In the long run, however, too much emphasis on amicable agreement may contribute to an increase in hostility among subcultures. In the following diagram I would like to introduce three intervening variables between amicable agreement and intersubcultural hostility: the perceived equity among subcultures, the perceived innovation capacity of the system, and the perceived opportunities for the articulation of dissent.

So far as equity among subcultures is concerned, I am dealing not with an objective criterion of equity, but with the perception of equity.[8] Members of a subculture may well perceive themselves as discriminated against even if an objective criterion—per capita income, for example—is presented as contradictory evidence. On the other hand, members of a subculture may not perceive themselves as discriminated against even if an objective criterion indicates discrimination. Similarly,

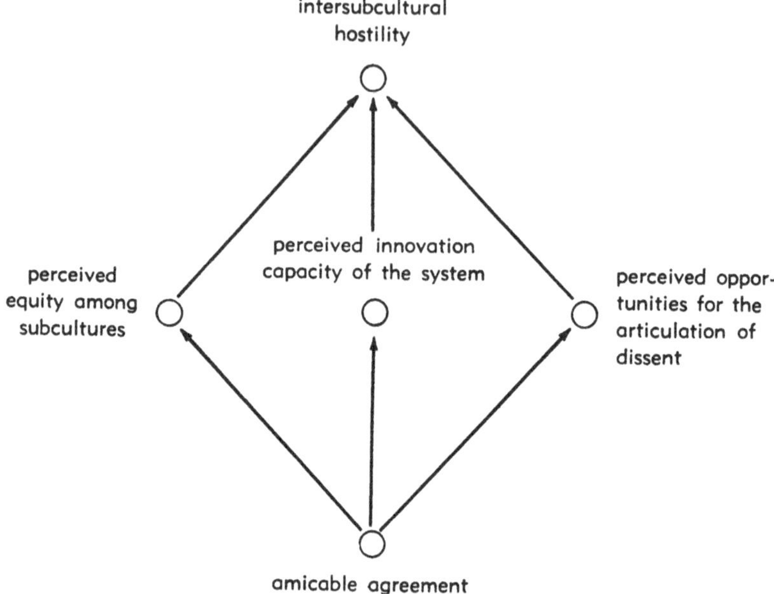

perceptions rather than objective criteria are being considered in the analysis of the innovation capacity of the system and the opportunities for articulation of dissent. As indicated in the diagram, the relationship between the perception variables and intersubcultural hostility is as follows:

Hypothesis 8:

The greater the perceived equity among subcultures, the greater the perceived innovation capacity of the system, and the greater the perceived opportunities for the articulation of dissent, the more probable is a low level of intersubcultural hostility.

The relationship between the perceived equity among subcultures and intersubcultural hostility is self-evident and needs no further explanation. But it may not be immediately cleaı why a low innovation capacity and few opportunities for the articulation of dissent should lead to a high level of intersubcultural hostility. This phenomenon may be explained by frustration-aggression theories. Most of the people who perceive that their political system has a low innovation capacity and that the opportunities for dissent are severely restricted are probably frustrated. This frustration leads to aggressive feelings. Frustration-aggression theories have demonstrated that there are many different ways to handle aggressive feelings. They may be sublimated or directed against all sorts of targets. In this case, other subcultures may easily be chosen as such targets even if they have nothing to do with the original frustration.[9]

How does amicable agreement affect the perceived equity among subcultures, the perceived innovation capacity of the system, and the perceived opportunities for the articulation of dissent? Hypotheses 9 through 11 will deal with this question.

Hypothesis 9:

The more often the pattern of decision-making is amicable agreement, the higher is the perceived equity among subcultures.

This hypothesis may seem a bit tautological. It is not certain, however, that decisions by amicable agreement always mean that none of the subcultures perceives itself as discriminated against. A subculture may perceive a particular solution as unfair, but may accept it nevertheless because it anticipates that all other solutions would result in even greater discrimination. Thus decisions by amicable agreement do not necessarily mean that no subculture perceives itself as discriminated against. It is also doubtful that majority rule automatically leads to the discrimination of some subcultures. The advocates of the majority principle argue exactly in the opposite direction, namely, that a regular change in the majorities guarantees that no subculture is discriminated against in the long run. The foregoing discussion shows that Hypothesis 9 is not at all tautological, but that it needs to be tested empirically. The rationale for Hypothesis 9 is the assumption that the application of the majority principle does not guarantee that all subcultures get power at regular intervals. Blacks in the United States and Catholics in Northern Ireland are examples of this inequity. As I have argued above, the principle of amicable agreement may also lead to discrimination against minorities, since they may be offered no solutions that would not discriminate against them. However, I expect that such cases are rare. A subculture that perceives itself as permanently discriminated against will refuse to take part in decisions by amicable agreement after a certain time. It will, so to speak, quit playing the game. If the other subcultures have a real interest in maintaining a strategy of amicable agreement, they will tend to make decisions so that no subculture perceives itself as permanently discriminated against.

Hypothesis 10:

> The more often the pattern of decision-making is amicable agreement, the lower is the perceived innovation capacity of the system.

If strategies of amicable agreement prevail, innovative political behavior is difficult to maintain because the consensus of all participants is always needed. Therefore, many decisions may be delayed for a considerable amount of time. More important, though, is that each subculture practically has a veto power in the sense that it can prevent any innovation by opposing it. An objection to Hypothesis 10 may be that majority rule does not increase the innovation capacity either if the majority is strongly status quo oriented. This is certainly true, but in such cases decisions by amicable agreement would be marked by a similar handicap. If the majority is not innovative, it can prevent innovations no matter which pattern of decision-making is being used. What Hypothesis 10 is saying is that the opportunity for innovation is lowest with amicable agreement because the least innovative group always has a kind of veto power.

Hypothesis 11:

> The more often the pattern of decision-making is amicable agreement, the lower are the perceived opportunities for the articulation of dissent.

In a political system in which the majority principle dominates, dissatisfaction with the government can be articulated by a vote for the opposition. A good showing by the opposition may lead to the overthrow of the government. Even if the opposition remains in a minority position, an increase in its electoral strength may easily be interpreted as dissatisfaction with the government, which may then change its policies. If, on the other hand, the principle of amicable agreement dominates, dissent can hardly be voiced through elections. In Switzerland, where all major parties are represented in the government, the citizenry can express dissatisfaction with government policy only by abstaining from voting or by voting for one of the small parties. Both forms of dissent are so difficult to interpret that they usually have no major consequences. However, the referendum and the popular initiative are highly developed forms of expressions of dissent in Switzerland, and they compensate for the lack of meaningful opportunity to express dissent in elections. If such a corrective mechanism is missing in a society (the Great Coalition in the Federal Republic of Germany during 1966–69 is an example in point), a consequence of frequent decisions by amicable agreement among the major parties may be that many citizens feel that they have no real opportunities to articulate dissent.

Hypotheses 8 through 11 and the diagram on page 276 are evidence that the decision-making pattern of amicable agreement has conflicting effects on the level of intersubcultural hostility. To determine the overall effect, it is necessary to specify the relative weight of the three intervening variables. I assume that this cannot be done in a general way, but that the weight of the three intervening variables depends at least on the following two conditions: the political interest by the general public and the number of new political problems. Combining these two conditions, I would like to offer the following two models because they seem particularly interesting for the present discussion:

> *Model A:* The general public has little interest in politics. There are few new political problems.
>
> *Model B:* The general public has a strong interest in politics. There are many new political problems.

In Model A the innovation capacity of the system is relatively unimportant because most political problems are structured in a traditional way. Because the public has little interest in politics, the opportunities for articulating dissent are not important either. However, it is crucial to Model A that no subculture perceives itself as discriminated against. According to Hypothesis 9, this goal can best be reached through a strategy of amicable agreement. Consequently, under the conditions of Model A, the relationship between amicable agreement and the level of intersubcultural hostility can be stated according to the terms of Hypothesis 12.

Hypothesis 12:

> If the general public has little interest in politics and if there are only few new political problems, a strategy of amicable agreement will most probably lead to a low level of intersubcultural hostility.

In Switzerland in the 1950s and the early 1960s the political interest of the general public was relatively low and most political problems were structured in a traditional way. In order to maintain low hostility among subcultures, the government's main concern was to make sure that no subculture perceived itself as discriminated against. This goal was attained relatively easily by a strategy of amicable agreement. In the last few years Switzerland has moved in the direction of Model B: political interest, especially among the younger generation, has increased, and there has been a sharp increase in new political problems. Switzerland's relationship with the European Community, the high number of foreign workers, and difficulties with pollution are some of the new problems that have recently beset the government. The political decision-making process, however, is still strongly dominated by the principle of amicable agreement. This pattern of decision-making has led to increased frustrations because more and more people are realizing that amicable agreement prevents innovations and makes the articulation of dissent difficult. There have also been indications that such frustrations may be projected onto other subcultures, thereby leading to higher intersubcultural hostility. It could be concluded that, under the conditions of Model B, amicable agreement may even be the *cause* of hostility among subcultures because the innovation capacity and the opportunities for the articulation of dissent receive an increased importance. Majoritarian strategies under Model B would also probably lead to intersubcultural hostility because some subcultures might perceive themselves as discriminated against (Hypothesis 9). I suggest that a combination of majority rule and amicable agreement may minimize the negative effects of either of the two strategies. This suggestion is expressed in Hypothesis 13.

Hypothesis 13:

> If the general public has a strong interest in politics and if there are many new political problems, a combination of majority rule and amicable agreement will most probably lead to a low level of intersubcultural hostility.

This hypothesis does not yet answer the question of what a combination of majority rule and amicable agreement may mean in practical terms. The decision-makers in Switzerland are confronted with this problem and are making serious efforts to include more majoritarian elements in the current decision-making structure. Thus in its platform in the national election of 1971 the Christian Democratic party demanded that the principle of having all major parties represented in the federal government be abandoned. However, the other parties felt that this proposal would be going too far in the direction of the majoritarian model. Currently, the parties are trying to come up with other solutions that would better guarantee an equilibrium between amicable agreement and majority rule. A close observation of these developments should clarify what a combination of amicable agreement and majority rule would mean in practical terms and enable us to further refine Hypothesis 13.

3. SOME APPLICATIONS TO THE EUROPEAN COMMUNITY

The theoretical model presented in this paper was mainly developed with Switzerland and some Swiss cantons as the empirical base. Tests with other countries will reveal the value of this model as an interpretive tool. As Rokkan states in the foreword to this study, "Switzerland presents a microcosm of Europe. . . . every . . . study of Switzerland is a contribution to the study of the political structure of Europe." It would seem to be of particular interest, then, to test the European Community against this model, since the Community is certainly a subculturally strongly segmented political system. I would like to use the model developed so far to give tentative answers to the following two questions:

1. *Should* the European Community choose the model of amicable agreement?
2. *Could* the European Community choose the model of amicable agreement?

These questions need not necessarily be answered in the same ways. It may be that the European Community *should* practice amicable agreement; however, contextual conditions may prevent it from doing so. It is also possible that the European Community *could* easily practice amicable agreement, but should not do so. First of all, are conditions in the European Community such that amicable agreement could be practiced? We have to look both at the cleavage structure and the political role structure of the Community. With regard to the cleavage structure, the most favorable condition for amicable agreement would be a multitude of crosscutting cleavages giving rise to a great many subcultures with none of them having a hegemonial position. The most unfavorable condition for amicable agreement would be a single cleavage line dividing two subcultures with one of them having a strongly hegemonial position. The unfavorable condition could come about, for example, if the cleavage between socialist and nonsocialist parties was to become the only salient cleavage and if one of the two groups were to hold a strongly hegemonial position. Another unfavorable condition could be if the only salient cleavage were between the Romance- and Germanic-language groups with one of them having a strongly hegemonial position. The same argument could be made with religion as the only salient cleavage. Conditions favorable to amicable agreement would be met by these cleavages having roughly equal importance and crosscutting one another. This cleavage structure would give rise to a great number of subcultures—"German-speaking Catholics" or "French-speaking Socialists," for example. It would also be important for conditions of amicable agreement that none of these subcultures develop a hegemonial position.

It would seem that the present cleavage structure and the political role structure of the European Community favors amicable agreement. Its decision-making process is narrowly restricted to top leaders and more or less excludes the activists. The main decision-makers keep their positions for relatively long periods of time. It also seems that the number of political role accumulations is quite high. The most unfavorable condition for amicable agreement is probably that role expectations in the political arena in Brussels are often not very congruent with role expectations in other social arenas—the business world, for example. Overall, the present cleavage and political role structure of the European Community seem to favor amicable agreement. There are also indications that decision-making in the European Community often operates by amicable agreement in the sense that discussion is continued until a solution is found which is acceptable to all participants. Of course, these few observations cannot be considered tests of the theoretical model. Nevertheless, it may be significant that this first brief overview has revealed nothing that would clearly contradict the conditions for amicable agreement set forth in the hypotheses.

Let me now address myself to the question of whether the European Community *should* practice amicable agreement. An answer cannot be given in absolute terms, but only in view of certain normative goals. Let us assume that a low level of hostility among the subcultures of the Community is an important normative goal. The model should then allow us to judge whether decision-making strategies using amicable agreement contribute to this goal. If Hypothesis 12 were viable, amicable agreement would contribute to this goal only if the input of new political problems is low and if the general public has little interest in politics. The first condition seems to apply to a certain extent because many problems are still dealt with in the Community at the national level. The second condition probably applies because public interest in Community matters seems relatively low. The presence of these two conditions could explain why intersubcultural hostility in the Community is relatively low.

However, things are changing rapidly. The Community is burdened with increasing problems—monetary questions, foreign policy, and so on—and there are also indications that the general public is becoming more concerned with what is going on in Brussels. Under these changed conditions strategies of amicable agreement may damage the innovation capacity and the opportunities for the articulation of dissent so much that in the long run intersubcultural hostility may develop. According to our model, majoritarian strategies would also present severe shortcomings in a political system with strong subcultural segmentation because some subcultures would never be able to be part of a winning majority. A combination of the two models seems to be a third alternative for the solution of conflicts.

Unfortuantely, such a recommendation would be much too abstract for the politicians. Should all important subcultures be represented permanently in a European government? Must the criterion of unanimity or near-unanimity apply to certain decisions? Should the referendum and the popular initiative be introduced to counterbalance the effects of strategies of amicable agreement as they are in Switzerland? Research-based answers to such concrete questions are not yet available. It should be rewarding to continue research along these lines with concentration not only on the majoritarian model and the model of amicable agreement but also on various models that combine strategies of amicable agreement and majority rule.

At the same time, a closer linkage should be made with normative questions of democratic theory. We have assumed that low hostility among subcultures is an important normative goal for the European Community. But this particular goal may conflict with other valuable goals. One may argue, for example, that a high level of political participation is a more important value than a low level of intersubcultural hostility. Those who make this point argue that taking part in political decision-making processes contributes to the self-actualization of human beings.[10] Thus political participation would be such an important goal that it could not easily be sacrificed to the goal of a low level of hostility among subcultures.

If empirical research could clearly demonstrate the causal relationship between such variables as political participation, decision-making strategies, intersubcultural hostility, and so on, it would become easier for normative theories to take account of the possible costs of their policy recommendations.

APPENDIXES
NOTES
INDEX

APPENDIXES

IMPORTANT SWISS INSTITUTIONS

A. *Political Parties*

Anti-Alien party: Nationale Aktion gegen die Ueberfremdung von Volk und Heimat
Christian Democratic party: Christlich-demokratische Partei
Communist party: Partei der Arbeit
Democratic party: Demokratische Partei
Farmer, Artisan, and Bourgeois party: Bauern-, Gewerbe- und Buergerpartei
Free Democratic party: Freisinnig-demokratische Partei
Independent party: Landesring der Unabhaengigen
Liberal Democratic party: Liberal-demokratische Partei
Protestant party: Evangelische Partei
Republican party: Republikanische Bewegung
Social Democratic party: Sozialdemokratische Partei
Swiss People's party: Schweizerische Volkspartei

B. *Economic Interest Groups*

Swiss Farmers' Union: Schweizerischer Bauernverband
Swiss Federation of Clerical Employees' Unions: Vereinigung Schweizerischer Angestelltenverbaende
Swiss Federation of Employers' Organizations: Zentralverband Schweizerischer Arbeitgeberorganisationen
Swiss Federation of Trade Unions: Schweizerischer Gewerkschaftsbund
Swiss National Federation of Christian Trade Unions: Christlich-Nationaler Gewerkschaftsbund der Schweiz
Swiss Union of Artisans: Schweizerischer Gewerbeverband
Swiss Union of Commerce and Industry: Schweizerischer Handels- und Industrieverein
Swiss Union of Protestant Employees: Schweizerischer Verband Evangelischer Arbeitnehmer
Union of Free Swiss Workers: Landesverband Freier Schweizer Arbeiter

C. *Departments in the Federal Administration*

Department of Defense: Militaerdepartement
Department of Economic Affairs: Volkswirtschaftsdepartement
Department of Finance and Customs: Finanz- und Zolldepartement
Department of Foreign Affairs: Politisches Departement
Department of the Interior: Departement des Innern
Department of Justice and Police: Justiz-und Polizeidepartement
Department of Transport and Energy: Verkehrs- und Energiewirtschaftsdepartement

D. Other Governmental Units and Special Terms

Canton: Kanton
Convention: Delegiertenversammlung
Council of States: Staenderat
Executive Committee: Geschaeftsleitung
Federal Assembly: Bundesversammlung
Federal Council: Bundesrat
Federation: Bund, Eidgenossenschaft
Local community: Gemeinde
National Council: Nationalrat
Parliamentary group: Parlamentsfraktion
Popular Initiative: Volksinitiative
Referendum: Referendum

E. Translator's Note

Unless an English name is available for a canton or community, the language of the specific canton or community in question is used in this book.

TABLE 1. POPULATION IN SWITZERLAND SINCE 1850

Year	Population
1850	2,392,740
1860	2,510,494
1870	2,655,001
1880	2,831,787
1888	2,917,754
1900	3,315,443
1910	3,753,293
1920	3,880,320
1930	4,066,400
1941	4,265,703
1950	4,714,992
1960	5,429,061
1970	6,269,783

Source: *Statistisches Jahrbuch der Schweiz 1972*, p. 12.

TABLE 2. POPULATION IN SWITZERLAND BY LANGUAGE SINCE 1910 (IN PERCENTAGES)

Year	German	French	Italian	Romansch	Other
1910	69.1	21.1	8.1	1.1	0.6
1920	70.9	21.3	6.1	1.1	0.6
1930	71.9	20.4	6.0	1.1	0.6
1941	72.6	20.7	5.2	1.1	0.4
1950	72.1	20.3	5.9	1.0	0.7
1960	69.3	18.9	9.5	0.9	1.4
1970	64.9	18.1	11.9	0.8	4.3

Source: *Statistisches Jahrbuch der Schweiz 1972*, p. 29.

TABLE 3. POPULATION IN SWITZERLAND BY RELIGION SINCE 1910 (IN PERCENTAGES)

Year	Protestants	Catholics	Others
1910	56.1	42.5	1.4
1920	57.5	40.9	1.6
1930	57.3	41.0	1.7
1941	57.6	41.1	1.3
1950	56.3	42.2	1.5
1960	52.7	45.9	1.4
1970	47.8	49.7	2.5

Source: *Statistisches Jahrbuch der Schweiz 1972*, p. 30.

NOTES

CHAPTER I

1. Robert A. Dahl, ed., *Political Oppositions in Western Democracies* (New Haven: Yale University Press, 1966), p. 371.

2. This formula measures "how many pairs of members find themselves at odds over any given cleavage" (Douglas W. Rae and Michael Taylor, *The Analysis of Political Cleavages* [New Haven: Yale University Press, 1970], p. 3).

3. See, for example, Erwin Bucher, "Die Entwicklung der Schweiz zu einem politischen System," in *Das politische System der Schweiz*, ed. Jürg Steiner (Munich: Piper, 1971), pp. 13–50.

4. Stein Rokkan, "The Growth and Structuring of Mass Politics in Western Europe: Reflections of Possible Models of Explanation" (Paper delivered at the Round Table Conference on Comparative Politics of the International Political Science Association, Turin, 1969).

5. William R. Keech, "Linguistic Diversity and Political Conflict: Some Observations Based on Four Swiss Cantons," *Comparative Politics* 4 (1972): 387–404.

6. Eric A. Nordlinger, *Conflict Regulation in Divided Societies*, Harvard University Occasional Papers in International Affairs, no. 29 (Cambridge, Mass., 1972).

7. Gerhard Lehmbruch, "A Non-Competitive Pattern of Conflict Management in Liberal Democracies: The Case of Switzerland, Austria, and Lebanon" (Paper delivered at the Seventh World Congress of the International Political Science Association, Brussels, 1967).

8. Arend Lijphart, "Typologies of Democratic Systems" (Paper delivered at the Seventh World Congress of the International Political Science Association, Brussels, 1967); idem, *The Politics of Accommodation: Pluralism and Democracy in the Netherlands* (Berkeley and Los Angeles: University of California Press, 1968).

9. Arend Lijphart, "Cultural Diversity and Theories of Political Integration," *Canadian Journal of Political Science* 4 (1971):9.

10. William T. Bluhm, "Political Integration, Cultural Integration, and Economic Development: Their Relationship in the Nation-building Experience of Republican Austria" (Paper delivered at the Eighth World Congress of the International Political Science Association, Munich, 1970).

11. Lehmbruch, "Conflict Management."

12. Richard Reich, "Image und Stellenwert der schweizerischen Parteien in der heutigen Politik," *Schweizerisches Jahrbuch fuer Politische Wissenschaft* 9 (1969):7–20.

13. In the Peace of Westphalia in 1648 the term *amicabilis compositio* was used for the relationship between Protestants and Catholics.

14. I am not dealing here with models of nondemocratic decision-making such as minority rule by military means.

15. Anthony Downs, *An Economic Theory of Democracy* (New York: Harper & Row, 1957), p. 24.

16. William Levine, "Ethnicity and Integration in Tropical Africa: The Response to Colonial Penetration" (Ph.D. diss., University of Chicago, 1972).

17. William H. Riker, *The Theory of Political Coalitions* (New Haven: Yale University Press, 1962), p. 40.

18. Richard Rose, *Politics in England* (Boston: Little, Brown and Co., 1964), pp. 220–21.

19. For this hypothesis and those that follow the asterisk indicates an *initial* hypothesis. The *final* hypotheses of the study will stand without asterisks.

20. Lehmbruch, "Conflict Management"; Lijphart, *Politics of Accommodation.*

21. William Kornhauser, *The Politics of Mass Society* (New York: Free Press, 1959), pp. 230–31; Seymour Martin Lipset, *Political Man: The Social Bases of Politics* (New York: Doubleday & Co., 1960), p. 67.

22. David B. Truman, *The Governmental Process* (New York: Alfred A. Knopf, 1951), pp. 169, 535; Bernard R. Berelson, Paul F. Lazarsfeld, and William N. McPhee, *Voting: A Study of Opinion Formation in a Presidential Campaign* (Chicago: University of Chicago Press, 1954), pp. 318–23; Robert A. Dahl, *A Preface to Democratic Theory* (Chicago: University of Chicago Press, 1956), pp. 104–5; Talcott Parsons, "Voting and the Equilibrium of the American Political System," in *American Voting Behavior*, ed. Eugene Burdick and Arthur J. Brodbeck (Glencoe, Ill.: Free Press, 1959), pp. 92–93; Lipset, *Political Man*, pp. 86–90; V. O. Key, Jr., *Politics, Parties, and Pressure Groups* (New York: Thomas Y. Crowell Co., 1964), p. 144; Stein Rokkan, "Norway: Numerical Democracy and Corporate Pluralism," in *Political Oppositions*, ed. Dahl, pp. 113–14; Dankwart A. Rustow, "Democracy, Consensus, and the New States" (Paper delivered at the Seventh World Congress of the International Political Science Association, Brussels, 1967), p. 10.

23. Lijphart, "Democratic Systems," pp. 35–36; Lehmbruch, "Conflict Management," p. 8.

24. Quincy Wright, "The Nature of Conflict," *Western Political Quarterly* 4 (1951):196; Val R. Lorwin, "Belgium: Religion, Class, and Language in National Politics," in *Political Oppositions*, ed. Dahl, p. 187; Lijphart, "Democratic Systems," pp. 29–30.

25. Robert A. Dahl, *Modern Political Analysis* (Englewood Cliffs, N.J.: Prentice-Hall, 1963), p. 77; Lijphart, "Democratic Systems," pp. 29–30; Gerhard Lehmbruch, "Segmented Pluralism and Political Strategies in Continental Europe: Internal and External Conditions of Concordant Democracy" (Paper delivered at the Round Table Conference on Comparative Politics of the International Political Science Association, Turin, 1969), p. 4.

26. Francis G. Wilson, "The Inactive Electorate and Social Revolution," *Southwestern Social Science Quarterly* 16 (1936):76–84; W. H. Morris-Jones, "In Defense of Apathy," *Political Studies* 2 (1954):25; Berelson et al., *Voting*, pp. 305–23; Morris Janowitz, "Die soziologischen Voraussetzungen der Theorie der Demokratie," *Koelner Zeitschrift fuer Soziologie und Sozialpsychologie* 8 (1956):365; Eugene Burdick, "Political Theory and the Voting Studies," in *American Voting Behavior*, ed. Burdick and Brodbeck, pp. 136–49.

27. Werner Kaegi, *Direkte Demokratie in Gefahr*, Swiss Teacher's Association Series, no. 32 (Zurich, 1958), pp. 14–15; Carl Joachim Friedrich, *Demokratie als Herrschafts- und Lebensform* (Heidelberg: Quelle & Meyer, 1959), p. 78; Otto Woodtli, *Erziehung zur Demokratie: Der politische Auftrag des hoeheren Bildungswesens in der Schweiz* (Erlenbach-Zurich: Rentsch, 1961), p. 215; Hans Huber, "Die schweizerische Demokratie," in *Die Demokratie im Wandel der Gesellschaft*, ed. Richard Loewenthal (Berlin: Colloquium-Verlag, 1963), p. 108.

28. Harry Eckstein, *Division and Cohesion in Democracy: A Study of Norway* (Princeton: Princeton University Press, 1966), p. 234; Giovanni Sartori, "European Political Parties: The Case of Polarized Pluralism," in *Political Parties and Political Development*, ed. Joseph LaPalombara and Myron Weiner (Princeton: Princeton University Press, 1966), pp. 137–76; Gabriel A. Almond and G. Bingham Powell, *Comparative Politics: A Developmental Approach* (Boston: Little, Brown and Co., 1966), pp. 69–70.

29. Almond and Powell, *Comparative Politics*, p. 82; Ted Robert Gurr, *Why Men Rebel* (Princeton: Princeton University Press, 1970), p. 365.

30. Lijphart, "Democratic Systems," pp. 39–40; Lehmbruch, "Segmented Pluralism," p. 6.

31. Lipset, *Political Man*, pp. 48–60; Dahl, *Modern Political Analysis*, p. 79; Phillips Cutright, "National Political Development: Social and Economic Correlates," in *Politics and Social Life*, ed. Nelson W. Polsby, Robert A. Dentler, and Paul A. Smith (Boston: Houghton Mifflin Co., 1963), pp. 569–82; Lijphart, "Democratic Systems," p. 30.

32. Lijphart, "Democratic Systems," pp. 37–38; Lehmbruch, "Conflict Management," p. 4.

33. Lipset, *Political Man*, p. 45; Dahl, *Modern Political Analysis*, pp. 83–84; Arnold S. Feldmann, "Violence and Volatility: The Likelihood of Revolution," in *Internal War: Problems and Approaches*, ed. Harry Eckstein (Glencoe, Ill.: Free Press, 1964), p. 123; Almond and Powell, *Comparative Politics*, p. 91; Lijphart, "Democratic Systems," pp. 29, 36–37; Lehmbruch, "Conflict Management," pp. 5–6; Gurr, *Why Men Rebel*, pp. 360–67.

34. Lipset, *Political Man*, pp. 78–79.

35. Ibid., pp. 79–80.

36. Almond and Powell, *Comparative Politics*, p. 29.

37. Elsewhere Almond and Powell take the same position: "Communication pervades the entire political process, and we cannot adequately consider the interest articulation structures without noting the specific communication structures available for the expression of political demands" (*Comparative Politics*, p. 80).

38. Ibid., pp. 25–27.

39. David Easton, *A Systems Analysis of Political Life* (New York: John Wiley & Sons, 1965), pp. 153–70; see also John C. Wahlke, "Public Policy and Representative Government: The Role of the Represented" (Paper delivered at the Seventh World Congress of the International Political Science Association, Brussels, 1967).

40. David E. Apter, "Political Systems and Developmental Change" (Paper delivered at the Seventh World Congress of the International Political Science Association, Brussels, 1967), p. 5.

41. Jürg Steiner, *Die Beziehungen zwischen den Stimmberechtigten und den Gewaehlten in laendlichem und staedtischem Milieu: Versuch einer staatssoziologischen Untersuchung am Beispiel des Grossen Rates des Kantons Bern* (Berne-Stuttgart: Paul Haupt, 1959).

42. Jürg Steiner, *Die Anteilnahme der Stimmbuerger am politischen Leben ihrer Gemeinde: Eine staatssoziologische Untersuchung am Beispiel der Gemeinde Belp im Kanton Bern* (Berne-Stuttgart: Paul Haupt, 1961).

43. Jürg Steiner, "Die Beziehungen der schweizerischen Stimmbuerger zur eidgenoessischen Politik," *Koelner Zeitschrift fuer Soziologie und Sozialpsychologie* 16 (1964):680–702.

44. Jürg Steiner, *Buerger und Politik* (Meisenheim am Glan: Anton Hain, 1969).

45. Florence Kluckhohn, "Die Methode der teilnehmenden Beobachtung in kleinen Gruppen," in *Beobachtung und Experiment in der Sozialforschung*, ed. René Koenig (Cologne: Verlag fuer Politik und Wirtschaft, 1956), p. 97.

46. René Koenig, "Die Beobachtung," in *Handbuch der Empirischen Sozialforschung*, ed. René Koenig (Stuttgart: Ferdinand Enke, 1962), p. 128.

47. Maurice Duverger, *Méthodes de la science politique* (Paris: Coll. Thémis, 1959), p. 285.

48. Koenig, "Die Beobachtung," pp. 128–29.

49. For a description of the research design see Jürg Steiner, "Teilnehmende

Beobachtung des Entscheidungsprozesses in der Freisinnig-demokratischen Partei des Kantons Bern," *Wirtschaft und Recht* 22 (1970):162–74.

CHAPTER II

1. Giovanni Sartori, "Typologies of Party Systems: A Critique" (Paper delivered at the Seventh World Congress of the International Political Science Association, Brussels, 1967), p. 10.
2. Ibid., pp. 4–5.
3. Ibid., p. 5.
4. Ibid., p. 7.
5. Ibid., p. 13.
6. In 1971 the Farmer, Artisan, and Bourgeois party and the Democratic party united into the Swiss People's party (Schweizerische Volkspartei). Before 1971 the seat in the federal government belonged to the Farmer, Artisan, and Bourgeois party. On the cantonal level the Farmer, Artisan, and Bourgeois party and the Democratic party have kept their old names. Today the Democratic party is represented only in the cantons of Graubuenden and Glarus where the Farmer, Artisan, and Bourgeois party has no cantonal sections.
7. Articles 89, 119, and 121 of the Federal Constitution.
8. *Statistisches Jahrbuch der Schweiz 1972* (Basel: Birkhaeuser, 1972), pp. 560–61.
9. See, for example, *Schweizerische Politik im Jahres 1965–*, University of Berne Publications in the History and Sociology of Swiss Politics (Berne, 1965–) (hereafter cited as *Schweizerische Politik im Jahre 19–*).
10. François Masnata, *Le parti socialiste et la tradition démocratique en Suisse* (Neuchâtel: Coll. Fondation nationale des sciences politiques, 1963). Similar estimates are found in Gerhard Kocher, *Verbandseinfluss auf die Gesetzgebung* (Berne: Francke, 1967), p. 193; Kurt Mueller, "Der Einfluss der Interessenverbaende," in *Die politische Willensbildung im Bunde, Neue Zuercher Zeitung* Publications, no. 1 (Zurich, 1968), p. 62; Erich Gruner, *Die Parteien in der Schweiz* (Berne: Francke, 1969).
11. For the Democratic party in the cantons of Graubuenden and Glarus see note 6.
12. Roger Girod, "Geography of the Swiss Party System," in *Cleavages, Ideologies, and Party Systems*, ed. E. Allardt and Y. Littunen, *Transactions of the Westermarck Society* (Helsinki, 1964), pp. 132–61.
13. Sartori, "Party Systems," p. 24.
14. This position is also taken by Girod, "Swiss Party System," p. 137: "Opposition, of course, is always possible. . . . This formula has therefore nothing in common with the authoritarian versions of the one party system."
15. Ibid., p. 138.
16. Ibid.
17. See, for example, *Statistisches Jahrbuch der Schweiz 1972*, p. 550.
18. Ibid., p. 549.
19. Girod, "Swiss Party System," p. 137
20. Ibid.
21. Ibid.
22. Gerhard Lehmbruch, "A Non-Competitive Pattern of Conflict Management in Liberal Democracies: The Case of Switzerland, Austria, and Lebanon" (Paper delivered at the Seventh World Congress of the International Political Science Association, Brussels, 1967), p. 26.
23. Gerhard Lehmbruch, *Proporzdemokratie: Politisches System und politische Kultur in der Schweiz und in Oesterreich* (Tuebingen: J. C. B. Mohr [Paul Siebeck], 1967), pp. 7–8.

24. Arend Lijphart, "Typologies of Democratic Systems" (Paper delivered at the Seventh World Congress of the International Political Science Association, Brussels, 1967), p. 26.

25. Jürg Steiner, *Die Beziehungen zwischen den Stimmberechtigten und den Gewaehlten in laendlichem und staedtischem Milieu: Versuch einer staatssoziologischen Untersuchung am Beispiel* des *Grossen Rates des Kantons Bern* (Berne-Stuttgart: Paul Haupt, 1959), *passim*. For the name of the Swiss People's party, see note 6.

26. Girod, "Swiss Party System," pp. 139–40.

27. Sartori, "Party Systems," pp. 22–23.

28. Ibid., p. 22.

29. *Statistisches Jahrbuch der Schweiz 1972*, pp. 550–51.

30. Girod, "Swiss Party System," pp. 140–41.

31. Ibid., p. 141.

32. Recently the Independent party was founded as a fourth party in the canton of Solothurn.

33. *Statistisches Jahrbuch der Schweiz 1972*, pp. 550–51.

34. This concerns a participant observation in the study described in Jürg Steiner, "Teilnehmende Beobachtung des Entscheidungsprozesses in der Freisinnig-demokratischen Partei des Kantons Bern," *Wirtschaft und Recht* 22 (1970): 162–74.

35. There are also some exceptions to the principle of amicable agreement on the local level.

36. Sartori, "Party Systems," p. 7.

37. Ibid., pp. 7–8.

38. Roger Girod, "Milieux politiques et classes sociales en Suisse," *Cahiers Internationaux de Sociologie* 39 (1965):53.

39. Lehmbruch, *Proporzdemokratie*, *passim*.

40. Lehmbruch, "Conflict Management," p. 10.

41. Girod, "Swiss Party System," p. 132.

42. Ibid., p. 143.

43. Ibid.

44. For the influence of the electoral system on the pattern of government formation see my article, "Typologisierung des schweizerischen Parteiensystems," *Schweizerisches Jahrbuch fuer Politische Wissenschaft* 9 (1969):71.

45. Stein Rokkan, "The Structuring of Mass Politics in the Smaller European Democracies: A Developmental Typology" (Paper delivered at the Seventh World Congress of the International Political Science Association, Brussels, 1967), p. 6.

46. Ibid., p. 61.

47. Ibid.

48. Ibid.

49. For a further discussion of the developmental approach of Rokkan see my article, "Die Bedeutung der Geschichte fuer die Theorienbildung in der Politischen Wissenschaft," *Wirtschaft und Recht* 21 (1969): 131–40.

50. Girod, "Swiss Party System," *passim*.

51. Max Weber, "Die soziale Schweiz," *Schweizerische Zeitschrift fuer Volkswirtschaft und Statistik*, nos. 1–2 (1964), p. 190.

52. *Statistisches Jahrbuch der Schweiz 1972*, p. 388.

53. Ibid., p. 389.

54. Ernst Steinmann, *Geschichte des Schweizerischen Freisinns*, vol. 1 (Berne: Paul Haupt, 1955).

55. Cited in Lehmbruch, *Proporzdemokratie*, p. 10.

56. Ibid., p. 19.

57. Erich Gruner, "Opposition und Regierung in der Schweiz im Hinblick auf die Bedeutung der Parteien" (Paper delivered at the annual meeting of the Swiss Political Science Association, Lucerne, 1968).

58. For a fuller development of this historical argument see Erwin Bucher, "Die Entwicklung der Schweiz zu einem politischen System," in *Das politische System der Schweiz,* ed. Jürg Steiner (Munich: Piper, 1971), pp. 13–50.

59. The "common dependent areas" were territories that were ruled by all or some of the cantons.

60. Lehmbruch, *Proporzdemokratie,* p. 17.

61. Unpublished campaign document of the Free Democratic party, written in connection with the general election of 1967, and made accessible to the author.

62. *Schweizerische Politik im Jahre 1967,* pp. 93–94.

63. Ibid., pp. 63–64.

64. Willi Geiger, "Der Mirage-Konflikt: Seine Entstehung, Loesung und grundsaetzliche Bedeutung," in *Schweizerisches Jahrbuch fuer Politische Wissenschaft* 5 (1965):90–99.

65. François-L. Reymond, "La votation fédérale du 28 février 1965 sur les arrêtés conjoncturels," in *Schweizerisches Jahrbuch fuer Politische Wissenschaft* 6 (1966):115–38.

66. Erich Gruner, "Le fonctionnement du système représentatif dans la confédération Suisse" (Paper delivered at the Seventh World Congress of the International Political Science Association, Brussels, 1967), p. 16.

67. Masnata, *Le parti socialiste,* p. 61.

68. Ibid., p. 244.

69. Girod, "Swiss Party System," p. 133.

70. Masnata, *Le parti socialiste,* p. 244.

71. This observation is based on the study described on p. 12.

72. See also Gruner, *Die Parteien in der Schweiz,* p. 33.

73. Reymond, "La votation fédérale," p. 131.

74. The Communist party in the canton of Geneva is an exception as we have already indicated.

75. *Statistisches Jahrbuch der Schweiz 1972,* pp. 550–51.

76. Cited in Masnata, *Le parti socialiste,* p. 179.

77. Geiger, "Der Mirage-Konflikt," p. 96.

78. Ibid., p. 97.

79. On this point see also Gruner, *Die Parteien in der Schweiz,* p. 39.

80. *Schweizerische Politik im Jahre 1966,* p. 20.

81. Christopher Hughes, *The Parliament of Switzerland* (London: Cassell & Co., 1962), p. 80.

82. Ibid., p. 82.

83. Ibid., pp. 82–83.

84. Ibid., p. 70.

85. Lehmbruch, "Conflict Management," p. 10.

86. Hermann Boeschenstein, *Wir waehlen den Nationalrat: Ein staatsbuergerliches ABC* (Berne: Paul Haupt, 1967), pp. 77–85.

87. Erich Gruner in *Schweizerische Politik im Jahre 1966,* pp. 148–49.

88. "Im Kampf der Interessen," campaign leaflet of the Independent party, n.d.

89. The Republican party split from the Anti-Alien party in 1970. James Schwarzenbach, the former leader of the Anti-Alien party, became the leader of the Republican party. It seems that the Republican party is somewhat more moderate on the question of foreign workers than the Anti-Alien party.

90. "Im Kampf der Interessen."

91. *Nationalratswahlen 1967,* ser. Qa9, vol. 436 (Berne: Federal Bureau of Statistics, 1968), p. 25.

92. *Statistisches Jahrbuch der Schweiz 1972,* pp. 550–51.

93. Erich Gruner and Juerg Siegenthaler, "Die Wahlen in die eidgenoessischen Raete im Oktober 1963," *Jahrbuch der Schweizerischen Vereinigung fuer Politische Wissenschaft* 4 (1964):116–17.

94. Reymond, "La votation fédérale," p. 131.

95. Robert A. Dahl, ed., *Political Oppositions in Western Democracies* (New Haven: Yale University Press, 1966), p. 340.

96. Ibid., p. 341.

97. For this hypothesis see the literature cited in note 21 of chapter I.

98. Gruner, *Die Parteien in der Schweiz*, pp. 228–30.

99. For the Swiss People's party see note 6.

100. *Nationalratswahlen 1967*, pp. 112–14. In 1972 a national survey showed that 45 percent of the farmers identify with the Swiss People's party and that 29 percent of the persons identifying with the Swiss People's party are farmers (Dusan Sidjanski and Henry H. Kerr, Jr., *L'électeur suisse*, forthcoming).

101. Girod, "Milieux politiques et classes sociales," pp. 40–50.

102. Masnata, *Le parti socialiste*, p. 35. In 1972 a national survey showed that 36 percent of the workers identify with the Social Democrats and that 49 percent of the persons identifying with the Social Democrats are workers (Sidjanski and Kerr, Jr., *L'électeur suisse*).

103. *Nationalratswahlen 1967*, p. 139.

104. Girod, "Milieux politiques et classes sociales," p. 32.

105. Masnata, *Le parti socialiste*, p. 270.

106. Ibid., pp. 259–60.

107. Ibid., p. 260.

108. Ibid.

109. Ibid., p. 261.

110. Karl Martin Bolte, *Deutsche Gesellschaft im Wandel* (Opladen: Westdeutscher Verlag, 1966), pp. 313–14.

111. Steiner, "Die Anteilnahme der Stimmbuerger," pp. 64–80.

112. Jürg Steiner, *Buerger und Politik* (Meisenheim am Glan: Anton Hain, 1969). These data are not included in this publication.

113. Masnata, *Le parti socialiste*, p. 261.

114. Ibid., p. 259.

115. Ibid., pp. 187–88.

116. For the research design see chapter I, p. 12.

117. In Lucerne the cantonal section of the Free Democratic party is called the Liberal party, which has nothing to do with the Liberal Democratic party in other cantons.

118. The educational system of Switzerland is hardly comparable to the system in English-speaking countries. In the present context it may be enough to say that the secondary school is a higher level than the primary school and that higher education is the highest level. The three levels are as follows: primary school (Primarschule); secondary school (Sekundar-oder Bezirkschule); higher education (Hochschule, Seminar, Technikum, Gymnasium).

119. See also Gruner, *Die Parteien in der Schweiz*, pp. 18–21.

120. *Statistisches Jahrbuch der Schweiz 1972*, p. 40.

121. Ibid., pp. 552–58.

122. *Nationalratswahlen 1967*, pp. 148–49.

123. Press release of the Free Democratic party, October 23, 1967.

124. *Der Schweizer Waehler 1963: Wissenschaftliche Analyse der Nationalratswahlen Oktober 1963* (Basel: Verlag der Nationalzeitung, 1963), pp. 10–11.

125. *Schweizerische Politik im Jahre 1965*, p. 208. In May, 1973, a referendum was held concerning the Exception Clause. It was only by a small margin that the people decided to take the Exception Clause out of the Federal Constitution.

126. For the research design see chapter I, p. 12. In 1972 a national survey showed that 52 percent of the Catholics and 7 percent of the Protestants identify with the Christian Democratic party. The survey also showed that identification

with the Christian Democratic party is particularly high among the regular churchgoing Catholics. Of the Catholics who identify with the Christian Democrats, 72 percent attend church every Sunday, 57 percent attend church nearly every Sunday, 32 percent attend church occasionally, 26 percent attend church rarely, and 6 percent never attend church (Sidjanski and Kerr, Jr., *L'électeur suisse*).

127. Regular churchgoers are those who go to church at least twelve times a year.

128. *Statistisches Jahrbuch der Schweiz 1972*, pp. 552–58.

129. *Nationalratswahlen 1967*, pp. 144–45.

130. Beat Junker and Rudolf Maurer, *Kampf und Verantwortung: Bernische Bauern-, Gewerbe- und Buergerpartei 1918–1968* (Berne: Verbands-druckerei, 1968). See also note 6.

131. *Nationalratswahlen 1967*, pp. 35–37. Urban communities are defined as communities having more than 10,000 inhabitants.

132. *Schweizerisches Kaufmaennisches Zentralblatt* 71 (October 20, 1967). At that time the Farmer, Artisan, and Bourgeois party and the Democratic party were not yet united in the Swiss People's party. The recommendation went to two candidates of the Farmer, Artisan, and Bourgeois party and to two candidates of the Democratic party.

133. Erich Schmid, "Politische Parteien und Wirtschaftsverbaende," *Neue Zuercher Zeitung*, September 22, 1967.

134. See also Gruner, *Die Parteien in der Schweiz*, pp. 177–78.

135. *Das Gewerbe und die Nationalratswahlen* (Burgdorf: Swiss Union of Artisans, 1967). This was a pamphlet published by the canton of Berne's branch of the Swiss Union of Artisans.

136. Arend Lijphart, *The Politics of Accommodation: Pluralism and Democracy in the Netherlands* (Berkeley and Los Angeles: University of California Press, 1968), p. 17.

137. *Statistisches Jahrbuch der Schweiz 1972*, pp. 392–93.

138. Masnata, *Le parti socialiste*, pp. 237–39.

139. Ibid., p. 69.

140. Steiner, "Die Anteilnahme der Stimmbuerger," p. 43.

141. *Statistisches Jahrbuch der Schweiz 1972*, p. 526.

142. Gruner and Siegenthaler, "Die Wahlen in die eidgenoessischen Raete," p. 141.

143. Circular from the Sports Fishing Club of Berne, October, 1967.

144. Mueller, "Der Einfluss der Interessenverbaende," pp. 60–61.

145. Rokkan, "Mass Politics," p. 26.

146. Masnata, *Le parti socialiste*, pp. 127–29.

147. Ibid., p. 129.

148. Steiner, "Die Beziehungen der schweizerischen Stimmbuerger." These data are not included in this publication.

149. Masnata, *Le parti socialiste*, p. 250.

150. Leon Festinger, A *Theory of Cognitive Dissonance* (Evanston: Northwestern University Press, 1957).

151. Cited in Masnata, *Le parti socialiste*, p. 150.

152. The best-known work about the history of Swiss neutrality is Edgar Bonjour, *Geschichte der schweizerischen Neutralitaet*, 6 vols. (Basel: Helbing and Lichtenhahn, 1965–70).

153. See also Gruner, *Die Parteien in der Schweiz*, pp. 33, 206.

154. Boeschenstein, *Wir waehlen den Nationalrat*, p. 85.

155. Masnata, *Le parti socialiste*, p. 151.

156. Ibid.

157. Ibid.

158. *Schweizerische Politik im Jahre 1968*, p. 45.

159. For a research project more like this one see note 34.

160. To indicate that the present propositions are tested again later in the book I have marked them with an asterisk (*). See pp. 85–95.

161. "University president" is the English translation of the German "Universitaetsrektor." Since the university system in Switzerland is very different from the system in the English-speaking countries the two positions are not entirely comparable.

162. For some hypotheses about the conditions of amicable agreement and majority decisions see my articles, "Conflict Resolution and Democratic Stability in Subculturally Segmented Political Systems," *Res Publica: Review of the Belgian Political Science Institute* 11 (1969):775–98; "The Principles of Majority and Proportionality," *British Journal of Political Science* 1 (1971):63–70.

163. For the term "optional referendum" see p. 18.

164. For a further development of this approach see note 34.

165. Masnata, *Le parti socialiste*, pp. 280–82.

166. Ibid., pp. 63–64.

167. Ibid., p. 83.

168. Ibid., p. 64. See also Erich Gruner, "Parteien und Verbaende," in *Schweizerische Politik im Jahre 1966*, pp. 145–46.

169. Masnata, *Le parti socialiste*, pp. 65–66.

170. Ibid., p. 94.

171. Ibid., p. 85.

172. Ibid., p. 87.

173. Ibid., p. 88.

174. Gruner, "Parteien und Verbaende," pp. 145–46.

175. Masnata, *Le parti socialiste*, p. 88.

176. Ibid., p. 89.

177. Ibid.

178. Ibid., p. 37.

179. Ibid., p. 149.

180. Ibid., p. 84.

181. There is, however, a recent tendency for the average member of the Social Democratic party to demand more from the party leadership. See *Schweizerische Politik im Jahre 1968*, pp. 155–57.

182. Masnata, *Le parti socialiste*, p. 96.

183. Ibid., p. 98.

184. Ibid., pp. 68, 91. See also Gruner, *Die Parteien in der Schweiz*, p. 205.

185. Masnata, *Le parti socialiste*, p. 237.

186. Ibid., p. 91.

187. Ibid., p. 170.

188. Ibid.

189. Ibid., p. 169.

190. Ibid., p. 80.

191. Ibid., p. 241.

192. Ibid., p. 244.

193. Ibid., p. 61.

194. My study referred to in note 34 is a beginning in this direction.

195. *Nationalratswahlen 1963*, ser. Qa8, vol. 34 (Berne: Federal Bureau of Statistics, 1964), p. 23.

196. Steiner, *Buerger und Politik*, pp. 42–50.

197. Steiner, "Die Anteilnahme der Stimmbuerger," p. 16.

198. Steiner, "Die Beziehungen zwischen den Stimmberechtigten." These data are not included in this publication.

199. Urs Jaeggi, *Berggemeinden im Wandel: Eine empirisch-soziologische*

Untersuchung in vier Gemeinden des Berner Oberlandes (Berne-Stuttgart: Paul Haupt, 1965), p. 221.

200. Gruner, *Der Schweizer Waehler 1963*, p. 13. See also Gruner, *Die Parteien in der Schweiz*, p. 210.

201. The study referred to in note 34 will hopefully result in some data concerning this question.

202. Steiner, *Buerger und Politik*. These data are not included in this publication.

203. Ibid., pp. 32–153.

CHAPTER III

1. See also Erich Gruner, *Die Parteien in der Schweiz* (Berne: Francke, 1969), pp. 169–74.

2. Jürg Steiner, "Die Beziehungen der schweizerischen Stimmbuerger zur eidgenoessischen Politik," *Koelner Zeitschrift fuer Soziologie und Sozialpsychologie* 16 (1964):680–702. These data are not included in this publication.

3. François Masnata, *Le parti socialiste et la tradition démocratique en suisse* (Neuchâtel: Coll. Fondation nationale des science politiques, 1963), p. 74.

4. These statistics are for the year 1971; see *Statistisches Jahrbuch der Schweiz 1972* (Basel: Birkhaeuser, 1972), p. 392.

5. *Das Gewerbe und die Nationalratswahlen* (Burgdorf: Swiss Union of Artisans, 1967). This was a pamphlet published by the canton of Berne's branch of the Swiss Union of Artisans.

6. *Nationalratswahlen 1967* (Berne: Swiss Union of Artisans, 1967). This was a pamphlet published by the city of Berne's branch of the Swiss Union of Artisans.

7. Roger Girod, "Milieux politiques et classes sociales en Suisse," *Cahiers Internationaux de Sociologie* 39 (1965):32–33.

8. Masnata, *Le parti socialiste*, p. 265.

9. François-L. Reymond, "La votation fédérale du 28 février 1965 sur les arrêtés conjoncturels," in *Schweizerisches Jahrbuch fuer Politische Wissenschaft* 6 (1966):119–21.

10. *Schweizerische Politik im Jahre 1967*, pp. 94–95.

11. Masnata, *Le parti socialiste*, p. 240.

12. Circular of the Sports Fishing Club of Berne, October, 1967.

13. Girod, "Milieux politiques et classes sociales," p. 52.

14. Ibid., p. 49.

15. Ibid., p. 47.

16. *Neue Zuercher Zeitung*, August 28, 1967.

17. *Statistisches Jahrbuch der Schweiz 1972*, p. 526.

18. My father, Werner Steiner, was of great help to me in this part of my study.

19. Erwin Bucher, "Die Entwicklung der Schweiz zu einem politischen System," in *Das politische System der Schweiz*, ed. Jürg Steiner (Munich: Piper, 1971), pp. 13–50.

20. Andreas Thommen, *Die Schweizer Presse in der modernen Gesellschaft* (Zurich: Orell Fuessli, 1967), p. 36. If not otherwise stated, Thommen's figures refer to the year 1967.

21. Ibid.

22. A new study by the Swiss Cartel Committee shows the following readership figures for the three largest newspapers: *Blick*, 201,347; *Tages-Anzeiger*, 192,071; *Neue Zuercher Zeitung*, 87,440 (*Die Konzentration im schweizerischen Pressewesen* [Berne: Swiss Cartel Committee, 1969], 3:178).

23. Thommen, *Die Schweizer Presse*, p. 146.

24. Ibid., p. 147. Not included here are the head systems restricted to advertisements.

25. Ibid., pp. 135–37.

26. Ibid., p. 61.

27. *Die Konzentration im schweizerischen Pressewesen,* 3:225.

28. Thommen, *Die Schweizer Presse,* pp. 53–54. See also Gruner, *Die Parteien in der Schweiz,* p. 222.

29. Reymond, "La votation fédérale," pp. 121–22.

30. Thommen, *Die Schweizer Presse,* p. 52.

31. *Die Konzentration im schweizerischen Pressewesen,* 3:179.

32. François-L. Reymond, "La question jurassienne et l'évolution du mouvement séparatiste 1959–1964," in *Schweizerisches Jahrbuch fuer Politische Wissenschaft* 5 (1965):35–36.

33. Ibid., p. 34. In the three northern districts of the Jura, where the separatists are particularly strong, 81 percent of the population is Catholic; see Kurt B. Mayer, "Einige soziologische Aspekte des Jura-Problems," *Schweizerische Zeitschrift fuer Volkswirtschaft und Statistik* 105 (1969):235.

34. Up to the present the cantons have been the electoral districts.

35. For the Jura question see also *Bericht zur Jurafrage* (Biel: Committee of the 24, 1968).

CHAPTER IV

1. Jürg Steiner, *Die Beziehungen zwischen den Stimmberechtigten und den Gewaehlten in laendlichem und staedtischem Milieu: Versuch einer staatssoziologischen Untersuchung am Beispiel des Grossen Rates des Kantons Bern* (Berne-Stuttgart: Paul Haupt, 1959), p. 63.

2. Ibid., p. 70.

3. Peter Gilg, "Die berufs- und interessenpolitische Gliederung des neuen Nationalrates," in *Der Bund,* November 16 and 17, 1967.

4. Steiner, *Die Beziehungen zwischen den Stimmberechtigten,* p. 72.

5. Gilg, "Die berufs- und interessenpolitische Gliederung."

6. This case concerns Eduard Zellweger of Zurich; see *Schweizerische Politik im Jahre 1967,* pp. 11–12.

7. Dusan Sidjanski, "Les groupes de pression et la politique étrangère en Suisse," in *Schweizerisches Jahrbuch fuer Politische Wissenschaft* 6 (1966):34.

8. Ibid.

9. Ibid., p. 35.

10. *Staatskalender der Schweizerischen Eidgenossenschaft* (Berne: Federal Chancellery, 1965), pp. 254–55.

11. *Schweizerische Politik im Jahre 1967,* p. 125.

12. *Schweizerische Politik im Jahre 1966,* p. 61.

13. Kurt Mueller, "Der Einfluss der Interessenverbaende," in *Die Politische Willensbildung im Bunde, Neue Zuercher Zeitung* Publications, no. 1 (Zurich, 1968), p. 61.

14. Erich Gruner, "Le fonctionnement du système représentatif dans la confédération Suisse" (Paper delivered at the Seventh World Congress of the International Political Science Association, Brussels, 1967), p. 2.

15. Hermann Haeberlin, "Altvertraute Unkenrufe," in *Neue Zuercher Zeitung,* August 25, 1967.

16. Gruner, "Système représentatif," p. 2.

17. Roger Girod, "Milieux politiques et classes sociales en Suisse," *Cahiers Internationaux de Sociologie* 39 (1965):30.

18. Gilg, "Die berufs- und interessenpolitische Gliederung."

19. Steiner, *Die Beziehungen zwischen den Stimmberechtigten,* p. 66.

20. William Kornhauser, *The Politics of Mass Society* (New York: Free Press, 1959), p. 228.

CHAPTER V

1. *Bericht der Eidgenoessischen Expertenkommission fuer Fragen der Hochschulfoederung* (Berne: Federal Chancellery, 1964), pp. 154–55.
2. For development until 1963–64 see ibid., pp. 191–93. For development since 1963–64 see *Statistisches Jahrbuch der Schweiz 1972* (Basel: Birkhaeuser, 1972), p. 466.
3. *Bericht der Eidgenoessischen Expertenkommission*, p. 478.
4. *Statistisches Jahrbuch der Schweiz 1972*, p. 484.
5. *Schweizerische Politik im Jahre 1966*, pp. 117–19.
6. *Schweizerische Politik im Jahre 1968*, p. 125.
7. *Bericht der Eidgenoessischen Expertenkommission*, pp. 153–54.
8. Ibid., p. 13.
9. Ibid., p. 153.
10. For the concepts of "lead" and "lag" see Karl W. Deutsch, *The Nerves of Government* (Glencoe, Ill.: Free Press, 1963), pp. 188–90.
11. *Botschaft des Bundesrates an die Bundesversammlung ueber die vorlaeufige Regelung von Beitraegen an die Ausgaben der Kantone fuer die Hochschulen, November 29, 1965* (Berne: Federal Chancellery, 1965), p. 6.
12. Deutsch, *Nerves of Government*, p. 129.
13. *Statistisches Jahrbuch der Schweiz 1972*, p. 417.
14. For the term "university president" see chapter II, note 166.
15. Deutsch, *Nerves of Government*, p. 163.
16. *Botschaft des Bundesrates . . . November 29, 1965*, pp. 9–10.
17. For the term "university president" see chapter II, note 166.
18. The committee defended its refusal by stating that it had promised the universities to treat their answers confidentially.
19. After the present case study was finished some efforts were made to build up such a staff within the Federal Chancellery (*Schweizerische Politik im Jahre 1967*, p. 10).
20. After the present case study was finished some efforts were made to give a scientific staff to Parliament (*Schweizerische Politik im Jahre 1968*, p. 12).
21. *Bericht der Eidgenoessischen Expertenkommission*, p. 158.
22. Ibid.
23. Ibid., p. 147.
24. Ibid., p. 182.
25. Ibid.
26. The author was given access to this letter by the Aargau Chamber of Commerce.
27. *Botschaft des Bundesrates . . . November 29, 1965*, p. 20.
28. Ibid., pp. 19–20.
29. Ibid., p. 20.
30. *Schweizerische Politik im Jahre 1968*, p. 12.
31. Advertisement in *Der Bund*, February 2, 1968.
32. To indicate that the present propositions are tested again later in the book I have marked them with an asterisk. Propositions 19* through 72* are a continuation of Propositions 1* through 18* (see pp. 82–84).
33. *Der Regierungsrat des Kantons Aargau an den Grossen Rat, April 23, 1964*, no. 1144 (Aargau: Cantonal Chancellery, 1964), p. 3.
34. Cited in ibid.
35. *Beitrag des Aargaus an das schweizerische Hochschulwesen* (Aarau: Cantonal Chancellery, 1967), pp. 65–68.

36. For reasons of discretion the members of Parliament are indicated by capital letters.
37. In the educational system of Switzerland the "gymnasium" is the highest level of school below the university level.
38. *Beitrag des Aargaus an das schweizerische Hochschulwesen.*
39. *Der Regierungsrat des Kantons Aargau an den Grossen Rat, October 2, 1969*, no. 2806 (Aarau: Cantonal Chancellery, 1969).
40. Christopher Hughes, *The Parliament of Switzerland* (London: Cassell & Co., 1962).
41. Beat Alexander Jenny, *Interessenpolitik und Demokratie in der Schweiz: Dargestellt am Beispiel der Emser Vorlage* (Zurich: Polygraphischer Verlag, 1966).
42. Gerhard Kocher, *Verbandseinfluss auf die Gesetzgebung* (Berne: Francke, 1967).
43. At the Department of Political Science of the University of Geneva several decision-making case studies are currently in progress. They seem to confirm, in general, the propositions of this study. A conclusive judgment, however, is not yet possible.
44. Hughes, *Parliament of Switzerland*, p. 103.
45. Jenny, *Interessenpolitik*, pp. 18–20.
46. Kocher, *Verbandseinfluss*, pp. 30–32.
47. Hughes, *Parliament of Switzerland*, p. 103.
48. Kocher, *Verbandseinfluss*, p. 100.
49. Jenny, *Interessenpolitik*, pp. 7–11, 27.
50. Kocher, *Verbandseinfluss*, pp. 29–30.
51. Hughes, *Parliament of Switzerland*, p. 103.
52. Ibid.
53. Ibid., pp. 106–8; Jenny, *Interessenpolitik*, pp. 23–25; Kocher, *Verbandseinfluss*, pp. 164–67.
54. Jenny, *Interessenpolitik*, pp. 23, 29.
55. Kocher, *Verbandseinfluss*, pp. 164–67.
56. Ibid., pp. 35–37.
57. Jenny, *Interessenpolitik*, p. 25.
58. Erich Gruner, "Le fonctionnement du système représentatif dans la confédération Suisse (Paper delivered at the Seventh World Congress of the International Political Science Association, Brussels, 1967), p. 2.
59. Hughes, *Parliament of Switzerland*, pp. 103–5.
60. Jenny, *Interessenpolitik*, p. 29.
61. Kocher, *Verbandseinfluss*, p. 204.
62. Jenny, *Interessenpolitik*, p. 12.
63. Kocher, *Verbandseinfluss*, p. 35.
64. Ibid.
65. Ibid., p. 59.
66. Ibid., p. 245.
67. *Expertenbericht ueber Verbesserungen in der Regierungstaetigkeit und Verwaltungsfuehrung des Bundesrates erstattet dem Schweizerischen Bundesrat, November, 1967* (Berne: Federal Chancellery, 1967), p. 40.
68. Hughes, *Parliament of Switzerland*, p. 104.
69. Modified according to Proposition 50*.
70. Kocher, *Verbandseinfluss*, p. 68.
71. Ibid., p. 57.
72. Ibid., pp. 46–48.
73. Jenny, *Interessenpolitik*, p. 22.
74. Kocher, *Verbandseinfluss*, p. 190.
75. See, for example, ibid., p. 100.

76. Ibid., p. 194.
77. Ibid., pp. 203–4.

CHAPTER VI

1. Hermann Weilenmann and Karl W. Deutsch, "The Political Integration of Switzerland: Conditions and Possibilities for the Making of a Multilingual Nation," quoted from the unpublished manuscript by permission of the authors.
2. Bruce M. Russett, Hayward R. Alker, Jr., Karl W. Deutsch, and Harold D. Lasswell, *World Handbook of Political and Social Indicators* (New Haven: Yale University Press, 1964).
3. Weilenmann and Deutsch, "Political Integration of Switzerland."
4. Ibid.
5. Ibid.
6. Francesco Kneschaurek, "Kritische Bemerkungen zu den Prognosen ueber die Entwicklung des Hochschulstudiums in der Schweiz und Schlussfolgerungen in bezug auf den notwendigen Ausbau unserer Hochschulen," *Wirtschaft und Recht* 15 (1963):155–67.
7. Jürg Steiner, *Die Anteilnahme der Stimmbuerger am politischen Leben ihrer Gemeinde: Eine staatssoziologische Untersuchung am Beispiel der Gemeinde Belp im Kanton Bern* (Berne-Stuttgart: Paul Haupt, 1961), p. 43.
8. Urs Jaeggi, *Berggemeinden im Wandel: Eine empirisch-soziologische Untersuchung in vier Gemeinden des Berner Oberlandes* (Berne-Stuttgart: Paul Haupt, 1965), p. 219.
9. Ibid.
10. Jürg Steiner, *Die Beziehungen zwischen den Stimmberechtigten und den Gewaehlten in laendlichem und staedtischem Milieu: Versuch einer staatssoziologischen Untersuchung am Beispiel des Grossen Rates des Kantons Bern* (Berne-Stuttgart: Paul Haupt, 1959).
11. Steiner, *Die Anteilnahme der Stimmbuerger*, pp. 40–42.
12. Jürg Steiner, *Buerger und Politik* (Meisenheim am Glan: Anton Hain, 1969). These data are not included in this publication.
13. Ibid.
14. Ibid., pp. 43–51.
15. Ibid. These data are not included in this publication.
16. Ibid.
17. Jürg Steiner, "Die Beziehungen der schweizerischen Stimmbuerger zur eidgenoessischen Politik," *Koelner Zeitschift fuer Soziologie und Sozialpsychologie* 16 (1964):683.
18. Dusan Sidjanski and Henry H. Kerr, Jr., *L'électeur suisse*, forthcoming.
19. Steiner, *Buerger und Politik*, pp. 37–73.
20. Ibid., pp. 74–153.
21. Steiner, "Die Beziehungen der schweizerischen Stimmbuerger." These data are not included in this publication.
22. Steiner, *Buerger und Politik*, p. 75.
23. Steiner, *Die Anteilnahme der Stimmbuerger*, pp. 33–35.
24. Steiner, *Buerger und Politik*. These data are not included in this publication.
25. Ibid.
26. Ibid., pp. 105–12.
27. Hans Huber, "Die schweizerische Demokratie," in *Die Demokratie im Wandel der Gesellschaft*, ed. Richard Loewenthal (Berlin: Colloquium-Verlag, 1963), p. 109.
28. Daniel Frei, "Sendungsgedanken in der schweizerischen Aussenpolitik," *Schweizerisches Jahrbuch fuer Politische Wissenschaft* 6 (1966):98–113.
29. Steiner, *Die Anteilnahme der Stimmbuerger*, p. 76.

CHAPTER VII *has no notes.*

CHAPTER VIII

1. Arend Lijphart, *The Politics of Accommodation: Pluralism and Democracy in the Netherlands* (Berkeley and Los Angeles: University of California Press, 1968).

2. Harry Eckstein, *Division and Cohesion in Democracy: A Study of Norway* (Princeton: Princeton University Press, 1966).

3. Hermann Weilenmann, *Pax Helvetica oder die Demokratie der kleinen Gruppen* (Erlenbach-Zurich: Rentsch, 1951); André Siegfried, *La Suisse: Démocratie-témoin* (Neuchâtel: Coll. helvétique, 1956); Christopher Hughes, *The Parliament of Switzerland* (London: Cassell & Co., 1962): Kenneth D. McRae, *Switzerland: Example of Cultural Coexistence*, Contemporary Affairs, no. 33 (Toronto: Canadian Institute of International Affairs, 1964); Roger Girod, "Geography of the Swiss Party System," in *Cleavages, Ideologies, and Party Systems*, ed. E. Allardt and Y. Littunen, *Transactions of the Westermarck Society* (Helsinki, 1964); Gerhard Lehmbruch, *Proporzdemokratie: Politisches System und politische Kultur in der Schweiz und in Oesterreich* (Tuebingen: J. C. B. Mohr [Paul Siebeck], 1967); Kurt B. Mayer, "The Jura Problem: Ethnic Conflict in Switzerland," *Social Research* 35 (1968):707–41, Wiilliam R. Keech, "Linguistic Diversity and Political Conflict: Some Observations Based on Four Swiss Cantons," *Comparative Politics* 4 (1972):387–404; James A. Dunn, "Consociational Democracy and Language Conflict: A Comparison of the Belgian and Swiss Experiences," *Comparative Political Studies* 5 (1972):3–39; Hermann Weilenmann and Karl W. Deutsch, "The Political Integration of Switzerland: Conditions and Possibilities for the Making of a Multilingual Nation," unpublished manuscript. In 1972 the respondents in a national survey were asked: "Which of these terms *best* describes the way you usually think of yourself? (1) Genevois (for example), (2) Swiss Romand (for example), (3) Swiss." Of the Swiss Romands, 31 percent identify mostly with the canton, 30 percent with the linguistic group, and 40 percent with the nation. Of the German-speaking Swiss, 31 percent identify mostly with the canton, 16 percent with the linguistic group, and 53 percent with the nation. The author of the study comments that "the self-concept of many Swiss in the two major language groups is as much bound up with a sense of cantonal or linguistic identity as with identification with the nation" (Henry H. Kerr, Jr., "Social Cleavages and Partisan Conflict in Switzerland," Paper delivered at the Ninth World Congress of the International Political Science Association, Montreal, 1973).

4. The literature cited in note 3 verifies this statement.

5. Seymour Martin Lipset, *Political Man: The Social Bases of Politics* (New York: Doubleday and Co., 1960), pp. 45–46.

6. Ibid., p. 46.

7. William Kornhauser, *The Politics of Mass Society* (New York: Free Press, 1959), p. 230.

8. Lipset, *Political Man*, pp. 88–89.

9. Arend Lijphart, "Typologies of Democratic Systems" (Paper delivered at the Seventh World Congress of the International Political Science Association, Brussels, 1967), p. 35.

10. Ibid., pp. 33–34.

11. Ibid., p. 34.

12. *Statistisches Jahrbuch der Schweiz 1972* (Basel: Birkhaeuser, 1972), p. 39.

13. Ibid., p. 41.

14. Lijphart, "Democratic Systems," p. 33.

15. Val R. Lorwin, "Belgium: Religion, Class, and Language in National Politics," in *Political Oppositions in Western Democracies,* ed. Robert A. Dahl (New Haven: Yale University Press, 1966), p. 187.

16. Lijphart, "Democratic Systems," pp. 29–30.

17. Carl Joachim Friedrich, *Demokratie als Herrschafts- und Lebensform* (Heidelberg: Quelle & Meyer, 1959), pp. 83–84.

18. Jürg Steiner, *Buerger und Politik* (Meisenheim am Glan: Anton Hain, 1969), pp. 35–36.

19. Ibid., p. 36.

20. Gabriel A. Almond and G. Bingham Powell, *Comparative Politics: A Developmental Approach* (Boston: Little, Brown & Co., 1966), p. 82.

21. Ibid.

22. Cited in Weilenmann and Deutsch, "Political Integration of Switzerland."

23. Sidney Verba, "Organizational Membership and Democratic Consensus," *Journal of Politics* 27 (1965):470.

24. Lijphart, "Democratic Systems," p. 39.

25. Lipset, *Political Man,* p. 48.

26. Hans Nabholz and Paul Klaeui, *Quellenbuch zur Verfassungsgeschichte der Schweizerischen Eidgenossenschaft und der Kantone* (Aarau: Sauerlaender, 1947), p. 4.

27. Erwin Bucher, "Die Entwicklung der Schweiz zu einem politischen System," in *Das politische System der Schweiz* ed. Jürg Steiner (Munich: Piper, 1971), pp. 13–50.

CHAPTER IX

1. G. Bingham Powell, *Social Fragmentation and Political Hostility: An Austrian Case Study* (Stanford: Stanford University Press, 1970), p. 1.

2. In another publication an attempt was made to operationalize the three levels for the Free Democratic party in the canton of Berne; see Jürg Steiner and Robert G. Lehnen, "Political Status and Norms of Political Decision-making," *Comparative Political Studies,* in press.

3. Moshe M. Czudnowski, "Sociocultural Variables and Legislative Recruitment: Some Theoretical Observations and a Case Study," *Comparative Politics* 4 (1972):561–87.

4. I accept Riker's definition of rationality: "Given a social situation in which exist two alternative courses of action leading to different outcomes and assuming that participants can order these outcomes on a subjective scale of preference, each participant will choose the alternative leading to the more preferred outcome." As Riker says, this definition of rationality simply asserts that "if a person can decide what action will suit him best, then he will choose that action" (William H. Riker, *The Theory of Political Coalitions* [New Haven: Yale University Press, 1962], pp. 18–19).

5. History offers obvious deviant cases to this general hypothesis (Hitler, for example). It would be interesting to use these cases to refine the hypothesis.

6. See, for example, Samuel J. Eldersveld, *Political Parties: A Behavioral Analysis* (Chicago: Rand McNally & Co., 1964).

7. Hypothesis 4 was confirmed in the study that is reported in Steiner and Lehnen, "Political Status."

8. The point that it is the *perception* of equity that matters is also made by William R. Keech, "Linguistic Diversity and Political Conflict: Some Observations Based on Four Swiss Cantons," *Comparative Politics* 4 (1972):387–404.

9. It would be interesting to further develop this hypothesis and to specify the conditions under which other subcultures are chosen as targets of aggressive feelings.

10. Jack L. Walker, "A Critique of the Elitist Theory of Democracy," *American Political Science Review* 60 (1966):285–95; Lewis Lipsitz, "If, as Verba Says, the State Functions as a Religion, What Are We to Do to Save Our Souls?" *American Political Science Review* 62 (1968):527–35.

INDEX

www.ingramcontent.com/pod-product-compliance
Lightning Source LLC
Chambersburg PA
CBHW020336270326
41926CB00007B/203

9780807897867